Breakthroughs and Integration in Psychotherapy

John Rowan

Psychotherapy Series

Series Editor: Windy Dryden

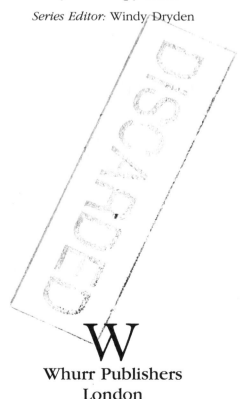
W
Whurr Publishers
London

Psyd

First published 1992 by
Whurr Publishers Ltd
19b Compton Terrace, London N1 2UN, England

British Library Cataloguing in Publication Data

Rowan, John
  Breakthroughs and integration in psychotherapy.
  I. Title
  616.89

  ISBN 1-870332-18-0

Composition by Scribe Design, Gillingham, Kent
Printed and bound in the UK by Athenaeum Press Ltd, Newcastle upon Tyne

Preface

The selection of papers for this book has been mine, with a little help from Windy Dryden, and I have found it necessary to split up the work into four parts. Each part has its own introduction, but it seems worth while to give a sense of the whole.

The first part gives a general overview to indicate where I am coming from generally. I think it is always useful to know what the biases of a writer are, so as to allow for wind, so to speak, in knowing how to take it all. One or two people have suggested to me that this section is 'too honest' in saying too much about my personal life, but I do not agree.

The second gives a selection of papers about theory. My interest in theory preceded my interest in psychotherapy, so it is appropriate to have this first, even though some of the later papers are quite recent. I always resent it when I am told that there is little theory in humanistic psychology – perhaps these papers will go some way towards refuting that.

The third part is all about humanistic psychotherapy, and this has been close to my heart for a number of years now. I think it is very important to be clear about what humanistic therapy is and is not, what it can and cannot do, and where it does and does not come from.

The fourth and final part is about transpersonal psychotherapy, and this is something I have only really come into since about 1982, although there were a number of glimpses and precursors before then. This is something that is even less understood and appreciated than the broad humanistic approach from which it emerged, and it is good to be able to present some useful material about it here.

Running all through this, although not amounting to a separate part, is a concern for the social context within which all psychotherapy takes place, and in particular, a concern with sexual politics and the questioning of patriarchy. It hurts me when I see, as happens about once every five years, an attack on psychotherapy as socially illiterate or even harmful. But let the papers speak for themselves.

John Rowan

Contents

Chapter 7

The self: One or many   72

Part III   Humanistic psychotherapy   79

Chapter 8

The concept of a breakthrough   81

Chapter 9

Humanistic psychotherapy and psychoanalysis   84

Chapter 10

Against feelings   91

Chapter 11

Siding with the client [abridged version]   93

Chapter 12

Counselling and the psychology of furniture   100

Chapter 13

Hypnotherapy and the humanistic   106

Chapter 14

Early traumas: A dialectical approach   111

Chapter 15

Integrative encounter   118

Part IV   Transpersonal psychotherapy   131

Chapter 16

The real self and mystical experiences   133

Chapter 17

Chapter 18

Chapter 19

Chapter 20

Chapter 21

Chapter 22

Index

Part I
Setting the Scene

Chapter 1
A Late Developer

Why I became a Psychotherapist

When I was born we were living in the married quarters of the RAF station at Old Sarum. My father was a squadron leader, and throughout my childhood he was moving from station to station. My mother was placid and stable, and adapted efficiently to all the moves and changes. We would move with him, but there was usually a period when he was away in the new place before we could join him, so that he was often not around in the home. It was as if he were the engine that kept everything going, but down in the hold somewhere out of sight. When he appeared, he was a strict disciplinarian, and believed in punctuality and the 24-hour clock. We had a nanny called Nurse Jacob, and a spaniel called Joseph. I was an only child until I was six and a half years old, when my brother was born.

Perhaps unusually, my father was the emotional one and my mother the cool, contained one. I experienced him as manipulative and emotionally blackmailing and guilt-inducing. So in my adolescence I resolved to be different from him, and to be straightforward emotionally. At sixteen I adopted the phrase 'education of the emotions', by which I meant having only those emotions that were convenient. The word 'love' in particular became very suspect, because of its associations with my father.

I did not know at the time that at an unconscious level I had made quite a similar decision for quite different reasons: this was that my mother had thrown me out of her womb, and taken away her breast, and cut off her love from me, and that I had to get revenge on all women, and all men too. My 'educated emotions' and straightforwardness turned out to consist largely of hate. I think it altogether probable that my mother, for reasons of her own, found it impossible to give love in any warm or personal way

From J. Rowan (1989). A late developer. In: W. Dryden and L. Spirling (Eds), *On Becoming a Psychotherapist*, pp. 148–168. London: Tavistock/Routledge, with permission.

to me, and perhaps to others too. It felt to me as if I made various attempts to get her love, failed several times to do so, and retired hurt and lonely (the final shot in this coming with the arrival of my brother), in the end turning loneliness into a virtue by claiming not to need people. In that way I could observe people in a way that was basically external, and calculated to cut me off from them very successfully. I then wondered why I never had much success with women. In other words, I had developed what I would now call the schizoid defence that I later found characteristic of so many men.

My father was interested in psychology, and particularly enthusiastic about the scientific approach of Cyril Burt. So at an early age I had some inkling of what psychology was all about, although I did not follow it up until much later.

So what I am saying is that my approach to psychotherapy came from roots which were not really about caring at all. I was deeply suspicious of caring, partly because my father used words such as love and care to manipulate and use others, and I was frightened of closeness, because I had tried to get close to my mother and failed and got hurt.

My approach to psychotherapy was rooted in a different concept: I was always more interested in the notion of freedom. As I grew up, I had no interest in doing good or in helping people and, although this has changed now, it is still true that my main interest is in enabling people to realise their potential, and this may well be painful rather than soothing in most cases.

So there was no tendency towards psychotherapy in my early adulthood. Because of my father's occupation, and because then I was called up in World War II, I lived in 30 different places in my first 30 years. This increased my schizoid tendency, in that it meant that I never allowed myself to get too attached to anyone or any place, because I knew I would have to leave it and lose things and people sooner or later. Then when I came to start work, I did not know who I was or what I wanted to be. My jobs included tutor, agricultural engineering clerk, electrical factor's clerk, supply teacher, telecommunications engineer, telecommunications instructor, encyclopaedia salesman, office manager, library research editor, marine insurance clerk and accountant.

During my Army service I spent some time in India, and was there introduced to the philosophy of Spinoza, which I found very exciting and liberating. Then when I came back to England, I was introduced to the work of Hegel by a friend of mine now dead, Harold Walsby. He pointed out that the work of Hegel was all based on the idea of freedom as the highest value, and he pointed out the connection between Hegel's famous statement 'Being and Nothing are one and the same' and the scientific value of taking nothing for granted. I joined a small Marxist party, and soon became the editor of its internal theoretical journal. All these influences made me very suspicious of psychotherapy, although Christopher Caudwell, a Marxist theoretician I had some use for, did have something to say about the importance of the unconscious, and Harold Walsby wrote about the connections between Marx and Freud.

It was about this time that I got married. I met my wife when I was teaching a course on cybernetics at Braziers Park Adult School, and Neilma was recording lectures by Joseph Needham on the same weekend. We played table tennis together, and it all started from there. We got married at a registry office in Burnt Oak, and Peri was born a little over a year later.

The turning point in my discovering what I wanted to do really came, I suppose, when four of us, who had been expelled from the same political party at the same time, started to study together for the London University Diploma in Sociology. This was a 4-year course, one evening a week, and at the time we did it, the 4 years were entitled 'Social history', 'Social structure', 'Social psychology' and 'Social philosophy'. Our main intention was to know more about society so that we could start a political movement of our own. We had tried to start a movement under the title 'Social integration', but this had failed and we wanted to know why.

I found that I was particularly good at social psychology and social philosophy, found it interesting and got good marks and awards. I even had a scientific article published in *Penguin Science News*. At the same time I had discovered that a possible career was in consumer research, and this quite appealed to me. It would develop my skills as a researcher very fast; it would pay well – I had a wife and two children to think of; it would give me a lot of knowledge of society and how it actually operated at grassroots level. Two social scientists had particularly impressed me – Mary Parker Follett and Ernest Dichter; both of these said that academia was slow and conservative, and that it was in commerce and industry that the live work of real change was pursued. Both of them took up the dialectical position I had learned from Hegel.

So I tried to get into consumer research, but none of the companies would have me without a degree. I decided, with a lot of help and prompting from the lecturers and my friends, to take a degree. I didn't have the required entrance qualifications, however, so in 1959, at the age of 34, I took the philosophy examination and the final examination for the Diploma, an 'A' level examination in logic and another one in English literature, and a scholarship examination to Birkbeck College. I passed all these satisfactorily, and duly enrolled for the Joint Honours degree in Philosophy and Psychology at Birkbeck College, under Richard Peters; I spent about three evenings a week for the next 4 years going to lectures and writing essays.

By the time I finished and got my degree, my wife and I had four children, so the pressure was even greater to get a well-paid job, and I duly went into consumer research. I liked the work very much, as I specialised on the psychological side, and this meant that I could use all my skills – in negotiating, in logic, in interviewing, in statistics, in writing – all at the same time. The views of Follett and Dichter that business people are much more alive, much more interested in experimenting than anyone in academia became truer for me than ever. I liked the feeling that my work was being used immediately, not placed on some shelf or dragged out with years of delays in the manner of some of my academic friends.

I went up the ladder quite fast, never staying in one job longer than 2 years, and at the beginning of the process described in this chapter I was Managing Director of the Bureau of Commercial Research and at the same time the London representative of Ernest Dichter International (interestingly enough, Dichter was a psychoanalyst who had gone over to market research – I was going to move in the opposite direction). I was well respected in the business, and had written papers and articles that had been published in the relevant magazines and journals. My main interest was in the objective measurement of attitudes and attitude change.

But I was not purely a businessman, as most of those in market research undoubtedly are. I had been a revolutionary, very much influenced by the ideas of Hegel and Marx, but had been disillusioned by the emphasis, in the small Party I had joined, on having the correct case at all costs, and seeing the essence of the matter as winning arguments. As already mentioned, I had tried with others to set up something better, but all our efforts foundered, and the group broke up. So I had been spending my spare time on the arts, working with Bob Cobbing to set up the Barnet Borough Arts Council, writing poems with the Writers' Forum group, exhibiting collages and constructions with Group H, taking part in drama with Arena Theatre, helping to organise 'Happenings', getting together a magazine called *AND* and organising a poetry-reading group called Soundabout.

Three phases

The process of becoming a psychotherapist took 12 years in all, and went in phases. My going-in position was that I was interested in social change, but was frustrated because I could not see any way to achieve this. Phase 1 (1969–1971) was what could be termed a 'mid-life crisis', where I understood a new notion of politics, that it didn't have to be just about having the ideal political case, or just about getting out and acting militantly: it could be about feelings and relationships and the way you lived. Phase 2 (1970–1979) was where the crisis resolved itself and I found that groups were the best places for personal and political change. Group therapy was one of the main roads to freedom. Phase 3 (1978–1981) was where I found that one-to-one work was equally satisfying and more regular and reliable.

The only time I had any sort of ideal model of what a therapist should be like was in phase 2, and here it was entirely a model of the group leader, not the individual psychotherapist. I was fascinated by group leaders such as Fritz Perls and Will Schutz and the Esalen Flying Circus – people who would fly in, do their week or weekend group and fly out again. I still feel that this is much more exciting than one-to-one work, and I do it three or four times a year.

What tends to happen in such intense groups is that people who have been working for months or years in their individual counselling or psychotherapy, and have got really stuck and grooved in their method, may come to the event and allow themselves to be stimulated and shaken into some kind of breakthrough. So the visiting group leader harvests a crop that has been nurtured and tended elsewhere. This is great for the visiting leader and great for the participants, although it may be a bit disappointing for the regular counsellor or therapist, who sees his or her patient or client valuing something that is outside the regular meetings. This is the model that had real magic for me, although I later came to see that the regular therapist deserved just as much credit and acclaim as the visiting leader. I now feel that the ideal set-up for the client is to go to an intensive workshop to stir up deep and valuable material, and then go to an individual therapist to work through all the implications of this in detail over time.

So it was not really a question of why did I want to become a psychotherapist, as if that were the explanation of why I did become a psychotherapist, because the desire to be an individual therapist and the action of becoming one were all part of phase 3, and happened more or less at the same time. Until I actually became an individual psychotherapist, I did not really want to be one at all. By the time I wanted to be a one-to-one therapist, I actually was one. I was thrown into being a therapist.

How did I become a Psychotherapist?

It all started with going to see a play. The play was 'Paradise Now', when it was put on by the Living Theatre at the Roundhouse in June 1969. This was an extraordinary play, which was partly scripted and partly improvised, and the improvised bits took up most of the time and involved the audience a great deal, either by the players coming into the audience, or by the audience coming on to the stage. It was highly political, but also had a spiritual aspect to it, mainly based on the Kabbalah and Tantra.

> The revolution of which the play speaks is the beautiful, nonviolent anarchist revolution. The purpose of the play is to lead to a state of being in which nonviolent revolutionary action is possible.
>
> (Rostagno, 1970)

Joseph Chaikin once said: 'The Becks perform that special function which very few books and movies, some love affairs and great losses do – they can actually change your life' (Chaikin, 1968). Well, I don't know how many people that is true for, but I am certainly one of them.

B NOW

I went with two friends who were also poets, Ulli McCarthy and Keith Musgrove. One of the lines in the play was 'Form a cell', so we thought we would. My loft had just been opened up, so we could meet there. We formed a group called B NOW, the B standing for 'Best society humanly possible'. Some of the best bits in the play had been the actions, which often took the form of the things done in encounter groups or microlabs – for example, one was the flying, where players and members of the audience had to get up on to a platform on the stage, and dive off into the arms of the waiting people, arranged in two lines with arms joining the lines. 'Breathe. . . breathe. . . breathe. . . FLY!!' – I remember it so vividly still (Malina and Beck, 1971).

The meetings of B NOW all took the same basic form: part 1 was a series of non-verbal exercises, which went on for anything up to an hour (the exercises were devised at first by Keith Musgrove, who was working as a group leader at Centre 42 in Kensington, the first growth centre in London; and later by Rupert Cracknell and John Henzell, both of whom were art therapists); to open part 2 I would say 'All right: the revolution has happened; the world outside is just the way you always wanted it to be; what do we do now?' (we would go on from there into some very fascinating fantasies about Utopia, where we took nothing for granted about the way things had to be); and part 3 was the eating, where we all brought food and fed each other – the rule was that you must not feed yourself. This turned into a very sensual and delightful part of the meeting.

This was really my first experience of group work and, because it was my house we met in at first (although we went to others later), I could put in any of my own ideas that I wanted to; so in a sense I was a co-leader right from the start. Some of the experiences I had in that group stay with me today, and some of them were turned into poems, and it was an emotionally shaking thing to go through. The exercises often stirred up early traumas and were quite cathartic on occasion. My wife and parents-in-law and children (who lived downstairs) hated the group because of the strange noises (people crying, shouting, groaning, screaming and so on) coming from the group. That was the main reason why we met in other places later. It may have been partly due to this beginning that Neilma always disliked my involvement with group work and therapy.

This group went on for about 6 months, meeting almost every Friday night, and then it gradually died – fewer and fewer people came regularly, and it petered out altogether. I got interested in groups at that point – What made groups live and die' How did groups work exactly? What really happened in groups? So I started going to groups: I went to encounter groups, gestalt groups, psychodrama groups, Tavistock groups, psychosynthesis groups, T-groups, bioenergetic groups, movement groups – you name it, I did it. I read about groups, I studied groups. As a social psychologist, I was supposed to have read all the literature on groups, but I found I knew hardly anything, and in fact some of the best books on groups had not been written by then.

In the process of all this I came across the Association for Humanistic Psychology. This was an organisation that had only been created in this country in 1969, although it had originated in the USA in the early sixties. It existed to put across the theory and practice of just the kinds of groups I had been going to, at growth centres and elsewhere. The idea of a growth centre, I discovered, had come from humanistic psychology, as had the whole idea of having direct methods of developing human potential. So I found it very congenial, and invited myself to a committee meeting: within 2 years I was Chairperson.

It seemed to me that humanistic psychology was implicitly revolutionary, in that it was totally dedicated to the idea of freedom. It was quite scornful of the idea that therapy was about nurturing people or supporting people – it was all about enabling people to take personal power and take charge of their own lives. It was very sympathetic to the ideas in the play, and indeed some of the exercises in the play had been taken from humanistic psychology in the first place. And yet there was something very solid about humanistic psychology – it worked.

What had been happening to me in the groups I had been to was that I had taken enormous steps in self-discovery. The first thing I discovered was that I was completely out of touch with my feelings – I really did not know I had such things, still less what they were. I remember how at one of the first encounter groups I went to, at one point the leader said: 'Let's just go round and see how we are feeling. How are you feeling right now?' When it came to my turn, I didn't know; I just had no idea of how to answer the question. If it happened now, and I had the same feelings, I would say 'I feel blocked', but I just did not have that vocabulary in those days.

The real self

The first clear and definite feeling I came up with in that first year was anger – I learned how to be angry, and how to express anger. The second feeling I discovered was grief – I cried and cried – I remember crying for 45 minutes about how sad it was, all the tears I had never shed! Later came other feelings, such as love, hurt, neediness and fear. Later still came the ability to open myself up to another person's feelings, and be intimate with them.

With the healing of the split between thinking and feeling came, one time in a group following a cathartic experience, a sense of being a whole person, of seeing people quite straight and undistorted. This only lasted for about half an hour, but it was something quite new, and I sensed that it was important for me. Later I had this experience again and again, as other splits were healed, and I started to label it as an experience of getting in touch with the real self.

The idea of the real self is very important in humanistic psychology, and it is always tied to actual experience, rather than being just a theoretical construct. I have written about it at some length elsewhere (Rowan, 1983). It is the result of healing splits in the personality, and of the integration of the person which results from that. I have seen it happen many times in groups, and it is a marvellous experience to participate in in any way. The person can go round the group and say something to each person, and each of these interactions is completely unique and appropriate – no clichés, no old tapes playing, just fresh and direct perception and communication.

One of the most confusing things about the whole business was that in the growth movement there was this great emphasis on autonomy – on moving from other support to self-support. Gestalt therapy was particularly strong on this, and I loved gestalt therapy. Fritz Perls (1970) was the great facilitator of autonomy. Now I was great on autonomy, which to me was another name for freedom – I had specialised in autonomy, I was brilliant at autonomy, and so leapt at this and loved it. The whole idea of the real self even promised more autonomy. It was only later that I discovered that there is a pathology of autonomy, the same as there is a pathology of dependence, and I had been feeding my pathology as much as doing genuinely good work in self-development. Autonomy is good, but emotional nourishment is important, too. With real intimacy I could get both of these things in a proper balance. This realisation took a long time to dawn.

Of course all this led to an increasing interest in psychotherapy, although I still saw this as best done through group work. I was very suspicious of one-to-one therapy, as an expensive, middle-class, establishment sort of thing. I was also very suspicious of the Tavistock type of group, which I went to in 1970. I wrote up my experiences in that group in a series of 38 poems, which I then delivered as a scientific paper on groups at the Annual Conference of the Occupational Psychology Section of the British Psychological Society, and which later became most of one chapter in my book *The Power of the Group* (1976b). This group, it seemed to me, was all about reinforcing the power of authority to put people down and keep them where they are. But what interested me was the process of change. How do people change? That was the question.

Radical psychology

At the same time my intellectual interests had expanded and taken a new turn. I still pursued humanistic psychology, which was my positive path, so to speak, but now I also started taking a parallel negative path. I went in 1970 to the first Radical Psychology conference, organised by Keith Paton at Keele University, and out of that came a magazine called *Red Rat*. I helped to produce the first issue, and stayed with it until it was overtaken by a better radical psychology magazine, *Humpty Dumpty*, which I later helped to originate and produce. I got involved in other activities – some of us produced a big pamphlet called *Rat, Myth and Magic*, and started to invade and militantly disrupt various psychology conferences. We were very critical of the way in which academic psychology misled and demeaned people, reducing them to the level of stooges or inanimate things in order to study them. We felt that no human psychology could be developed in that way, and that it was all a big confidence trick.

I remember the excitement I felt on picking up, on a second-hand bookstall, the original American edition of Charles Hampden-Turner's (1971) book *Radical Man*. This was an account of what personal growth was and how it took place, right within the boundaries of humanistic psychology as I understood it. Later I met Charles, and liked him very much, although we have never seen eye-to-eye on the question of patriarchy. What the book said was that the personal and the political are one – that personal growth leads to political radicalism. The book also made it clear that authenticity in the existential sense (a combination of self-respect and self-enactment) was the major factor in any real self-development; it was the key to where one was going and also the key to getting there. The strong feeling of the real self which I had had in groups connected up with the philosophical idea of authenticity, and I felt a real connection there – that authenticity was one place where the personal and the political came together. It was not possible to be authentic and experience alienation or anomie at the same time. This brought together the two paths (the positive path of personal growth and the negative path of radical psychology) in a way that I found very satisfying.

At first all this apparently made no difference to my daily life. In 1970 I moved to a better job in market research, as Director of Psychological Research for one of the biggest companies. But the thing was working beneath the surface, and it came to the top when the company asked me to conduct an investigation of the validity of a big survey that was on a yearly contract and one of the biggest sources of regular income. My answers were so disturbing (showing that the figures we published were in certain ways seriously misleading) that the crucial lines in my report were reworded by the Managing Director and buried in a remote part of the report, not being mentioned in any of the summaries issued to the client. After some discussion of this, I resigned.

The year 1971 was an extraordinary one for me. I left my job, and did not take up another one, but went freelance. I got a contract to write a four-volume textbook of social psychology. I left my wife and went to live with a revolutionary woman in a political commune in Holloway, and wrote a series of poems about the experience (Rowan, 1973). I spent a good deal of the summer doing street theatre, where I played the role of Mr Busy Bigness, in a piece called 'The Allo Allo Allo Show: An Everyday Story of Ghetto Folk'. I went to more groups and found out more about myself. I was investing myself very intensely in my own life. Mid-life crisis, here I was!

Phase 2

At the end of 1971 the political group I had been working with fell apart, and I broke up with the woman I had been with. This was an extremely painful time for me. I went back to my wife, and the whole story which is unfolded in my book *The Horned God* began. I started to take a much more intense interest in group work as such. It seemed to be a natural development, as if one chapter had closed and another one opened. I started leading groups, just following the methods I had picked up bit by bit, as we all used to do in those days, because there were no training courses to speak of. My first paid workshop was at Kaleidoscope in 1972, and was specifically on creativity: since then I have done many workshops around that topic, and still regard it as one of the central issues in all growth and self-development.

It is marvellous to see people in these groups dropping their assumptions about what they are capable of, and finding their own creative centre. I find this one of the greatest satisfactions in the whole field, just of seeing people blossom and come forth. You can see their whole body change and become more open, more energised, more relaxed, more approachable. Very often there is an experience of ecstasy, and I myself had more and more peak experiences around this time. I found I could even lay myself open to experiences of ecstasy quite deliberately, along the lines suggested by Joanna Field (1952) in *A Life of One's Own*. It was as if I had hit bottom and could now start coming up again.

This is perhaps a suitable point to say that I regarded then, and still do now, personal growth, counselling and psychotherapy as all really the same thing under different labels. They are all based on the twin ideas of unhindering and unfolding. Unhindering is about removing the blocks that people have put up in the way of contacting their own centre, and unfolding is about encouraging people to allow that centre to take over and to follow their own process of self-development with confidence and trust.

Along the way the issues around existential choice arise again and again – as Maslow (1973) used to say, at every moment we have a choice between the joys of safety and the joys of growth; and as Mahrer (1978) was to say later, it is all a question of doing justice to our deeper potentials, and really choosing to do that.

So in the second phase of my development into a psychotherapist, I was mixing with highly experienced and trained people, some of whom were certainly quite radical, and learning as much from them as possible. One of the most exciting events I attended was in 1973, when I went to the AHP Annual Meeting in Montreal. Here I met some of the people I had been reading about and admiring, and actually saw them in action. In the same year I also went to an international workshop on co-counselling, where I met Harvey Jackins, and again learnt a great deal about myself. I was really getting in among a stimulating crowd.

The Council of Group Studies was an interesting group of such people, who decided in the end to start up a Diploma course. This was adopted by the Polytechnic of North London, under the able and continually innovative leadership of John Southgate, and I duly joined this course and eventually (in 1975) got my Diploma in Applied Behavioural Science. This covered group work, individual counselling, theory and research, organisation development and so on. This was my first introduction to one-to-one work, which took the form of co-counselling, because that was more politically acceptable than any other form. In the same year I had an important breakthrough in therapy, all about my mother, which I wrote up (Rowan, 1975; see chapter 19) in *Self and Society* a little later, and which made a big difference to my whole life. I could now relate to women as real people.

At this point I wrote a book called *Ordinary Ecstasy: Humanistic Psychology in Action,* which put a lot of what I had discovered into print and made a sort of milestone in my progress so far. In a way it put me on the map as a person seriously interested in the whole area of personal growth, counselling and psychotherapy. I had already written a critical chapter on research methodology for a book edited by Nigel Armistead (one of the other people on *Humpty Dumpty*) which came out from Penguin (Armistead, 1974).

Red Therapy

At the same time (1973–1978) I was working intensively with a self-help group called Red Therapy, which was dedicated to finding out more about the relationship between therapy and politics. It had started as a result of a meeting put on by Quaesitor, then the biggest growth centre in Europe, and was an interesting example of personal growth and radicalism coming together once again. In 1978 it produced a big pamphlet about its work, which I helped to write and put together. I learned a great deal in this group, both about myself and about the political implications of psychotherapy. Many of the lessons of this group were written up later in the excellent book by Sheila Ernst and Lucy Goodison, *In Our Own Hands* (1981).

What I finally learned from this group was that personal change and political change could both be worked on in the same group. Often it seems that the growth person is opposed to the political person, and the politico is opposed to the groupie – in the USA they called it the conflict between the Wheelies and the Feelies. I also learned the same thing in another organisation that existed at about the same time, called Alternative Socialism. Here again we found that the two things could be combined, rather than having to be contrasted with one another. Of course the women's movement had discovered this for themselves long ago, but men were rather left out of this, and had to make their own (our own) discoveries.

So at the end of this phase I had run the full gamut of group work, and had made many discoveries there. I was by now a fully developed and functioning encounter group leader, specialising in work on creativity, sex roles and subpersonalities. I was also a researcher, now having seen that the old paradigm of empirical research most used in psychology actually reduced people to something less than human, so that anything that might be discovered in that way could not really be about human beings at all. In 1977 I initiated the New Paradigm Research Group to push forward this insight, and this later led to the production of a big book (Reason and Rowan, 1981).

Phase 3

But it was in 1977 that an important turning point came, when I interviewed Bill Swartley for a special primal issue of *Self and Society.* It was as a result of that meeting that I discovered that he was just about to start a training course in primal integration therapy in London; I promptly joined it, and found it an absolutely extraordinary experience. The course was a very intensive one, with one weekend every 2 weeks; these later became residential, which made them even more intense. On the Friday night there would be a lecture or seminar, where we would examine some theoretical points, do tests, look at a case or whatever, usually with written notes supplied by Swartley. The Saturday and Sunday would be simply an experiential group, where we would work spontaneously with whatever came up out of the initial go-round. As well as seeing Swartley in action himself, plus guest leaders such as William Emerson, Jim Diamond and Paco, we worked with each other in small groups, learning how to do it ourselves. I did some deep primal work which was very important to me, including a lot of work on my father, and perhaps most of all working through my Oedipal material in a vivid, face-to-face way.

Primal integration therapy is a holistic approach, which says that the four functions that Jung speaks of – sensing, feeling, thinking and intuiting – all have to be dealt with and done justice to in any therapy worthy of the name. So we all had to work in all four of these modes, learning how to use body work, cathartic work, analytic work and transpersonal work, all in their proper place at their proper time. It was a deep and far-reaching discipline which put tremendous demands upon all of us. I have described it at length elsewhere (Rowan, 1988).

This training seemed to put together everything I knew and give it a coherent framework. As a result of this training, I felt ready now to work on my own. But I was working hard at other things, first of all as a freelance market researcher, then spending a year as a researcher for the British Psychological Society located in the Occupational Psychology Department at Birkbeck College, and then another year and a half heading up the Behavioural Science Unit at the Greater London Council's headquarters in County Hall. In 1978 the radical psychotherapist Giora Doron had the idea of starting up a psychotherapy training centre running a 3-year part-time course, and very kindly asked me to take part in running seminars for it. This I did, and quickly found myself more and more involved in the Institute which it later became. But it was still difficult to have more than a very minor private practice as a psychotherapist, because of the demands of my work and other interests. For example, I was on the committee of the Association for Humanistic Psychology, and also helping to produce the magazine *Achilles Heel* at this time, as I still am.

It was also at this time that I was meeting and going out with Sue, and at the end of 1978 I moved in with her. This relationship has proved to be one of the most important parts of my life, and Sue has encouraged me enormously at all the turning points that came from then on. This was helped very much by another breakthrough which came about in my own therapy in the primal integration group.

What happened was that I seemed to go back down the channel of time to a fork in the road where I had made a decision about how to live my life. It was as if I had decided to do without other people, and to make it on my own. It was a lonely, thumbsucking sort of a decision, and had led to what I called earlier 'the pathology of autonomy'. It seemed incredibly early, as if it were the first decision I had ever made, not to rely on anyone else. And I just went back to that fork in the road, and took the other path. The phrase that came into my mind was 'I don't want to be alone', and it even came with a tune – an old tune from the 1930s called 'We don't want to go to bed'. As I came back up, clutching as it were this tune, it became louder and louder, and I could feel as it were relays clicking and connections making and unmaking themselves all through my brain and my body – as if the implications of that changed decision were working their way through the system. And when I came back from that weekend I found that my relationship with Sue was much more meaningful; that I could let her in to my deepest places in a way which I had not known was possible before. I could experience intimacy with her.

This may not sound very impressive. What is so new or remarkable about intimacy? But for me it was an enormous change. It was like opening up a whole other side of my brain and body, so to speak. The ability to let go of my fixed boundaries, which I first found with Sue, later extended to others too, and I found it extremely valuable in my work as a therapist. I could actually allow myself to know what other people were feeling, from the inside, as it were. So that when later I discovered a form of psychotherapy which necessitated just this opening of boundaries (Mahrer, 1986) I was able to take it on and practise it with relatively little difficulty.

But let us get back to the story and see how all this fitted in with my becoming a psychotherapist.

The thing happens

The big breakthrough took place at the end of 1980, when the GLC decided it no longer needed a Behavioural Science Unit, and I was suddenly out of a job. This was a very painful experience, and the actual sacking took place in a hurtful way. I developed a bad back which ached so much that I could hardly walk. I went to my psychotherapy group with my bad back, and we discovered that I felt as if I had been stabbed in the back, and also that I had a burden of responsibilities which also weighed heavily on my back. So I dealt with both of these things, and my back went back to normal.

I wrote off for job after job, but nothing seemed to turn up, and it became clear that my age (55) was a problem. I did not fit neatly into any of the pay scales that people seemed to have. In January I spent more than I earned; in February I spent more than I earned; in March I spent more than I earned. But in April I turned the corner. I had found that the absence of a job had freed up my time so that I could go into psychotherapy full-time, and after one or two false starts this is exactly what happened. I took on more work with the Institute, starting to run groups and do supervision as well as leading the seminars on humanistic psychology. So now I was acting as a full-time therapist, and also teaching psychotherapy. I had arrived. It was 1981.

When did I become a Psychotherapist?

I became a psychotherapist proper in November 1980, when the tenant downstairs moved out, and I took over his room and turned it into a therapy room. It still had the old wardrobe and chest of drawers in there, but I installed a mattress and a futon and two chairs and some big cushions and a tennis racquet and a baby's bottle and some massage oil and some boxes of tissues, and I was in business. Before that I had taken individual sessions in various hired premises, but this was now my own place, and I began to see more people more regularly.

It seems that I was already regarded as a therapist by many people, so it did not make any great ripples in my circle of acquaintances. It was more or less expected. It was as if the only question was 'What took you so long?'.

As an individual therapist, I did all the same things I had done in groups. In the kind of groups I was most involved with, much of the work is done with one person at a time, with the rest of the group looking on and sometimes participating in various ways. So there was no fundamental difference between working with one person in a group and working with one person on their own.

In theoretical terms there is an important point here, in that it is generally laid down that people shall not practise any form of therapy that they have not been through themselves. I had not been through the long-term one-to-one therapy that I was now offering. But it seems that there are exceptions to every rule, and I found no difficulty in adapting what I was doing in the way required. I had certainly done several years of work on myself in co-counselling, which is a one-to-one method, and I suppose this must have helped too, although the assumptions are significantly different. I do not really know why it worked so well, but I seemed to find that I could do it adequately. However, there are some qualifications, which we shall come to shortly.

One of the main ways in which I learned more about psychotherapy was by teaching it, through seminars, group leadership and the supervision of trainees. In a way there is no quicker way of learning something than by teaching it. As I learned the lessons, I tried to pass them on again. In this way my 1983 book came about, which was all about how to be a humanistic counsellor or psychotherapist. People keep telling me that it is a very practical and useful book, and it was certainly very useful for me to write it.

However, it came home to me after a while that there were certain clients I did not like or do very well with. It seemed that I did not do well with them because they did not respond to the dramatic techniques that I prefer. They seemed unable or unwilling to take up more active roles, and insisted on staying passive and being the victim. Now of course this was not their fault, and I began to wonder if the reason I was so bad with them was that I had not myself experienced the extended one-to-one therapy that I was trying to practise. I seriously considered going into some very orthodox therapy just to see whether this were the case. It seemed that a Jungian analyst might be the most suitable.

So that is what I did, and I am still carrying this on. It is too early to say whether this is the answer to the problem, however.

I suppose one of the main changes that took place between starting to be a therapist and now is that I acquired, from 1982 onwards a new appreciation of spirituality. I began to acknowledge myself as a spiritual being with a path to be followed. This has led to an increase in the extent to which I work in a transpersonal way, using symbols rather than words. I actually believe that this ability to use symbols and to live and breathe symbols is what is meant by the phrase 'Opening the third eye'. It really is a different way of perceiving the world. I found Ken Wilber the best guide into the whole field of spirituality, and have continued to gain benefit from his thinking, although I do not believe that his map is quite complete or adequate.

But I combined this with my continuing interest in sexual politics, and what came out was a deep appreciation and some understanding of paganism. The old religion of paganism holds the Great Goddess to be primary, and links her with the earth and with the underworld. I particularly liked the approach of Monica Sjöö (Sjöö and Mor, 1987), who also links feminism with paganism. Seen in this way, many of the usual transpersonal symbols are unwittingly patriarchal: for example, the identification of height with spirituality and depth with the primitive unconscious is a patriarchal distortion of the earlier conception of spirituality being essentially a downward movement. I have written about this at length elsewhere (Rowan, 1987).

In the earliest days when I started to practise psychotherapy people came through word of mouth, and they still do. One of the biggest differences between what I was doing then and what I am doing now is that I have much greater ability to empathise and get inside another person's experience. I also think I have become more adventurous and imaginative, as I have explained in some detail elsewhere (Rowan, 1987b).

What Sustains Me as a Psychotherapist?

I would need much more sustaining if I were to become the kind of psychotherapist who sees client after client all day every day. But I do not need much sustaining because my practice is very varied in all sorts of ways. On Mondays at the moment I start writing at about 5.15 a.m., have a bath and breakfast, have one 2-hour session in the morning, then a staff meeting at the Institute, then a seminar there on humanistic psychology, then a 2-hour session in the afternoon, and a 1½-hour session in the evening. Except that once every 3 weeks I have someone from Swansea who comes for a 3-hour session in the morning. On Thursdays after my writing stint I have a lecture for the London University Diploma in Psychology, followed by two 1-hour clients, and some reading, followed by a 2-hour session. On Fridays I generally spend some time reading and writing, and going somewhere with Sue. My other days are equally varied; usually I spend most of the weekend with Sue, but sometimes there is a group workshop at the weekend as well. Then there are committee meetings and magazine collective meetings to fit in once a month or so.

Another thing that sustains me is the feeling of success I often have, when something goes well. I can really see people changing in front of my very eyes, and that is very cheering. I remember one woman I worked with for a long time had a very dark undertone to her complexion, as if there were a sort of greyness under the surface. I said to myself that I would really believe she had got somewhere when this greyness disappeared. And sure enough, when she had worked through a particularly horrific and very early bit of her personal trauma, her whole complexion changed, quite dramatically and obviously. But more common are changes of mood, where people feel much more relaxed and able to take more risks in life.

What I do not like, however, are experiences of failure, where I go on week after week with someone and see no change at all, or where the person balks at the same point time after time. My worst times have been with very quiet people who insist on taking the passive position all the time – they have an internal persecutor, but will not take the position of the persecutor, insisting on taking the position of the victim. Nowadays I try not to take on any clients such as these, because it seems to me that some other therapist might be able to do something much better with them. But perhaps if my project, mentioned above, of going into therapy myself works out, as I hope it will, I may be able to handle these clients as well.

Something else that sustains me is my membership of the International Primal Association, which was founded by Bill Swartley and others. I read the journal and newsletter of that association, and get tapes of important presentations, and this makes me feel that I am part of something bigger – a network of people with similar interests to my own, with whom I can share my practice. It is very sad, however, that not only Swartley, but also David Freundlich, whose ideas seemed very similar to my own, have both now died.

Another thing that sustains me is my membership of the Association of Humanistic Psychology Practitioners. This was something I helped to start in 1980, and it is the professional group within the Association for Humanistic Psychology. I have learned a great deal from this group over the years, starting with the Self and Peer Assessment programme initiated by John Heron and carrying on through various seminars and workshops – perhaps most of all through my work on the membership committee, which put me in touch with the work of most of the best people working today, and led to my involvement with the accreditation of counsellors and supervisors in the British Association for Counselling, and to my work with the Rugby Conference on the whole future of psychotherapy in this country.

Perhaps the thing that sustains me most is my work at the Institute. It was set up as a radical course, concerned not only with the technicalities of therapy but also with the social and political context within which all counselling and psychotherapy are carried out. We make sure that students are exposed to all the issues around exploitation, alienation and oppression, not only on the global scale but also in the nitty-gritty details of therapy itself. One of the prime areas where this becomes obvious is sexism – the oppression of women by men. My own work in sexual politics (Rowan, 1987a) becomes very relevant here. Therapists can put down women just as much as can any other authority figure – and even more effectively, in some cases, due to the closeness of the influence. Alice Miller (1985) has written eloquently about the 'poisonous pedagogy' that can take place in the therapy session, reproducing and enforcing the oppressive relationships that all too often occur in childhood. Hopefully the students we turn out from the Institute will not repeat these patterns. Racism, of course, introduces similar issues.

But because I recognise that the personal is political, I see all therapy as liberating. To the extent that a client can be enabled to work through to the stage of getting in touch with the real self, he or she will begin to see through the sham of roles and masks, and insist on authentic relationships. This is bad news for oppressors, because all oppression is based on mystification. Also because the outcome of any adequate therapy is autonomy and the taking of personal power, it cannot be used to manipulate. There is no way that manipulation can produce genuine autonomy – and if by some miracle it did, the first task of that autonomy would be to confront the manipulator.

Of course the liberation that comes through psychotherapy or counselling is slow and small in scale. But it is very sure, because it produces irreversible changes in people. I believe that owing to the availability of co-counselling and self-help groups, any time it needed to spread more quickly and speed up the process, this could be achieved.

I do not try to conduct my own therapy through my clients, and would feel that to be quite wrong. I have my own therapist, who I see twice a week, and also a supervisor, who I see regularly on a peer-sharing basis. It is essential to me to have somewhere to go with my distress or my lack of understanding, and be enabled to work through it and come out with some better awareness of what has been going on.

My main relationship is with Sue, and this sustains me considerably. I do not discuss the details of my cases with her, but I can exclaim about any particular triumphs or trials that I have had in the day, and she will listen sympathetically and share in whatever happens. And of course I listen to her day in the same way. The only strain is over time, when she has complained every now and then that we do not have enough time together, but we have that reasonably well sorted out at the moment.

I see myself as being a therapist for the rest of my life, because I am 62 now and this is a job that can be done even at an advanced age – it might even be that there is an advantage in being older for this kind of work. There is a feeling of stability and security that is quite useful in therapy, and which comes very naturally from an older person. But at the same time I want to make a bigger proportion of my income from writing, because writing is something that can be done at even older ages, and gives much more flexibility about where to live. I would like to run a live encounter group on television, but no one has yet asked me to do so.

Psychotherapy seems a good choice for me, especially in the varied way in which I carry it out. It gives me enormous interest and satisfaction. I only wish I could do more groups and less one-to-one work. But groups are much harder to set up and run, and I cannnot bear the hassle of organising them myself, so I can only do them when someone else organises them for me. I find groups much more stimulating and much more satisfying than one-to-one work; usually in my groups a lot of things happen and people change a lot, and social issues come up much more. I particularly like the more extended residential group of 5 days or so, where people can really get down to deeper pieces of work on themselves with open-ended time to go through them fully, and other people to help out in various ways. And recently I have been co-leading groups with Sue, which has been marvellous and even better than running them on my own. It has been even more satisfying to see her growing and developing as a leader under my very eyes, and some of her comments and questions have deepened my own practice.

Implications for Other Psychotherapists

The one main thing I would like people to learn is a negative one – do not put all your eggs in one basket. I hate the narrow kind of therapist who was trained in one school, analysed by one analyst, and practises in one mode. I hate even more the narrow kind of 'therapist' who has never done any self-therapy at all. I very much like the open kind of therapist who has had many teachers and tried many modes, and has then settled on his or her own combination.

This is not just a personal preference – there is a theoretical rationale for it too. It is that, as Freud said, therapists can only operate up to the limit of their own resistances. These resistances tend to be strongest in the areas that have not been reached by the type of therapy they did in their training. So when they get clients bringing up material that they did not cover in their training, they distort it and treat it as something else, which must be ineffectual.

It seems crystal clear to me that the most important influence on any therapist is the personal therapy they have experienced themselves, on themselves and for themselves; the second most important influence is the supervision they have had; and the third most important influence is the clients they have had. However, this third one can be crucially and sometimes cruelly limited by the first two.

I would argue that every therapist who works in depth must be able to handle infant stuff when it comes up, must be able to handle perinatal stuff when it comes up, must be able to handle prenatal stuff when it comes up, must be able to handle spiritual stuff when it comes up. Many training courses avoid some of these areas, and the beginning therapist will just have to get them somewhere else, or face being inadequately equipped.

Similarly, many training courses have quite an inadequate coverage of group work, and the aspiring therapist will probably need to go elsewhere for work on psychodrama, encounter, T-groups and so on. This work is needed to produce the kind of authentic human being which I think the therapist had better be. It has often been pointed out (Marmor, 1974) that certain problems, as for example insensitive talkativeness, are never going to come out in one-to-one therapy, and need a group to become at all accessible. So I feel very strongly that a good training course absolutely needs to cover group work in some detail. If an otherwise good course is not adequate in this respect, the aspiring therapist is just going to have to go elsewhere for such training and experience.

On the whole, the therapists I know myself are very conscientious in this respect, and do continue to work on themselves and expose themselves to new ideas and new experiences. But there should be more facilities for established therapists and counsellors to be properly taught about the new work as it comes along. Probably today there are more therapists who have never enabled their clients to go back to their early experiences of before 5 years of age than of any other kind, and yet all the implications of the work that has come along in the past few years, both in psychoanalysis and in the humanistic approaches, is that clients often need to go further back than that if we want to see substantial changes in the basic character structure.

Further, it seems to me that any course that avoids any discussion of the social context is going to let its students down. There is so much opportunity for manipulation by psychotherapists that it is crucially important to make sure that students are aware of the necessity for this not to happen in their work. I believe that psychotherapy is a political act, and has to be taken seriously as a political act if it is not ultimately to do more harm than good. I have elsewhere (Rowan, 1983) gone into this in some detail, in a chapter entitled 'Listening with the fourth ear'. This ear – the ear for the social and political aspects of the work – is more and more necessary each year. Good psychotherapy must do justice to this.

Possibly the biggest challenge is the spiritual aspect of the work. If we can take Wilber and his co-workers (1986) seriously, we have to devote much more attention than we normally do to this type of approach. The argument is that people operate on something like nine different developmental levels, some of which are completed, some of which are still in process, and some of which are not as yet visible at all. My own belief at present is that anyone who wants to be a good psychotherapist has to have his or her own spiritual discipline to follow. Otherwise there are important and crucial human areas he or she cannot help their clients with. This is to cheat people of part of their humanity, and it will not do.

As I go around the world, I often find myself introducing people to the idea of self and peer assessment (Heron, 1981), which entails watching people do short sessions of 15–20 minutes using their own form of psychotherapy or counselling. I am struck by the almost uniformly dismal level of expertise that I see and hear. I have come to believe that most psychotherapy and counselling that goes on in the world is pretty bad. I want it to be better. But it seems obvious to me that unless psychotherapists and counsellors are continually and quite humbly working on themselves to improve and develop further as professionals no improvement will happen. As far as I can see, the reason for the lack of quality is that people do not really question themselves very much, once the training years are over. Kottler (1986) remarks on the way in which a depressing self-satisfaction seems to settle over so many therapists, such that they become blind and self-deceiving.

As can be seen from the narrative just completed, I had my first important breakthrough in therapy after 5 years of working on myself, and other major breakthroughs in the 5 years following. From that point on I was what Rogers (1961) calls a 'fully functioning person' and my spiritual path and growth became more important than my therapy. It seems to me that therapy really does take this long – something like a 10-year stint. Also I think the experience of Jenny James (1983), who had almost continuous access to psychotherapy for long periods, and who still took 10 years about it, bears out this view.

Obviously, no training course could take this long, and this means that any psychotherapist, no matter how well trained, must continue to engage in personal growth work for a considerable time after the end of any training course. What I am arguing for is a substantial change in the way this further work is regarded – not as further deepening in the same method, but rather an extension into new and different methods and approaches that were not covered, or hardly covered, in the original training. Only in this way can we get the fully trained, fully functioning psychotherapists that clients so desperately need.

References

ARMISTEAD, N. (Ed) (1974). *Reconstructing Social Psychology*. Harmondsworth: Penguin.

CHAIKIN, J. (1968). A play on the stage *Village Voice*, Oct. 17.

ERNST, S. and GOODISON, L. (1981). *In Our Own Hands*. London: The Women's Press.

FIELD, J. (1952). *A Life of One's Own*. Harmondsworth: Penguin.

HAMPDEN-TURNER, C. (1971). *Radical Man*. London: Duckworth.

HERON, J. (1981). Self and peer assessment for managers. In: T. Boydell and M. Pedler (Eds), *Management Self-development*. Aldershot: Gower.

JAMES, J. (1983). *Room to Breathe*. London: Caliban.

KOTTLER, J.A. (1986). *On Being a Therapist*. San Francisco: Jossey-Bass.

MAHRER, A.R. (1978). *Experiencing*. New York: Brunner/Mazel.

MAHRER, A.R. (1986). *Therapeutic Experiencing*. New York: W.W. Norton.

MALINA, J. and BECK, J. (1971). *Paradise Now: Collective Creation of the Living Theatre*. New York: Vintage Books.

MARMOR, J. (1974). *Psychiatry in Transition*. London: Butterworths.

MASLOW, A.H. (1973). *The Farther Reaches of Human Nature*. Harmondsworth: Penguin.

MILLER, A. (1985). *Thou shalt not be Aware*. London: Pluto Press.

PERLS, F. (1970). Four lectures. In: J. Fagan and I.L. Shepherd (Eds), *Gestalt Therapy Now*. Palo Alto: Science & Behaviour Books.

REASON, P. and ROWAN, J. (Eds)(1981). *Human Inquiry: A Sourcebook of New Paradigm Research*. Chichester: John Wiley.

ROGERS, C.R. (1961). *On Becoming a Person*. London: Constable.

ROSTAGNO, A. (1970). *We, the Living Theatre*. New York: Ballantine Books.

ROWAN, J. (1973). *The Clare Poems*. London: Writers Forum.

ROWAN, J. (1975). A growth episode. *Self and Society* 3(11), 20–27.

ROWAN, J. (1976a). *Ordinary Ecstasy*. London: RKP.

ROWAN, J. (1976b). *The Power of the Group*. London: Davis-Poynter.

ROWAN, J. (1983). *The Reality Game*. London: RKP.

ROWAN, J. (1987a). *The Horned God*. London: RKP.

ROWAN, J. (1987b) Siding with the client. In W. Dryden (Ed.), *Key Cases in Psychotherapy*. Beckenham: Croom Helm.

ROWAN, J. (1988) Primal integration. In J. Rowan and W. Dryden (Eds), *Innovative Therapy in Britain*. London: Harper & Row.

SJÖÖ, M. and MOR, B. (1987). *The Great Cosmic Mother: Rediscovering the Religion of the Earth*. New York: Harper & Row.

VAUGHAN, F. (1986). *The Inward Arc*. Boston: New Science Library.

WILBER, K. ENGLER, J. and BROWN, D.P. (1986). *Transformations of Consciousness*. Boston: New Science Library

Part II
Humanistic Psychology

The first article here – 'Is the human potential movement narcissistic?' – was written at a time when there was a good deal of criticism floating around, particularly by some very capable psychoanalytic writers, of humanistic psychology generally. This article was circulated privately, and seemed so popular that I put it forward to a journal. I felt it was worth while to cast a much more more critical eye on the pretensions and assumptions of these writers than seemed usually to be done. On re-reading the article now, it seems eminently sensible, the only thing needing alteration being the price of a weekend group, then £20 and nowadays £60 or £65.

The next article – 'On being irrational' – started as a one-page handout which I produced about 1978 and gave to people attending my workshops etc. Then later Craig Newnes saw it somewhere and asked me to rewrite it with particular reference to cognitive therapy, which I happily did.

The third article – 'Hegel and self-actualisation' – was actually written in 1979, and the first draft of it was published in *Self and Society*. I also did a talk based on it at the Esalen Institute in the following year; but later I thought it was rather better than being left in the files, and rewrote some of it and submitted it to one journal which turned it down, a second journal which turned it down, and a third journal which I am still waiting to hear from.

The article after that – 'Nine humanistic heresies' – was also based on something earlier, which appeared originally in *Self and Society*. Tom Greening saw it, and suggested that I write an updated version, so I did, and think it turned out rather well. It is one of my favourite pieces.

The brief article called 'Two humanistic psychologies or one?' was written in genuine puzzlement, and Tom Greening sent it round to a number of other people who might be interested. As a result of that, an issue of the *Journal of Humanistic Psychology* came out with replies from Ken Wilber, Rollo May, Alvin Mahrer, Maureen O'Hara and Donald Michael.

This was fascinating, although of course I could not have waited for the replies before completing my own manuscript. It turned out that there were many different ways of looking at this question.

The final article in this section - 'The self: One or many' - was one of several I wrote while waiting for my book on subpersonalities to come out. I think it is the best of them, and it makes a good introduction to the whole question. It provoked a letter in *The Psychologist* from a philospher who objected to my using the word 'self' at all, on the grounds that there was no such thing. I replied, saying that although the title of the article might make it seem as if I were talking about the self, I was actually talking about the person, which is rather different. He never came back on that one, so I don't know if he was impressed. It has been pointed out to me that the whole idea of subpersonalities is very much in line with the recent ideas on constructivism and postmodernism, but I did not know that at the time.

Chapter 2
Is the Human Potential
Movement Narcissistic?

One of the things we are often accused of is being too self-indulgent. John Southgate (Southgate and Randall, 1978) once said that AHP really stood for the Association of Hedonistic Pursuits (hedonism is the philosophy of personal pleasure). It is an accusation which I believe deserves an answer. It really can give offence to political people, or to people with severe practical problems, when they see people paying £20 for a weekend with some such title as 'Turning Inwards', or 'Loving Your Body' or 'Integrative Holistic Macrosynthesis'. So what is the answer we can give?

The first step is obviously to get clear what we are talking about. There seem to be six things that are worth distinguishing: self-love; egotism; selfishness (exclusive); selfishness (inclusive); self-improvement; and self-actualisation.

Self-love

This is a general feeling of being convinced of one's own worth. It is also often called self-esteem, self-respect or having a good self-image or self-concept. This is a healthy thing, and most people in the helping professions would be only too pleased if their clients had more of it. It is one of the things that is aimed at by Rogerians when they aim at reducing the difference between the present self-image and the ideal self-image; by gestaltists when they aim at enabling people to give more love to themselves; by transactional analysis (TA) people when they aim at putting people in touch with their internal positive nurturing parent; by psychosynthesis people when they aim at putting people in touch with the transpersonal self. In all these instances, it is felt to be very desirable to help people to see that they don't need to be addicted to sucking love

From J. Rowan (1979). Is the human potential movement narcissistic? *Self and Society* July/August, 11–14, with permission.

off other people. If they can give more love to themselves, they are better able to give it to others, and to accept it from others in a genuine way which does not feel like a burden and a danger, So this is an important one, and a very positive one. In so far as we are teaching or facilitating this kind of self-love, we are doing something of value.

Egotism

This is a general feeling of being convinced of one's own pre-eminence. It has a lot to do with pride, with an inflated self-image, with a kind of self-importance. It really seems as though no one in the world is quite as deserving of attention as me. There is usually a great deal of defensiveness about it, although it comes across more as smugness and self-satisfaction. When well-meaning people go in for ego-boosting, for telling their children 'You are better than the rest – you should be coming top', or telling their husbands 'You should have got that promotion, you're better than the person who got it' they are feeding egotism rather than self-love. Egotism always sees things in terms of better and worse; self-love does not. There is always something edgy about egotism – it is always having to prove itself all over again. This is not something which anyone in the growth movement is trying to foster, and Karen Horney in particular is very clear about what she calls the 'Pride System' and its dangers.

Selfishness (exclusive)

This is looking after one's own self-interest with blinkers on. This kind of selfishness can only see what is straight in front of it. It is as if the rest of the world somehow did not exist. It is impulsive – if I feel a feeling, I have to express it straight away, without any consideration for the circumstances. If I want something, I have to have it now, without considering any other priorities. If we define rationality as taking account of all those values of mine that are relevant to a situation, then this kind of selfishness is irrational. This is not something that is encouraged by any form of therapy known to me – in fact, they would all try to help the person exhibiting this to change in some way. Sometimes some people think that the feeling therapies foster this, but this is because they have not been into the feeling therapies themselves. It is a false belief.

Selfishness (inclusive)

This is looking after one's own self-interest without blinkers, letting in everything from inside and from outside. It means going after what I really want, but with complete openness to experience. At my best, I am in touch with all my relevant feelings and all my relevant values and all the relevant information, and I can then act spontaneously in whatever situation I find myself. This kind of spontaneity is the most rational action of which I am capable. I don't deny my interests, my needs, my wishes or my fantasies, but take all of them into account – rather than focusing on just one and pursuing that. (From this point of view, we can see that the 'rational economic man' of the economist is in fact highly irrational, because he is only taking into account one value, and setting all the others aside!) Every kind of therapy or counselling I know helps people to move in the direction of this inclusive kind of selfishness, and I think this is highly defensible and thoroughly OK. The world would be a better place if there were more of this open and all-embracing selfishness around.

Self-improvement

This is about the attainment of long-range goals. It has to do with good self-management. How do I set goals for myself? How do I get the rewards I want to get? How do I avoid the traps I want to avoid? How do I acquire the skills I need to acquire? How can I be a good friend to myself? How can I make the best use of my time? This is a tricky area, because it can easily degenerate into a kind of self-separation, where one part of me is trying to improve another part of me – leading possibly to an unhealthy split in the personality. But if this can be avoided, self-improvement obviously makes sense at a commonsense level. Certainly someone who has been agoraphobic for 20 years, and starts to come out of it, would be well advised to go in for careful self-management, so as not to ask for trouble. John Heron says that it makes sense to talk of 'the directing self' as setting up projects – 'I must go on that workshop', 'I could take that course', 'Read that book' and so on. But there are certainly defensible and indefensible forms of self-improvement, and this is something that can do with careful scrutiny. If someone improves so as to be a better slavedriver, that would be a bad thing in my book. But on the whole, I think the human potential movement is a lot better in this area than a lot of other people one might go to in a search for self-improvement.

Self-actualisation

This is being all that I have it in me to be – being that self which I truly am. It is generally seen as a process of emergence – when I have done enough work on myself, I will get in touch with my real self, without having to search for it in any specific way. There is something deeply paradoxical about this whole thing. As one approaches self-actualisation, one leaves the realm of deficiency and enters the realm of being. So the self, which to most of us still means something limited to me and my interests and my needs, is now seen in quite a different light. It is not about my deficiencies, my needs, my addictions, my hang-ups – it is about being. Suddenly the whole universe opens up, and I have to recognise that this is me. I am not a narrow, petty, history-bound, conditioned thing, but a self-transcendent being, who does not have to think any more in terms of fixed categories. Yet, of course, at the same time, I do not actually stop being narrow, petty, history-bound and conditioned etc. This is the paradox (Rowan, 1976). And it is hard to understand, because we keep on trying to understand it in deficiency terms, in deficiency language, with deficiency logic. As long as we have not personally experienced self-actualisation, we are bound to go on doing this – we have little alternative. But most of us have in fact experienced self-actualisation, in those precious moments known as peak experiences. And if you can remember how the world seemed then, you have some good clues about how to cope with paradox – this or any other. The peak experience, as Maslow (1968) has said, is a good indication of what self-actualisation is all about.

Now obviously there are dangers here. As Maslow himself pointed out, we can start going after peak experiences in a programmed way which is basically deficiency-oriented, and also basically self-defeating. We can go to workshop after workshop and expect something to be handed to us. But this is another paradox: self-actualisation is easy and natural – we can be surprised by joy – and yet quite a lot of work and commitment seems to be necessary in practice before we can get to the point where we are really ready to allow it to happen, and to accept it and own it as ours.

Conclusion

To sum up, then, what I have been trying to suggest is that the human potential movement is certainly concerned with focusing attention on the self. But far from being self-indulgent or narcissistic, it is fostering something that is socially defensible and politically desirable.

Because, as Carl Rogers (1978) has pointed out, this kind of work gives people a sense of their personal power. It gives people the strength they need in order to start running their own lives. If at present this is mainly for the benefit of middle-class people, who are supposed to be well able to look after their own lives anyway (although of course they are not), the answer to this is not to stop doing it with such people, but to extend it and do it with more people.

There are various ways of doing this. Roger's way is to hold large meetings (anything up to 800 people) where people can discover that they are not powerless after all. Paulo Freire's (1972) way is to teach literacy in a way that puts people in touch with their own position as political beings. My own way is to teach the method of the barefoot psychoanalyst (Southgate and Randall, 1978), and to try to get the book more widely distributed and known.

References

ROWAN, J. (1976). *Ordinary Ecstacy: Humanistic Psychology in Action*. London: Routledge & Kegan Paul.

ROGERS, C. (1978). *On Personal Power*. London: Constable.

MASLOW, A. (1968). *Toward a Psychology of Being*, 2nd edn. New York: Van Nostrand.

FREIRE, P. (1972). *Pedagogy of the Oppressed*. Harmondsworth: Penguin.

SOUTHGATE, J. and RANDALL, R. (1978). *The Barefoot Psychoanalyst*, 2nd edn. AKHPC (12 Nassington Road, London, NW3).

Acknowledgement

Thanks to Dorothy Tennov, who gave me the idea for this article by a quite different one of her own given at the APA Conference in Washington in 1976.

Chapter 3
On Being Irrational

People accuse each other of being irrational when they disagree. It is bad to be irrational. But the funny twist comes when expressing feelings is called irrational, or when taking feelings into account is called irrational. This makes logical coolness the rational thing, and hot emotion the irrational thing. Sometimes we are tempted to accept this kind of putdown and say – 'All right, so I am irrational, so what?'. This is the wrong answer, because we should not agree to be put down in the first place. What I am saying is that feelings are not irrational.

A variation on this first view is to say that it is rational to feel those feelings that we want to feel. This seems to be the view of rational behaviour therapy, as described by Maultsby (Dryden and Golden, 1986). Another variation is to say that feelings are rational when they are in line with our conscious goals and purposes: this is the view of rational–emotive therapy, as described by Ellis (Dryden and Golden, 1986).

What I want to argue is that to be rational is to do justice to reality. The more of reality we are doing justice to, the more rational we are being. This applies to external reality – things, animals, other people – and it also applies to internal reality – my own sensations, feelings, thoughts, intuitions and so forth. If I am suppressing my awareness of part of the external world, I may be rightly accused of burying my head in the sand, of culpable ignorance, of irrationality. If I am suppressing my awareness of part of my internal world, it is much the same thing: it may make life simpler, but at the cost of being irrational. So I cannot be fully rational if I am suppressing awareness of my own feelings.

But we now need to look at the question of how rational it is to express those feelings, because this involves a choice of what is to be done at a particular place, with a particular person, at a particular time. Choices are

From J. Rowan (1989) On being irrational. *Clinical Psychology Forum* **24**, 27-28, with permission.

always being made in terms of our values. If I act on just one of my values, ignoring all the others, that is a narrow and blinkered kind of rationality. For example, if an economist acts only on his value to get the best goods for the smallest expenditure, this is a very low and inadequate kind of rationality. If I act on all my values, allowing them all in and integrating them, that is the most rational thing I can do. This power of total integration is one of the most remarkable abilities of the human mind, once we can acknowledge it and trust it.

Whether I express my feelings, and how fully, and in what way, therefore, are the outcome of a process that involves taking all these influences into account. If someone tells you that being emotional is irrational, tell them that it is leaving feelings out that is irrational, because it is ignoring an important part of the real situation.

Reality is a big place. Reality includes real aspirations, real dreams, real ideals, real feelings. If rationality is to do justice to all this, it must be big too. It is no use having a thin and limited rationality which can only take into account one value or one set of feelings or one way of looking at the world. We must have a conception of rationality that allows us to include all that needs to be included.

This way of thinking about rationality may seem strange at first, because we have been taught to link thought and intellect with rationality, as if rationality could be reduced to formal logic or scientific law, or as if rationality could be reduced to rationing – eking out our feelings in line with desirable standards. This teaching comes from an anxiety to get away from subjectivity and childish naïveté, and a desire to embrace an objectivity that will be free from bias and partiality.

But there is no need to get away from our deep and important subjectivity in order to be objective. We can go on to an objective subjectivity that does justice to the whole. There are in fact three levels involved here:

Primary level	Irrationality	Impulse	Subjectivity
Social level	Rationality	Control	Objectivity
Realising level	Rationality	Spontaneity	Objective subjectivity

We all start at the primary level, and are taught in our education to leave it behind and go on to the social level which is supposedly so objective. We learn about the difference between truth and falsity, we learn about scientific method, we learn how to put our feelings aside in the search for objectivity. This actually works quite well when dealing with things, but it does not work at all well when it comes to dealing with people. For that we need to go on to the realising level. But we are not taught to go on to the realising level, because when we go on to the realising level we are harder to control and predict.

What is also not told to us is that the feelings at the realising level are actually different from the feelings at the subjective primary level. At the primary level of consciousness our feelings sweep over us and take us over. We are sometimes 'at the mercy of our feelings'. At the social level we put our feelings aside, or cultivate only those feelings that are acceptable to others in our social milieu. But at the realising level we choose our feelings; we take responsibility for our feelings; we really have our feelings, instead of our feelings having us. It is always rational to take our feelings into account, but at the realising level our feelings are actually rational in themselves.

Some of us are now arguing that this is even so in the realm of scientific research itself (Reason, 1988), and that if research wants to have any rational understanding of human beings it has to move on to the realising level. But this would need a much fuller argument. Perhaps all we need to say here is that the cognitive-behavioural perspective makes it very hard to see these points and to do them justice. Poor Wessler, in his chapter in Dryden and Golden (1986), clearly wishes that feelings were cognitions. If only they were cognitions he could deal with them so easily, but they just will not fit in. He says:

> Of these various meanings of the word feeling, two are cold cognitions (perception of bodily sensation and opinion), one clearly a hot cognition (appraisal), and the remaining meaning indeterminate.   (p. 17)

This 'remaining meaning', by the way, includes things like (his example!) 'it scares me when I think the other side won't disarm'. To him this is indeterminate. To me it is a feeling, just the kind of feeling I have been talking about all along. I rest my case.

References

DRYDEN, W. and GOLDEN, W. (1986). *Cognitive-Behavioural Approaches to Psychotherapy*. London: Harper & Row.
REASON, P. (1988). *Human Inquiry in Action*. London: Sage.

Chapter 4
Hegel and
Self-actualisation

The idea of self-actualisation has always been slightly mysterious, and it is not easy to be clear about it, although I have tried (Rowan, 1983) to do so. It seemed obvious from that investigation that self-actualisation intimately involved the transpersonal and the mystical. There have been several attempts by other people, and I found the discussion by Donald Rothberg (1986) interesting, where he searches for clues about the transpersonal among modern philosophers, and comes to the conclusion that 'we have to explore both the truth and the limits of the claims of a hierarchical ontology'. It occurred to me that it would be interesting to go to one of the great philosophical classics to see what hints there might be there. So I went to Hegel's *Philosophy of Mind* (Hegel, 1971), which I had glanced at before, but never read properly, and also to an exposition of it by Murray Greene (1972). I have loved Hegel since 1950, when I was introduced to his work by Harold Walsby, and have related his work to personal growth before, running workshops on 'Dialectics as a felt experience'. Certainly he is the exponent of a hierarchical ontology if ever there was one.

What happened was that I found Hegel extraordinarily illuminating: much more powerful than the vague notions of 'energy' that are floating around at the moment, or the various ideas put together according to the whim of each individual practitioner – a dash of Zen, a touch of existentialism, a drop of Taoism, a smidgin of Seth, a flash of feminism, a pennyweight of Jung, a lashing of Lacan, a string of Perls.

Hegel says that there are three levels of mind: the primary level, the social level and the realising level*. Self-actualisation consists in moving up

From J. Rowan (1979) Hegel and Self-actualisation: *Self and Society* November/December, 129–138, 149–154, with permission.

*He actually talks about the Soul (Seele), the Consciousness (Bewusstein) and the Mind (Geist), but what I am trying to do here is to revise and update Hegel to be as relevant as possible. If you like, you can say that this is my philosophy, leaning heavily on Hegel, rather than an academic exegesis of his work in itself.

the levels from the primary level, through the social level, to the realising level. The primary level is mostly to do with one-sided subjectivity, the social level is mostly to do with one-sided objectivity, and the realising level is subjectivity on a higher level – a new kind of subjectivity that includes but surpasses one-sided objectivity – an objective subjectivity, in fact. What I want to say is that it is at the realising level that we achieve self-actualisation.

This is a rough outline, which is very abstract and unrevealing. Let us now try to put some flesh on the bones.

Running through the whole thing is an enormous respect for mind, which can also be translated as spirit, or rational spirit.* This mind or spirit runs through the whole thing – all the levels – and is at the base of them all. At the very centre and origin of the primary level, as it were, inform-ing it and perpetually creating it, is spirit, which Hegel says is 'absolutely restless being, pure activity' (p. 3). Some people might want to call it energy, but Hegel would not go along with this.

Primary Level

The primary level is by no means simple – it is extraordinarily rich. In the first place, it has the whole of heredity going into it. We are individuals within a family, within a nation, within a race, within a continent, within a climatic zone, and all these have had their effect, over many generations, in playing up some characteristics (physical and behavioural) and playing down others. Right from the start, all this is within us. (It is tempting for us to go back further into an evolutionary perspective, but Hegel's way of doing this is rather different.)

Also we have developmental processes all going on within us in a programmed way. The process of maturation builds on the hereditary constitution, uses it and unifies it within a particular womb at a particu-lar time and place. This is just a little more like us than the totally exter-nal and pre-existing hereditary matters previously mentioned, but the main emphasis is still on the external, the programmed, the unchosen.

Once again we have our senses developing from a very early stage. This is something physical, and to an extent programmed – we cannot decide, in the womb, not to have a sense of touch, a sense of hearing and so forth – but as soon as information starts coming in through the senses, it starts to have meaning and to arouse emotion.

So at the very base of the primary level, as it were, there are all these physical and rather programmed things going on. All these take their effect in the womb, long before we are born. They have to do with our very existence, our survival.

---

*Rationality is redefined by Hegel in an important way which we shall see later.

It is as if the right to exist came logically before every other right, and the need to exist came before every other need.

But we now go on to a second phase within the primary level. Hegel says that there is a very important *feeling* phase here too. This feeling phase is all about experiencing things *directly*, without any kind of mediation or interpretation. This we do in relation to our internal states. My own feelings of pain, rage or fear are not something I have to infer or judge, and my bodily reactions of screaming or pounding or shaking are not events that I have to construct or interpret. Hegel actually calls this a *magical* relationship: 'the magic which is devoid of any mediation whatever is that which the individual mind exercises over its own bodily nature...' (p. 97). We do not have to work out how to lift our arm – we just do it. This direct knowledge is not only magical in this sense, it is also extremely accurate. A baby is in no doubt as to whether it feels miserable or not, and in no doubt about how to scream if it does – and it is *right* about these things.

This, by the way, is the answer to those writers and researchers who say that emotions such as anger are mediated by cognitive factors. A baby does not have anything like the same cognitive apparatus that is conferred later by entry into the symbolic, and the acquisition of language. But anyone who says that babies cannot be angry has little acquaintance with babies. And it is not just anger: Bradley (1989) says babies have a 'basic propensity for misery' which shows itself as early as the first 3 months of life.

Hegel (1971) goes on to say that this kind of direct perception without any need for mediation (by fallible interpretation, attribution of meanings, judgement about what things are etc.) is a kind of clairvoyance – an openness to the internal world which is particularly sensitive. It can lead to a very interesting phenomenon in the adult, which is remarked on in the following way:

> ...in that state noble natures experience a wealth of noble feelings, their true self, their better spiritual side, which often appears to them as a special guardian angel.
>
> (p. 114)

Now this is fascinating and challenging, because what Hegel is obviously talking about here is the transpersonal self. He is, then, denying that such perceptions belong to the realising level, which is, I believe, where transpersonal psychology would like to locate them. Many things, in fact, which Assagioli or Jung would say belong to the higher levels of our nature are firmly placed by Hegel in this primary level.

One of the most crucial questions is the whole question of our knowledge of the world and of other people. We are often told today that we have amazing powers of intuition, clairvoyance, telepathy, telekinesis etc., if we would only cultivate them. Shirley MacLaine tells us that we can change even the weather if we want to badly enough. Hegel says firmly that this kind of magical knowledge only exists in relation to our own interior states; to think that we can know or control other people or the outside world in this same direct way is just an illusion. We have to go through all the pain and error of getting to know things and people in all the usual ways of coming-to-know which are very ordinary and basic.

There is one exception to this which is very interesting. Hegel says that we can sometimes get into someone else's mind. But this only happens when one person takes over another person's mind, and imposes their own mind upon the other person's mind. This happens in three main types of situation: first, in the womb, where Hegel says that the mother's psyche can invade that of the fetus, virtually taking it over. The fetus has so little sense of self that it finds it hard or impossible to tell which are its own thoughts, feelings, reactions etc., and which are those of its mother (this is fascinating reading to those of us who know of Frank Lake's (1980) extremely valuable work about how the fetus is virtually 'marinated' in the mother's feelings); secondly, this can happen in the case of certain very sensitive women friends, certain husbands and wives, certain brothers and sisters etc. (I would add to this, between therapist and client at times.) There can be a sense of what Hegel calls an 'undivided psychic unity' (p. 95) between the members of such couples (many of us have had such experiences at times, or know of people to whom this has happened, and there are even some scientifically attested cases now of this happening under laboratory conditions); and thirdly in the case of hypnotism, which has of course been studied and substantiated far more today than it was in Hegel's day.

All this ties in very much with the findings on telepathy, where it appears that the problem with telepathy is that you get spatial, temporal and symbolic scatter, i.e. for example, you get a strong impression of a tiger. But you cannot know if it is a tiger a thousand miles away or a few yards away; a tiger today or a month ago – or a month hence; a real tiger, or a symbol for your father. That is exactly what the case would be if telepathy were connected with the primary level, rather than with some more highly developed level of consciousness.

So the second phase of the primary level is very much to do with this kind of immediate apprehension, very accurate in relation to our own internal states, but very inaccurate in relation to the outside world. (The trouble is that it gives itself credit for being very highly accurate in relation to the outside world. It jumps to conclusions and takes them for facts.) But it also has to do with neurosis and psychosis.

Hegel's ideas about mental distress, formed at a time when today's knowledge of psychiatric diagnosis was hardly in its infancy (his book was mostly written over the first 30 years of the nineteenth century), make a surprising amount of sense. First, he says that the primary level of mind is a highly complex world – 'a totality of infinitely many distinct determinatenesses' (p. 90) – which come together in unity. 'We have within us a

countless host of relationships and connections which are always with us'
(p. 90) and these perpetually differentiate themselves and become distinct
entities. In other words, he is saying something that is highly compatible
with today's up-to-date notions of subpersonalities (Rowan, 1990), internal objects, complexes, ego states and so forth. His idea of mental distress
is that one of these takes over, separates itself from the rest, becomes flat
and one-dimensional and highly predictable. This one-sided self pretends
to be the whole person, 'thereby becoming a purely formal, empty,
abstract subjectivity' (p. 125).

On this reasoning, therapy would be mainly about overcoming this one-
sidedness, and restoring the connections with the other parts of the
person. In doing this, Hegel says, we can always appeal to the patient's
rationality, because spirit is always there and always rational, underlying
everything else. Good therapy, says Hegel, 'presupposes the patient's rationality, and in that assumption has the sound basis for dealing with him on
this side – just as in the case of bodily disease the physician bases his treatment on the vitality which as such still contains health' (p. 124).

This suggests what we have already hinted at, that Hegel sees the
connection between mind and body to be a very intimate one, particularly at this primary level of mind.

> Mind is not ... a soul-thing only externally connected with the body, but is inwardly
> bound to the latter by the unity of the Notion.   (p. 3)

It does not surprise us, then, when he says that 'The point is that insan-
ity must be grasped essentially as an illness at once mental and physical'
(p. 129). Again he is very up-to-date, because this is a point that is now
agreed both by the most orthodox and by the most unorthodox.

Where it is not agreed, of course, is by the existentialists (and by people
such as Szasz in his different way), who insist that neurosis/psychosis is a
free choice, and that it must be left to the patient to move out of it. Hegel
is much more with the Alan Watts (1961) of *Psychotherapy East and West*,
where he talks about the *upaya* of the *guru* – the ways in which the
student is tricked into insights.

> It is true that the insane are extremely distrustful when they notice that attempts
> are being made to wean them away from their fixed idea. Yet at the same time
> they are stupid and easily taken by surprise. They can therefore not infrequently
> be cured by someone pretending to enter into their delusion and then suddenly
> doing something in which the patient catches a glimpse of liberation from his
> imagined complaint.   (p. 138)

It is obvious from his language here that Hegel is no therapist, but rather
a philosopher looking at things from the standpoint of an outside specta-
tor, but, in spite of the offensiveness of his remarks, the basic point he is
making does run through most of the psychotherapy that works. We do go
along with the patient or client; we do then suggest role-reversal, or contra-

diction of a statement made, or linking the present feeling with some other situation, or whatever. We do trick the client into insight, or into catharsis, or into some new sensation, if we are using any of the techniques at our disposal (see Bergantino (1981) for a good discussion of this).

This issue of Hegel's language is worth a note in passing. He does seem to look down on the patient or client in a way that would seem unacceptable to us today, and yet what he says does often seem very accurate. For example, he says:

> The passion of vanity or pride is the chief cause of this psychical self-imprisonment.
> (p. 133)

This sounds awfully punitive, and is certainly not the kind of thing one wants to say to the person involved. However, it is not dissimilar to the kind of thing that Horney and Mowrer have both emphasised (and others too, of course) in pointing to the actual dynamics involved. I personally find it quite refreshing to have it spoken out so boldly. It does not tell us how to do therapy, but it does tell us how to clear our minds.

What is also of great interest here is the way in which Hegel makes it clear that we have to go down into the primary level, this level of immediate feeling and existence, in order to do effective and fundamental therapy. Not only is he supporting the basic idea that regression is necessary for effective therapy, but also he is asserting that transpersonal therapeutic work, too, takes place at this level.

He is even up-to-date in his ideas about the therapeutic relationship. Richard Schuster (1979) talks about the best empathy being based on the kind of mindfulness that can be attained through meditation. In this state, he says:

> It seems to rely heavily on direct-intuitive modes of perception. In addition the therapist must try to allow himself or herself to 'unite' with the client yet remain separate. The therapist must be alert and aware of all nuances that arise within or around him or her, yet must still be in experiential contact with the client
> (p. 73)

Hegel, for his part, talks about rapport as a phenomenon in which the person 'knows, sees and feels, not merely about someone else but in someone else and, without directly turning his attention to the individual, *immediately shares* his feelings, contains the other individual's feeling as his *own*' (p. 114). But what Hegel makes clear, and Schuster does not, is that this kind of empathy and rapport is very much open to illusion. It needs to be checked out and tested, because it can be wrong – just as the dream often has greater clarity than waking life, but is no more trustworthy for that reason.

Pressing on now, Hegel also says that in the Primary level we find all the habits and skills of a person – all those things that we have relegated to automatic pilot.

The habits, he says, have at the same time great advantages and disadvantages. On the one hand, they put an end to the dividedness of the self, and bring one to a state of being-at-home-with-oneself but, on the other, habit makes a person its slave. Habits are important to understand, because very often they express very well the intimate unity of body and mind which Hegel emphasises again and again. 'I must give my body its due, must take care of it, keep it healthy and strong, and must not therefore despise it or treat it as an enemy' (p. 145). Further than this, I have to *train* my body if I want to realise my aims through it – I have to learn to write, or drive a car, or use a computer, or speak or sing in public. And every time I do this, I gain freedom in one way, and lose it in another. At the moment when my mind *pervades* the activity most thoroughly, it also *deserts* it.

Also, of course, our bodily habits – the way we walk and talk, our expressive gestures, the way we hold our faces, our general postures and attitudes – are formed by the earlier self-divisions we have discussed. Hegel would agree very much with people such as Reich, Rolf and Feldenkrais that just by looking at someone standing, walking and talking it is possible to say a great deal about him or her. However, he also says that you cannot make a science out of this, because the relationship between mind and body is always complex and variable, by no means simple and fixed. Our conclusions should be treated as guesses, and checked out carefully.

So all the way through this discussion of the primary level, Hegel is saying that our knowledge at this stage is subjective rather than objective. We continually make the mistake of thinking that it is more objective than it really is, and because all the time we are talking about the mind, and because mind is essentially rational, we think we are being rational in our subjectivity. This leads to the phenomenon that Berne (1972) called 'the little professor', where we leap to conclusions and then proceed to justify them. Making up theories on the basis of thoroughly inadequate evidence, and then coming to decisions on the basis of these theories, is exactly what the subjective mind does. This, of course, is exactly what babies do, according to Klein, Laing, Lake, Janov, Grof, and numerous and sundry other people. As Berne says, the little professor can be extremely intuitive, can 'pick up' a great deal, but it can be right or wrong; and because the little professor is more intent on having a theory than checking it, there is never any real feedback on whether the theory is right or wrong. Consequently, the assumption that it is right gets perpetuated indefinitely.

Social Level

What rescues us from this state is our entry into the social level, and our invention of a social ego. This appears at first as a cataclysm.

Remember the whole thrust of the dialectical position, which stands behind everything Hegel says, is that development takes place through contradiction. Because the social level contradicts the primary level, entry into it is painful. It costs something.

We are leaving behind a realm where all the emphasis is on subjectivity, and entering into one where all the emphasis is on objectivity. Things are not what we thought they were. They have their own nature, which may be nothing to do with us – but at first this feels like 'opposed to us'.

We first enter this level by finding something that resists us. But resistance implies freedom (as Walsby (1948) has pointed out and elaborated on very fruitfully). Hegel makes it clear that he sees freedom as basic to human nature. The substance of mind is freedom, as he says. At the primary level, this is often lost sight of, because there may be nothing to contrast it with. As soon as it is contradicted, we become aware of our strong and fundamental need to assert our freedom.

> Whereas the animal is silent or expresses its pain only by groaning, the child makes known its wants by screaming. By this ideal activity, the child shows that it is straightway imbued with the certainty that it has a right to demand from the outer world the satisfaction of its needs...   (p. 59)

So the act of saying 'No' (as Reich and Lowen have urged) is crucial to entry into this new level of consciousness. By saying 'No' to the world, we become aware of our own need for freedom; and when the world says 'No' to us, we are forced to recognise its independent reality.

Once we accept its independent reality, we can start to control it. This is a new kind of control, which we do not have at the primary level. It is control by assuming that things are fixed, firm, constant and predictable. Piaget, Mahler and others have now traced the way in which the acquisition of this kind of control takes place in the child's development. But because they are looking from the outside, they miss the traumatic nature of the discovery that objects exist, that objects resist us, and that we are an object like other objects.

It is only now that we discover that we are not just an 'I' – we are also a 'me'. (This is the bit that Mead (1934) gets importantly wrong.) This may come about, as Duval and Wicklund (1972) suggest, at the first moment when we are first convinced that we have done something wrong. At this moment two ideas which are there already, but separate, come suddenly together – the idea of 'what I want' and the idea of 'bad' (or 'not OK', if we prefer). At that moment I become an object to myself. And ever after this, I am able to say 'No' to me, myself.

This social level type of approach now becomes our way of relating to the world more and more. It stands in front of the primary level, as it were, and eclipses it more and more.

This may well link with Winnicott's (1975) idea (for which there are many other parallels in many other investigators into this area) that what happens is that the subjective self gets pushed down into a safe but impotent place, and the social self gets pushed forward as a role-playing mask, ready to perform as required. I have explored this idea at length in my book on subpersonalities (Rowan, 1990).

These possible parallels in therapy and psychology do sometimes give the impression that the painfulness of this process is something culpable – something done by the parents to the poor unsuspecting baby. Now it is certainly true that the baby sometimes blames the parents – and this could certainly have implications for later life – but from our standpoint as philosophers such blaming would be wrong. Hegel says very clearly:

> The substance of mind is freedom... But the Other, the negative, contradiction, disunity, also belongs to the nature of mind. In this disunity lies the possibility of pain. (p. 15)

So Hegel, like Melanie Klein (but for different reasons), is saying that there is no way of avoiding the pain of having to create a social ego, distinct and split off from our primary ego. In fact, it is only the act of creating the social ego that also brings into being the primary ego which the object relations school of psychoanalysts have talked about. What is there at first in the primary level is what Hegel calls a 'world-soul' (p. 90). This then turns into the ego – what Guntrip (1961) calls the primary libidinal ego.

So we get the paradox that at the very moment when we first get a real sense of being an 'I' we also get the sense that this 'I' is not OK, and that we have to produce a 'me' which will be OK, or at least 'OK' in the sense of being acceptable. We discover the 'I' only to have to put it aside.

But in putting it aside we change it. It becomes open to argument and this changes it radically. As Hegel says:

> The 'I' is the lightning which pierces through the natural soul [the Primary level, as we have renamed it] and consumes its natural being. (p. 152)

So this loss of innocence (of Eden) is nothing to be sad about – it is part of a process of development (realisation, actualisation) that is dialectical, and therefore never really loses anything, but takes it up, at a later stage, into a higher level where it becomes in reality what it only wished to be in the first place. As Hegel says very well:

> In its immediacy [that is, at the Primary level] mind is free only implicitly, in principle or potentially, not yet in actuality; actual freedom... has to be brought into being by mind's own activity. (p. 16)

It is important, too, not to idealise the primary level and to regard it as some kind of repository for everything that is good or natural, as Washburn (1988) seems to do. It is very basic and very well worth understanding and coming to terms with, as we shall see later, but it is also very lacking in various ways:

> Since the 'I' [the ego at the Social level] enters into conflict with external objects, it is superior to the impotent natural soul [the ego at primary level] which is entrapped, so to speak, in a childlike unity with the world, to the soul in which, just because it is impotent, fall the states of mental disease we have previously considered.   (Hegel, 1971, p. 155)

What we have now reached is a state of consciousness to which objectivity is extremely important. 'A thing is what it is, and not another thing', as the positivists say. Rothberg (1986) has a spirited discussion of this position as it relates to the transpersonal. This is, of course, the type of consciousness that is pushed by our educational system. We are encouraged to be more and more objective, and to mistrust and push under our subjective nature.

In our schools we are taught not merely to recognise the existence of external objects and other people, but also that the right way to approach all these things is in a scientific way. Science becomes the essence, the exemplar, of objectivity. 'If you want to know what real objectivity is like', we are told, 'look at science.' And of course the highest kind of science, as we are also told, is that which is most mathematical. And so we get introduced to the idea of proof. We cannot only recognise things as independent of us; we must also prove that they must be as they are.

Then we proceed to adopt the same approach to the relationships between things – thus arriving at the idea of a scientific law.

We have gone rather fast over this, but in fact, of course, it requires a real obsession with the natural world – as Walsby (1948) has urged most strongly – to arrive at this point. We learn a tremendous amount by adopting this approach. We are genuinely engaged with this effort at overcoming our ignorance. It is an effort at getting back the freedom – the mastery – which we felt we had at the start. But because of the way in which we have excluded our subjectivity from the process, there is something lifeless about the result:

> The merely abstractive, intellectual consciousness [at the Social level] does not as yet . . . succeed in developing dialectically from one of these determinations its opposite; this unity still remains for this consciousness something dead...
> (Hegel, 1971, p. 164)

It is here that we find formal logic, and particularly mathematical logic, seeming to be the answer to everything. In fact, this is taken to be the essence of rationality at this stage. At the heart of science is mathematics, and at the heart of mathematics is symbolic logic. If only everything could be reduced to symbolic logic, we think at this stage, there would be world peace, because everybody would be able to understand everything clearly.

So at this social level, rationality is seen as being the answer to everything, and rationality is identified ultimately with some version of formal logic.

So far, we have only been concerned with the outside world, as it is understood at this social level; however, equally important, says Hegel, is our understanding of ourselves at this level. Let us go back, then, to the beginning of this level and remember the nature of the confrontation that takes place then. We are met by objects that resist us, and deny our freedom.

The first way in which we can overcome this opposition is by using it. In that way we can make it ours. We can take off the curse, as it were, by turning what was resisting us into something that works for us. And the classic way of doing this is by eating or drinking it.

Some American philosopher asked the question: 'How does everything that Miss Mary eats become Miss Mary?' Hegel actually answers this question (in Section 427), but the answer is too long to quote here, and would only distract us from our main purpose.

But it is interesting that Hegel, like Perls (1947), lays so much emphasis on appetite as aggressive, and as necessarily so: 'Thus, appetite in its satisfaction is always destructive, and in its content selfish' (p. 167). Again, like Perls, he teaches us that this action gives us satisfaction – it is a way of giving ourselves pleasure, of loving ourselves. It is the other side of the same process that split us in what seemed a bad way: there we had to suppress our subjectivity in its separation but now we are satisfying our subjectivity in its separation. (Here we are laying stress on the Jungian faculty of sensation, just as before in this level we were laying stress on the thinking faculty; sensation and thinking go together at this level.) There is still a split, but now we are using the split in a positive way. We can look on our own self as an other and say 'I know what will satisfy me'. This is the beginning of our self-knowledge.

But how about when we meet another person? How do we relate to another person at this stage? Hegel says by recognition. (Remember Berne's definition of a stroke as a sign of recognition.) Having first seen people as sources (of food, comfort, touch etc.), we now go on to see them as recognisably like ourselves. This is someone like me, capable of benefiting or harming me. And Hegel sees this very much as a relation of contradiction – I am opposed to the other. In a striking passage he contrasts this with the kind of relationships we had at the subjective stage, when we were open and vulnerable:

We face here the tremendous contradiction that, on the one hand, the 'I' is wholly universal, absolutely pervasive, and interrupted by no limit, is the universal essence common to all men, the two mutually related selves therefore constituting one identity, constituting, so to speak, one light; and yet, on the other hand, they are also two selves rigidly and unyieldingly confronting each other, each existing as a reflection-into-self, as absolutely distinct from and impenetrable by the other.

(p. 171)

This puts Perls' humanistic 'Gestalt prayer' (with its emphasis on separate-ness) and Ed Elkin's revision of it, the 'transpersonal gestalt prayer' (with its emphasis on connectedness) into the proper context; they are both true, both accurate, but they are talking about different positions, which Hegel regards as different levels of consciousness.

What can happen, of course, in this opposition of one person to another, is that one dominates the other. The archetypal expression of this relationship of dominance and submission, according to Hegel, is the relationship of master and slave. Here he makes another paradoxical point – because the slave is made to care about another human being, the slave learns an important lesson that the master can quite easily avoid. The slave learns self-control, learns how not to be selfish, learns how to serve others. If we want to arrive at what Hegel calls 'universal self-consciousness' we have to go through this painful experience, of dependence upon another. But obedience to the will of another person is only the beginning of wisdom, says Hegel, because ultimately what we have to learn is obedi-ence to what is universally rational – what that good Hegelian Mary Parker Follett (1941) called the law of the situation. And the master ultimately has to learn this just as much as the slave.

Once having learned these lessons, we can at last perceive the truth which Hegel offers in language that is crystal clear: 'I am only truly free when the other is also free and is recognised by me as free' (p. 171). But he does not offer any easy way to this kind of freedom. Because of the contradiction between us and others (which at times reminds us of Sartre's emphasis on the total and necessary isolation of each person) and because relationships of domination and submission are in practice so common (in his day as in ours), we may have to fight for our freedom:

> Only through struggle, therefore, can freedom [at this Social level] be won; the assertion that one is free does not suffice to make one so; at this stage, humanity demonstrates the capacity for freedom only by risking everything, even life itself.
> (p. 172)

Here he is talking about the struggle for individuality, for recognition as a person, as a group, as a nation or whatever. It applies to adolescents, to women, to blacks, to gays and lesbians, and to many liberation groups of all kinds. We have seen a burst of this kind of freedom recently in Eastern Europe. But it is important to see that this is a liberal kind of individual-ity and freedom. It does not have the awareness of what Charles Hampden-Turner (1971) has called the 'developmental left', or the ecological standpoint of Petra Kelly (Plant, 1989). It is the kind of approach to freedom which emphasises free trade, free speech, freedom of assembly and so forth. It asserts the freedom of each person to assert their own interests, except only in so far as they infringe the interests of others. But Hegel is sophisticated enough to see that just as things are seen as fully determined and as conforming to the laws of physics etc., so in a similar way people at this level are seen as social atoms, and also ultimately understandable in a scientific way (using a notion of social science which takes over all the assumptions of natural science).

So Hegel says that even at the highest reach of the social level, our understanding of things and people is still 'abstract and formal', it is still falling short of really doing justice to the fullness of humanity. It is all right to treat things or objects as relating to each other in deterministic ways. But it does matter with human beings, because they are living, growing and developing, and this kind of thinking cannot handle such matters. It is a one-sided objectivity which can only establish a formal correctness, not a fully rounded truth.

Nevertheless, going through this whole level is necessary. Without this detailed obsession with things, without this building of what Freud called a strong ego, without these painful struggles with oppression, we just do not know enough to go on to anything better.

Realising Level

So what is it we go on to? It is what we have called the realising level. Just as the social level contradicts the primary level, so the realising level contradicts the social level. If we wish to use such terms (which Hegel actually does not) we can say that the primary level is the thesis, the social level is the antithesis and the realising level is the synthesis. The realising level is thus the primary level raised to a new standard of consciousness. The way in which it emerges is by going back to the primary level, rescuing what is found there, and raising it to a new level of awareness. In other words, what we have here is a new kind of subjectivity – a subjectivity that has been through the social level, and is therefore much better informed and educated, much stronger and less vulnerable.

The example he gives at greatest length is the question of feeling. Feeling at the primary level, he says, is merely subjective – something that happens, that sweeps over us, that takes us unawares. Feeling at the social level is merely objective, and has to do with basic sensations of the outside world – contact with what is out there. At this level the value of intellect is upheld, and the value of emotion is denied. But feeling at the realising level is more appropriately called intuition, or intelligent perception. It is both objective and subjective. Here is what Hegel says about intuition:

> Mindful, true intuition... apprehends the genuine substance of the object. A talented historian, for example, has before him a vivid intuition of the circumstances and events he is to describe; on the other hand, one who has no talent for writing history confines himself to details and overlooks what is essential... Only thinking that is firmly based on an intuitive grasp of the substance of the subject-matter can, without deserting the truth, go on to treat the details.   (p. 199)

What we are doing, therefore, in moving to the realising level, is opening up the primary level in a new way. It is as if all our attempts to learn in the social level had the effect of pushing down and compressing the primary level, so that it took up less and less room, so to speak. We could almost forget it was there, were it not for dreams and mistakes to remind us. But now we are releasing material from the primary level and bringing it to light on the other side of the social level. As Freud put it, we are making the unconscious conscious. The social level negated the primary level, and now we are negating that negation.

We are now able deliberately to use images and symbols instead of being at the mercy of them, as we are with the dreams and daydreams of the primary level. What Hegel says about this is highly compatible with the idea of using guided fantasy (as in psychosynthesis) to rescue material from the primary level on purpose, and raise it to consciousness in such a way that it can be used for our further education on this new level.

Similarly, instead of just having memories pop up in no particular order, we can start deliberately to search for those memories that will be most useful to us – recovering all those events that we pushed down or thrust aside at some point in our past, and that are still significant for us. The ideas of Janov, Lake and Grof about trauma are highly relevant to this, as I have described elsewhere at length (Rowan, 1988). But in speaking of memory, Hegel attaches particular importance to words. Because words express the full power of the mind better than pictorial (or other sensory) images, memories that involve words in some way are more important for this realising level than those that are merely about images. This fits very well with all those forms of therapy that emphasise the decisions which the child or baby made, and seeks to enable new and better decisions to be made, using our new level of consciousness.

> Having been through these understandings, we are now able to think in a new way: We only know our thoughts, only have definite, actual thoughts, when we give them the form of objectivity, of a being distinct from our inwardness, and therefore the shape of externality, and of an externality, too, that at the same time bears the stamp of the highest inwardness. The articulated sound, the word, is alone such an inward externality.   (p. 221)

This sounds very close to some of the things that Lacan, in France, has been urging in recent years, but I think the context is very different. Hegel is talking here very much about adult thinking, not about the infant. 'Knowing now constitutes the subjectivity of Reason, and objective Reason is posited as a Knowing' (p. 227). In other words, theoretical thinking at this stage is now fully made a part of me. It is me, and I own it and take responsibility for it. It is not just the truth, out there somewhere; it is my truth, and I am committed to it. But in that case, it approaches very close to will. If I am choosing to think what I think, on the basis of my whole understanding, and all that I have experienced, then this is practical as much as it is theoretical. And this gives us a whole new view of what science is, and how it works, and how to evaluate it. Such thinking is very close to the recent ideas about new paradigm research (Reason and Rowan, 1981).

Now Hegel says that the will, when it first comes to fruition at the realising level, is still very one-sided. We start to feel our own nature – material rescued out from under the social level ('up from under', as the feminists say) and at first we tend to throw it around as if we were alone important in the world. Self-expression is all. At last we feel what it is really like to act for ourselves – not to fit in with some social norm, but to do justice to what we have discovered inside ourselves.

What happens is that, rather than exercising our fully developed will, what we are exercising are our passions. 'The special note in passion is its restriction to one special mode of volition, in which the whole subjectivity of the individual is merged, be the value of that mode what it may' (p. 235). Hegel is not condemning the passions, but merely seeing that they are not the whole to which we are ultimately moving. They may at times be most necessary:

> Passion is neither good nor bad; the title only states that a subject has thrown his whole soul – his interests of intellect, talent, character, enjoyment – on one aim and object. Nothing great has been and nothing great can be accomplished without passion.
> (p. 235)

The milder form that the will takes is that of interest, which Hegel carefully distinguishes from selfishness. It is really important to know and pursue my own interests – this is one of the best ways in which I can contribute to universal rationality, as Mary Parker Follett (1941) has shown in great detail.

This leads, as Hegel insists, to happiness – to a will that, because it includes all that is relevant, is genuinely free. This is very close, I think, to what Carl Rogers called 'the fully-functioning person'. The gestalt people, too, have been very clear that free choice feels good – as John Enright (1980) once said 'If you are not experiencing joy, you are being irresponsible'.

We have now reached a conception of a higher kind of rationality from that known at the social level. Because we have now incorporated all of the primary level into the realising level, bringing it to conscious awareness, we do not have any mysterious currents dragging us down. We can see clearly through our own eyes, instead of seeing everything as externally true or false, right or wrong, pleasant or unpleasant. So we are taking more into account than was possible at the social level – we are doing greater justice to the whole – hence we are being more rational. Being rational, we see at this stage, is doing justice to the whole – to all that is there, out in the world and inside ourselves. Hegel calls this realisation the achievement of free mind or free spirit – a spirit that has genuinely won for itself the freedom that it could only partially sense at first. This is the meaning of self-actualisation.

Practical Implications

Well, that is the general story – the philosophical theory that I think makes a lot of sense. I find this extremely inspiring and useful. At the same time, as it clarifies my mind, it contradicts a number of things that I and other people in the growth movement have said or written in the past. Let us look briefly at some of them, remembering that each one could be expanded to make a whole paper of its own.

The real self

I now feel that the ecstasy which comes when one 'contacts the real self' is the ecstasy of making the unconscious conscious. One has reclaimed another part of one's world, and made it possible to understand it and own it. But it is still only a part of one's inner world, which is why there is more than one breakthrough in therapy, for any given individual. What one has really done is to take some material from the primary level and move it straight into the realising level. This is a dizzying act, and can only be done if the social level is sufficiently well developed to permit it.

Therapy

All forms of therapy go into the primary level, but they explain it differently. Some only aim at improving performance at the social level, and do not recognise the realising level at all. If this is a temporary measure, aimed at strengthening the social ego until it can cope with the realising level's emergence, it may be justifiable, but otherwise it can actually hinder a person's self-development.

Therapy can be a powerful method of doing justice to the whole person, as I have tried to spell out in detail elsewhere (Rowan, 1988).

Spirituality

Sometimes it seems that spirituality thinks it can go beyond rationality, but it cannot. It can only do occasional magic, and on those occasions it is really working at the primary level. In reality, spirituality runs through the whole process, all the levels, and is rational throughout, in whatever way it can be. When it gets to the realising level, it is not chancy, not temporary and not surprising. This makes a huge difference to transpersonal work. Much of the agony in Grof and Grof (1989) can be understood as struggles with material from the primary level.

The persona

The main social ego is not a subpersonality. It is all too solid. Unless it is, we get real dissociation (Miss Beauchamp, Eve, Sybil, the troops for Truddi Chase) instead of just subpersonalities. So subpersonalities are all within the primary level. The super-ego is just one of the subpersonalities. But what I used to call the 'inner self', I would now call the emergence of the realising level (Rowan, 1990). This was something else which I got significantly wrong before.

Feminism

The primary level is not feminine any more than it is masculine, and it is an insult to women to say that one-sided subjectivity is female. The truth is that a male-dominated society has tried to keep women in an immature and undeveloped state, so that they will be attractively child-like rather than adult and possibly competitive. The idea of men 'cultivating their female side' is highly suspect for the same reason. The primary level is not female, but it is what men need to explore, and women too. All the stuff about male/female polarities has to be closely re-examined in the light of Hegel's insights. Starhawk (1989) has some useful remarks on this. The task for women is the same as for men – to develop in the social level until they have enough knowledge and skills (male-biased knowledge and male-distorted skills as they may be) and then go on into the realising level by recovering material that has been suppressed, repressed and denied and split off down in the primary level.

Social science

The third-person approach of the old paradigm is transformed into a first-person approach, but instead of sinking into the mere subjectivity of the primary level, we go on into the new and rigorous subjectivity of the realising level (Reason and Rowan, 1981). Research can never be neutral. The new paradigm is dialectical.

These are just a few of the first implications that come to mind. Others will emerge very fast, as the Hegelian insights become better known and more widely accepted. I hope this essay does something to help that happen.

References

BERGANTINO, L. (1981). *Psychotherapy, Insight and Style.* Boston: Allyn & Bacon.
BERNE, E. (1972). *What Do You Say After You Say Hello?* New York: Grove Press.
BRADLEY, B.S. (1989). *Visions of Infancy.* Cambridge: Polity Press.

DUVAL, S. and WICKLUND, R.A. (1972). *A Theory of Objective Self-awareness*. New York: Academic Press.

ENRIGHT, J. (1980). *Enlightening Gestalt*. Palo Alto: Pro Telos Press.

FOLLETT, M.P. (1941). *Freedom and Coordination*. London: Pitman.

GREENE, M. (1972). *Hegel on the Soul*. Leiden: Martinus Nijhoff.

GROF, S. and GROF, C. (Eds) (1989). *Spiritual Emergency: When Personal Transformation becomes a Crisis*. Los Angeles: Jeremy Tarcher.

GUNTRIP, H. (1961). *Personality Structure and Human Interaction*. London: Hogarth Press.

HAMPDEN-TURNER, C. (1971). *Radical Man*. London: Duckworth.

HEGEL, G.W.F. (1971). *Hegel's philosophy of mind* (being Part Three of the *Encyclopaedia of the Philosophical Sciences* (1830) translated by William Wallace, together with the Zusätze in Boumann's text (1845) translated by A.V. Miller). Oxford: The Clarendon Press.

LAKE, F. (1980). *Studies in Constricted Confusion*. Oxford: Clinical Theology Association.

MEAD, G.H. (1934). *Mind, Self and Society*. Chicago: University of Chicago Press.

PERLS, F.S. (1947). *Ego, Hunger, and Aggression*. New York: Random House.

PLANT, JUDITH (Ed) (1989). *Healing the Wounds: The Promise of Ecofeminism*. London: Green Print.

REASON, P. and ROWAN, J. (Eds) (1981). *Human Inquiry: A Sourcebook of New Paradigm Research*. Chichester: John Wiley.

ROTHBERG, D. (1986). Philosophical foundations of transpersonal psychology: An introduction to some basic issues. *The Journal of Transpersonal Psychology* **18**(1), 1–34.

ROWAN, J. (1983). The real self and mystical experience. *Journal of Humanistic Psychology* **23**(2), 9–27.

ROWAN, J. (1988) Primal integration. In J. Rowan and W. Dryden (Eds), *Innovative Therapy in Britain*. Milton Keynes: Open University Press.

ROWAN, J. (1990). *Subpersonalities: The People Inside Us*. London: Routledge.

SCHUSTER, (1979). Empathy and mindfulness. *Journal of Humanistic Psychology* **19**(1), 71–77.

STARHAWK (1989). *The Spiral Dance*, 2nd edn. San Francisco: Harper & Row.

WALSBY, H. (1948). *The Domain of Ideologies*. Glasgow: McClelland.

WASHBURN, M. (1988). *The Ego and the Dynamic Ground*. Albany: SUNY.

WATTS, A. (1961). *Psychotherapy East and West*. New York: Pantheon Books.

WINNICOTT, D. (1975). *Through Paediatrics to Psychoanalysis*. London: Hogarth.

Chapter 5
Nine Humanistic Heresies

Someone once defined a *heresy* as what happens when one bit of a coherent body of doctrine gets taken and blown up in size until it becomes something new, but distorted and one-sided, and harmful. I happen to think that humanistic psychology is a coherent body of doctrine, and I have tried to say (Rowan, 1976a) exactly how and why this is so. It scares me when I see bits of it taken and twisted.

The difference between now and the old days of heresies is that no one is going to go around today with an inquisition burning people at the stake. I can present these criticisms with an easy mind, knowing that no one is going to be excommunicated because of them. But I would like people to think about them, and maybe feel some of the pain I have felt at times when these things have come up.

Heresy No. 1: Instrumentalism

This is the one where people use the methods developed within humanistic psychology to oppress other people in new and more effective ways (Farson, 1978). In encounter and other growth groups, the leader can become something like a drill sergeant, initiating exercise after exercise without waiting for the spontaneous to happen. But as James Elliott (1976) has said well: 'Everything the group leader does will tend to deprive the group members of the opportunity of doing it on their own.' Techniques can be useful when a person wants to do something but genuinely doesn't know how to do it. Instrumentalism loves technique for the power it gives to the leader. I heard one leader recently saying with apparent pride that

From J. Rowan (1987). Nine humanistic heresies. *Journal of Humanistic Psychology* 27(2), 141–157, with permission.
Author's note: This is an expanded and updated version of an article, 'Heresy-hunting in the AHP' which originally appeared in *Self and Society: European Journal of Humanistic Psychology*, 8(1).

his music worked on people without their conscious awareness to take them deeper into feelings. This sort of manipulation is nothing much to do with humanistic psychology as I understand it, because the same technique could be used by thoroughly nasty people for thoroughly nasty ends. But it can also get more subtle than that. Instrumentalism is also to do with using thoroughly defensible methods in thoroughly appropriate ways, but within an indefensible system, which is resolutely not examined or questioned.

This can happen, for example, in management training. Wooton (1981) showed how Albert Speer, Minister of Armaments and War under Hitler, ran his ministry in accordance with the principles of organisation development, management by objectives, participative management, temporary organisation and matrix organisation. Wooton says that:

> this system of industrial self-responsibility parallels today's attempts to restructure the workplace by the use of autonomous work groups.

He warns that there is no guarantee that the ends will be good, because '90 percent of management education today is still the teaching of functional skills (very sophisticated skills, admittedly)'. I have discussed this sort of question at greater length elsewhere (Rowan, 1976b).

This can also happen in education. Bridges (1973) wrote an article a while ago in which he revealed his worries about this: Is telling people to touch their neighbour any better than telling them to get out their exercise books? Is getting people to visualise the ascent of a mountain any better than getting them to copy the sums off the blackboard? The content is different, but the form is the same – the teacher is the provider and the student is the consumer. This is perhaps using new ways to prop up the old style of top-down teaching, instead of offering an alternative to it. Romey (1972) has a similar idea when he gets worried about thinking of better questions to ask the students, instead of finding ways of encouraging the students to think of better questions themselves and better ways of finding answers. The point is that humanistic psychology is about the realisation of potential, not about its limitations or its guidance into some groove laid down by someone else.

But the further and deeper point is that even the best methods can turn sour if the context in which they are used is ignored. As Ruth Leeds (1970) once pointed out, established systems are very good at absorbing protest, and even better at absorbing new methods. We have to stand always for real freedom and real communication, and this will always be subversive of fixed systems.

Heresy No. 2: Feelingism

It is often said that humanistic psychology emphasises feelings. There are even Institutes of Feeling Therapy, and therapists who continually talk about the importance of feelings. As someone who uses primal integration as his main form of therapy (Rowan, 1988), I too see a lot of deep feelings expressed, and believe that to be a very important part of the process. But somehow there is a falsity here when this one clue is made into the whole game. I have seen people bullied and intimidated in groups because they were not expressing feelings, or even because they were not expressing the *right* feelings, such as anger. Miale (1973) suggests that this happens when the leader believes that feelings arise from the dynamic core of being, while thinking is an acquired process detached from and antithetical to the reality of self. I have even seen people criticised because they were not expressing feelings *all the time!* A kind of false picture of the 'natural person' seems to be behind this – someone who is continually coming out with spontaneous feelings and expressing them in an immediate and naïve way. I do not know where this comes from, but it is clearly a quite inadequate picture of what human beings could or should be.

Feelings are in reality no more important or central than sensing, thinking, intuiting, imagining, desiring, willing and so forth. All these things can be connected to the centre or disconnected from it. We are told, for example, that 'what blocks, limits and programmes people are uncontacted and unexpressed feelings'. True, but anything at all can block, limit or programme somebody, not just feelings. We are told that 'for genuine intimacy to take place, communication on a here-and-now feeling level is essential'. But that is not all that is essential: honesty on a conceptual level, freed energy on an organismic level, clear demands on a desire level – all these and other things too are necessary for full intimacy.

The truth of the matter seems to be that in therapy or in personal growth, we are trying all the time to encourage the real person to come out, and this means the whole person. We are encouraging the person to put his or her whole self behind life and action.

One-sidedly feeling people would be monsters, just as much as one-sidedly thinking (sensing, intuiting, imagining, desiring) people would be. What we are aiming at is integration, not feelings.

Of course, the epitome of feeling is catharsis, or the primal. This, too, can become the one narrow aim, the panacea for all ills. John Heider (1974) once said:

> Even though catharsis produces peaks easily, the effects of these peaks seem random; no one can tell who will really change, and who will merely taste the possibility for change. But, even worse, the emphasis on catharsis leads practitioners and participants alike to seek ever more potent blowouts in the illusory hope of finally discovering the permanent high.

Nor is this a criticism that simply comes from outside, from someone who has nothing to do with primal work. Those inside the primal camp say the same thing. The late David Freundlich (1974), for example, after discussing twelve types of primal experience, dismisses a thirteenth in this way:

> *Final Primal* The false hope that an overwhelming cataclysmic primal will magically change the personality. This contrasts with the attitude that primal experiences and personality growth are lifelong processes which hopefully only terminate with death.

Heresy No. 3: Autonomy-ism

One of the key things about humanistic psychology is the emphasis it places on taking responsibility for oneself, and on creating one's own world. As a therapeutic stance, and taken in a first-person way, this can be extremely valuable and indeed necessary. Hampden-Turner (1976) describes a project for dealing with some of the most damaged and difficult people in society, most with considerable jail experience. He says that the project was very successful for those who were able to grasp the key point:

> The system made you what you are, but if you want to change the system, you have to accept the responsibility for what you let the system do to you.

Those who got this point made it, those who did not, did not. But if this stance is idealised as a total answer to life, it can turn into a pathological wish to be totally independent of everyone else in the world. Such a person will become quite incapable of love, because this involves some element of dependency on the other person, whether we like it or not, and whether our theory says so or not. A sort of classic of autonomy was Fritz Perls, who found it best to have his wife live some 3000 miles away. This autonomy reached its peak at his death, as the story has it in the book put together by Jack Gaines (1979):

> He was giving us a bad time about being held down. He started to get up and the nurse said, 'Dr. Perls, you have to lie down! You're pulling out all these things.' She put him down. A minute later, he started to get up again. At this point she buzzed for me and I went in. As I came in he had almost swung his legs out of bed, and I said, 'Dr. Perls, you have to lie down,' He looked at me and said, 'Don't tell me what to do.' Then he collapsed and he was gone.

Gaines says rather carefully that this story may be a myth, but that it does have the ring of Fritz, and is a fitting commentary on the way he lived.

But this heresy does not only affect the person involved, because if autonomy is urged in a third-person way (they create their own world, they are responsible for their lives, and so on), it can become punitive and oppressive. It turns into something like 'pull yourself together', or 'stand on your own two feet', or 'don't expect any handouts from me, buster'.

This is very far from what humanistic psychology is all about (remember Maslow and *gemeinschaftsgefühl*), and it loses all sense of community or solidarity.

The point is that you alone can do it, but you do not have to do it alone. This slogan is adapted from Mowrer (1971). Both sides of the statement are true, and they must not be separated from each other. In fact, sometimes you cannot do it alone even in principle. Autonomy is important, but love and mutual support and nourishment are important too.

There is a rather nice diagram in Paul (1985), which shows the sequence of personal development as dependent (passive supporter) leading to counter-dependent (angry, rebellious) leading to independent (competitive, aloof) leading to interdependent (involved achieving team member). This is in an organisational context, but a similar process can be seen in couple relationships, as Campbell (1980) has suggested. Autonomy as a total ideal is for hermits.

Heresy No. 4: Peace-and-love-ism

This is the way in which group leaders and others aim at warmth, trust, and openness in a way that seems to suggest that if you're not being warm, trusting, open and loving you are not getting it right. This is just as harmful as any other attempt to tell people what to think and what to feel, and is quite absurd as a norm. We are not in the peace and love game, we are in the reality game. If we attend closely to reality and do justice to what is present, what is there, my experience is that a lot of peace and love does ultimately ensue, but when it does, it too is real.

I once heard a man say, 'I keep telling my wife that it's wrong to invalidate me, but she won't stop doing it.' This is using the jargon of the group to set up a norm that is clearly manipulative. In effect, he is saying, 'Be peaceful and loving – see it my way'.

But worse still, the group in which these norms are upheld now has to project all its badness onto the outside world. It is the world outside that becomes the source of all the problems, and we are off the hook, because we are trying so hard to be positive. Unfortunately, however, the attempt to be positive and not negative is unreal, and can only end in disaster. The reasons for this are spelled out at length in Charles Hampden-Turner's (1981) marvellous and very original book, which shows with a wealth of detail how one-sidedness is always evil, even if it is a would-be-good one-sidedness. Humanistic psychology stands for the synergy that comes from doing justice to both sides of any polarity, not settling for one pole or the other.

There would be no change and no development without negativity, without death, as Ken Wilber (1983) points out in his discussion of Eros and Thanatos in the process of psychospiritual development. There is a great deal of research to show that confrontation is just as important as support in group work, as Peter Smith (1975) has shown, and Egan (1982) has given an excellent set of rules to make sure that confrontation works well.

However, there needs to be a note of caution the other way, too. I have seen people dismiss certain workshops on love as 'peace-and-love-ism' when in fact what the workshop leader was doing was to use 'total love' exercises in an attempt to encourage people to explore what love really meant to them. The test is simple: What happens when hate, lust, fear or anger come out instead of love? If the leader welcomes them and works with them and helps the person to come to terms with these feelings or to work through them, that is fine. If they are ignored or shunted aside or wished away, then we are faced with the heresy of peace-and-love-ism.

Heresy No. 5: Peakism

In this aberration, people get hold of the bit about peak experiences being important (Maslow, 1973) and somehow turn it into something for which to strive hard. Instead of the emphasis being on opening oneself up so that peak experiences have a chance to get in, all the emphasis goes on pushing oneself to greater and greater heights. The recent craze for fire-walking is a good example of this. The trouble with it is that it does inevitably lead on to the idea of the superman – the guy who stands on top of the mountain defying the lightning. Ayn Rand's characters often approach this (Branden, 1984), and the tendency is quite obviously towards individualism and fascism: individualism if it is you who is doing it, fascism if someone else is doing it and demanding your support and followership. Nietzsche is perhaps the prime example of all this, and I think he has influenced many people in the human potential movement, including some of those who do not recognise his name. One example of this influence is to be found in Colin Wilson (1979), whose book on Maslow seems to me a wildly Nietzschean misreading.

It is also suspicious that peaks are always upward, as we shall see in the next section. Peak experiences are certainly important and valid events, as I have explained at length elsewhere (Rowan, 1983b), but they are not things to be sought after or programmed. In fact, as Maslow (1970) pointed out, if we do seek after them we may become not only selfish but also evil. A deficiency-motivated search for private peaks can become very narrow and nasty.

Heresy No. 6: Spiritual-ism

An inelegant word to describe an all-too-elegant reality. This is where one gets so very spiritual that one loses touch with the ground altogether. Funk (1983) has a nice phrase on this:

> In contrast (to Beethoven) New Age music. . .seems not fully in the world. It is,
> metaphorically, like the peak of a pyramid suspended in mid-air.

The usual description of this sort of state – and it is used by genuinely spiritual people themselves – is 'ungrounded'. To be ungrounded is to adopt what is essentially a dualistic position – that we have risen above the mere flesh to the supernal region beyond. People like this seem to confuse smiling with insight.

It is also curious how so many of those who consider themselves to be so highly evolved seem quite oblivious to their own sexism. There are an awful lot of perfect masters and not very many perfect mistresses, and these perfect masters seem to keep getting caught in financial and sexual exploitation that is quite hard to explain away. The women find themselves in service roles just the same as anywhere else.

Nobody seems to point out that all this emphasis on the upward direction is very patriarchal – always the phallus pointing up at the sky. But there is also a spirituality of the downward direction, entering into the underworld realm of the Great Goddess. Down there in the darkness – for the Goddess was usually approached through caves – the miracles of birth and creativity were honoured. The most sacred ceremonies of death and rebirth took place down there in the depths. At the entrance to the cave there was a maze, a labyrinth, presided over by a mythical woman. The initiate had to find the way through to the underworld – the womb of the Mother – going through symbolic death to be reborn again through her on a deeper psychic level.

> Simultaneously, by dancing the winding and unwinding Spiral, the initiate reached
> back to the *Still Heart of the Cosmos*, and so immortality, through Her.
>
> (Sjöö and Mor, 1981)

Seen from this perspective, the whole idea of a peak experience becomes much more problematic, and suggests the dualistic escape that we have noticed before in these heresies. It does not have to be that, but in a patriarchal society, it is hard for it to avoid the general tendency to put the best at the top.

Whether we go up or down or stay in the middle, one of the promises of spirituality is that we may in some way be or become a god or goddess. We shall lose our limited ego, and become That. There is a sort of double-talk about this that needs to be spelled out. I don't think we ever really lose our egos – they change and at some stage we may have to be *prepared to lose them*, but they do not really go away. As Marlan (1981) suggests, false images of the ego are abandoned, and we end up with a new and improved ego. Edinger (1960) says that this is the basic paradox of therapy – the real self is, on the one hand, non-ego and, on the other hand, the very core of the ego. Wilber (1980) is very clear about this, talking about the death-seizure of the mental ego. But the ego does not really die, it just has to change, by removing some of its boundaries, some of its assumptions, some of its identifications.

In fact, I think Wilber has done us all a great service by showing that most of what we do in humanistic psychology is all about one particular stage in psychospiritual development – what he calls the centaur level:

> This integrated self, wherein mind and body are harmoniously one, we call the 'centaur'. The centaur: the great mythological being with animal body and human mind existing in a perfect state of at-one-ment.   (Wilber, 1980)

What this achievement of integration brings with it is a great sense of what the existentialists have called *authenticity*. This is the stage of the existential self, the real self, the true self. What Wilber has done so well is to show how this relates to other definitions of the self and other versions of the ego. It turns out that the real self is at one and the same time the end of the road of personal development, and the beginning of the spiritual path. No wonder it was ambiguous and confusing.

Heresy No. 7: Expertism

One way out of ambiguity and confusion is to become the great expert on something. People usually do this by means of the written word. They invent new words, describe new processes, make new distinctions, develop new syntheses, and in general strive to enlarge their domain. They may even try to take out a registered name to protect their specialty. Journals are great places to make one's mark, and if no existing journal will take one's stuff, one can simply start one's own journal. People in the Reichian tradition seem particularly fond of expertism; here is an almost random quotation from *Energy and Character*:

> The distinction is similar to that which Reich makes between alternating or genetic antithesis, and antagonistic antithesis. In constructive catastrophe the system makes a qualitative leap to a higher level or order: it moves up the orgonomic potential.

A similar approach is found in Janov and Holden (1977), which really takes a medical education to understand properly, and in many of the transactional analysis (TA) books and papers, with their unique and specialised vocabulary. (The Freudians, Jungians, and Scientologists are, of course, notorious for this, but they are not really within the boundaries of humanistic psychology.)

The point is that humanistic psychology is essentially anti-mystification, and expertism can be mystifying. Obviously technical terms must sometimes be used, but it really is important to avoid them whenever possible. It is very noticeable how the most central figures in humanistic psychology are also those who use jargon least.

Heresy No. 8: Sexism

In terms of its overt wishes, humanistic psychology is clearly antisexist. Sexism involves, as we all know by now, reducing women to the rigid roles that represent the only proper ways of being in a patriarchal society: almost always service roles of some kind, but also idealised moralistic roles. This is all documented very well and wittily in Gray's (1982) book on patriarchy as a conceptual trap, which is well worth seeking out.

Humanistic psychology is dedicated to questioning all rigid roles whatsoever, because they represent one of the main ways in which potential is limited by self or others. I have been into this at length elsewhere (Rowan, 1976a). But somehow the patriarchal roles seem often to creep back into the work of humanistic practitioners. For example, in group after group, I have seen the heterosexual couple relationship underlined and supported and pushed, as if it were really the only way to be.

There are several reports, in journals such as *Humpty Dumpty*, of groups where the women were treated quite differently by the leaders, as compared to the men. Most group leaders – and a much bigger majority of the best-paid and most prestigious leaders – are men. And most group attenders (in all the cases I have seen where any statistics have been kept) are women. This is obviously an enormous question, which affects the whole culture, and it is not surprising that it should affect humanistic practice as well as everything else. But it is certainly depressing (or anger-provoking) to see a discipline that is dedicated to the questioning of fixed roles, and dedicated to personal awareness, often being so unaware of sex roles and the way in which they constrain the person's development.

My own belief is that sexism keeps on creeping back because it needs so much work at different levels to deal with it. It needs work at the conscious level of laws and regulations and rules and practices and personal conduct. It needs work at the unconscious level of hatred of women and all that is female, coming from deep early material, as people such as Dinnerstein (1978) and Chodorow (1978) have explained. And it needs work at the spiritual level of myths and archetypes – a good summary of some of this material is to be found in Whitmont (1983). I have gone into this matter at much greater length in my book *The Horned God* (Rowan, 1987).

In psychology, the rot has gone very deep. Even nice people such as Lawrence Kohlberg have unconsciously introduced patriarchal assumptions into their work, and it takes someone like Gilligan (1982) to show this up and supplement it by paying much more attention to the female experience and female approaches. The whole emphasis on autonomy, which we saw earlier had some difficult questions attached to it, seems very male when seen in this light. As Joanna Macy (1983) has pointed out, we need in the nuclear age much more emphasis on interdependence, on networking and on mutual support.

My own work on research methodology (Reason and Rowan, 1981) shows again and again how many of the assumptions made by social researchers about the nature of the research process are very masculine (see also Reinharz (1985), for some very pertinent points on this). Recently, I did a presentation of some of the new paradigm research material, both theoretically and practically, to a group of managers who were involved with research training. On the second day, one of the women came up to me and said: 'It's not fair. For ten years I've been trying to turn myself into a man, and now you come along and tell me I have to turn back into a woman again!'

If we want to question patriarchy, as I have urged elsewhere (Rowan, 1978), we have to work on many levels simultaneously. We in the field of humanistic psychology are in a good position to do this, because we work with individuals, with groups, with organisations, and with whole communities, and we work at conscious, unconscious and spiritual levels. It is just a question of doing it, and not forgetting.

Heresy No. 9: Eclectic Mish-mash-ism

One of the strengths of our general approach is its adventurousness – the way in which we are prepared to try things out and see whether they work or not. But pushed to a one-sided extreme, this becomes a nervous search for novelty and fads. It also results in a set of practitioners who are using mutually contradictory theories and practices and trying to turn them into a whole – which can only be a false whole, only held together by the idealised wish of the user, and revealing a lack of critical thinking. And so we get Rogerian–Reichians, and gestalt–regressionists – I have even come across a Bhagwan–Marxist! In their study of 154 eclectic psychologists, Garfield and Kurtz (1977) found that 145 of them used 32 different combinations drawn from a wide range of therapeutic schools. Quite common were neo-Freudian and Rogerian, learning theory and humanistic, and Rogerian and learning theory. Dryden (1984) has a good discussion of this whole issue. I do not know how to make sense of some of these combinations. Learning theory (which should more accurately be called conditioning theory) has quite different assumptions from the person-centred approach, and to put them together seems to me quite impossible.

If we put disparate approaches together in this unthinking way, the work of forging new theories and new unities of theory and practice is avoided and sidetracked. This is not what humanistic psychology is about.

Conclusion

So these are the heresies I'd rather like to pursue and root out – except that I do not suppose I have the power or the right to do that. All I can do is confess to my anxieties and difficulties about these tendencies.

Someone asked me what I wanted positively. I really think it's obvious, and I've said it elsewhere anyway (Rowan, 1983a), but just for the record, here goes. I am in favour of humanistic psychology, and I think it is about encouraging the development of human potential. This means questioning all those structures (whether internal or external) that limit and constrain people. The main internal constraints seem to be rigid patterns of thought and action that have been set up as answers to the problems of living; however effective these may have been at the time they were first used, they have now turned into handcuffs or blinkers that prevent movement or awareness. Through the process of therapy, counselling, personal growth, critical thinking, and general self-discovery, these patterns are questioned in such a way that they can undergo change. The self-image gets dismantled, and the rich realm of subjectivity that was pushed down as too dangerous and too weak is now opened up and entered into and allowed to exist and be used and transformed. There is a feeling of being real instead of unreal.

The main external constraints seem to be rigid social patterns that have been set up as answers to the problems of living; however effective they may have been in the past, they have now turned into hobbles and straitjackets that prevent change or awareness. Through the process of consciousness-raising, organisational work, social research and political activism, these patterns are questioned in such a way that they can start to move.

Now we are aware of another set of constraints. We have been deprived, and continue to deprive ourselves in so many cases, of access to our spiritual nature. But by opening our eyes (or our third eye) to the myths and symbols that surround us on all sides, we can see that change is necessary here too. The old mythical figures have been distorted and narrowed and desecrated. My book *The Horned God* (Rowan, 1987) is about this, focusing particularly on how men's consciousness has been diminished, and how it can be restored to life in a way that makes it a partner to the Goddess consciousness that has inspired so many women (e.g. Spretnak, 1982; Starhawk, 1982) and made them strong.

To the extent that all these changes go forward together – the internal and the external and the spiritual – we shall find ourselves entering a new kind of society with new kinds of people. Instead of doing repair jobs on damaged people, we can spend more time on encouraging people to experience and explore their highest or deepest fulfilment.

But we must not shut out the very great obstacles that stand in the way of this. If something as simple and obviously desirable as the Equal Rights' Amendment (ERA) cannot get passed, there must be a lot of people around who do not want the kind of changes that I do. Reagan and the radical right, Thatcher and the amazing story of the Falklands crisis, all seem to show that things are not necessarily going our way. We do have something to offer, on the large scale as well as on the small, but all my experience tells me that unless someone takes up the offer, nothing much is going to happen. If people ask me how they can change, I have tremendous power, and can work magic. But if it is just me wanting them to change, all my power disappears, and I am just the same as anyone else with something to sell.

Progress is not inevitable. It may not even be very likely. Maybe the whole idea of progress is suspect in any case. Maybe it is just a question of what we like and what we want. There are not many people who even know that much. If we can link up with people who think and feel and intuit the same sort of things that we do, maybe we can just ride out the storm and be ready if humanity survives and the time comes to play our part. In the meantime, we can just act locally in any way that seems to be possible.

One key point that needs to be made over and over again is that the way to regulate well in times of great uncertainty is by learning rather than by controlling. Not learning fixed answers, but learning as a continuous process of coming to know. This is what transforms control, or even mutual control, into a process of co-creation, where we genuinely take responsibility for our world. As Michael (1983) says: 'But its successful practice requires openness to the unexpected: vulnerability.' We cannot learn much when all our defences are up. It is the horror, and the shame, of the world we live in that so often we seem driven to defend ourselves, forced to raise our barriers. It takes real inner strength, and staunch allies, to keep on going for a beter world.

Moving towards the society we want is a step-by-step process, where at each step we shall know what we are doing, just because we are trained to look at reality and to be real ourselves. Humanistic psychology stands for this unafraid look at the personal, the social and the spiritual.

References

BRANDEN, N. (1984). The benefits and hazards of the philosophy of Ayn Rand: A personal statement. *Journal of Humanistic Psychology* **24**(4), 39–64.

BRIDGES, W. (1973). Thoughts on humanistic education, or, is 'teaching' a dirty word? *Journal of Humanistic Psychology*, **13**(1), 5–13.

CAMPBELL, S.M. (1980). *The Couple's Journey*. San Luis Obispo, CA: Impact.

CHODOROW, N. (1978). *The Reproduction of Mothering*. Berkeley: University of California Press.

DINNERSTEIN, D. (1978). *The Rocking of the Cradle and the Ruling of the World*. London: Souvenir Press.

DRYDEN, W. (Ed.) (1984). *Individual Therapy in Britain*. London: Harper & Row.

EDINGER, E. (1960). The ego-self paradox. *Journal of Analytic Psychology* **5**(1).

EGAN, G. (1982). *The Skilled Helper,* 2nd edn. Monterey, CA: Brooks/Cole.

ELLIOTT, J. (1976). *Theory and Practice of Encounter Group Leadership*. Berkeley, CA: Explorations Institute.

FARSON, R. (1978). The technology of humanism. *Journal of Humanistic Psychology* **18**(2), 5-35.

FREUNDLICH, D. (1974). What is a Primal? *Primal Experience Monographs*. New York: Centre for the Whole Person.

FUNK, J. (1983). Music and fourfold vision. *Re Vision* **6**(1), 57-65.

GAINES, J. (1979). *Fritz Perls Here and Now*. Millbrae, CA: Celestial Arts.

GARFIELD, S.L. and KURTZ, R. (1977). A study of eclectic views. *Journal of Consulting and Clinical Psychology* **45**, 75-83.

GILLIGAN, C. (1982). *In a Different Voice*. London: Harvard University Press.

GRAY, E. (1982). *Patriarchy as a Conceptual Trap*. Wellesley, MA: Roundtable Press.

HAMPDEN-TURNER, C. (1976). *Sane Asylum*. New York: William Morrow.

HAMPDEN-TURNER, C. (1981). *Maps of the Mind*. London: Mitchell Beazley.

HEIDER, J. (1974). Catharsis in human potential encounter. *Journal of Humanistic Psychology* **14**(4), 27-47.

JANOV, A. and HOLDEN, M. (1977). *Primal Man*. London: Sphere Books.

LEEDS, R. (1970). The absorption of protest: A working paper. In W.G. Bennis, K.D. Benne and R. Chin (Eds), *The Planning of Change,* 2nd edn. New York: Holt, Rinehart & Winston.

MACY, J.R. (1983). *Despair and Personal Power in the Nuclear Age*. Philadelphia: New Society.

MARLAN, S. (1981). Depth consciousness. In R.S. Valle and R. von Eckartsberg (Eds), *The Metaphors of Consciousness*. New York: Plenum.

MASLOW, A.H. (1970). *Religions, Values and Peak Experiences*. New York: Viking.

MASLOW, A.H. (1973). *The Farther Reaches of Human Nature*. Harmondsworth: Penguin.

MIALE, G. (1973). Is feeling more real than thinking? An analysis of an imagined encounter. *Journal of Humanistic Psychology* **13**(2), 53-60.

MICHAEL, D.N. (1983). Competence and compassion in an age of uncertainty. *World Future Society Bulletin* (January/February), 1-6.

MOWRER, O.H. (1971). Peer groups and medication: The best 'therapy' for professionals and laymen alike. *Psychotherapy: Theory, Research and Practice* **8**, 44-54.

PAUL, N. (1985). Increasing organizational effectiveness: A training model for developing women. *Management Education and Development* **16**(2), 211-222.

REASON, P. and ROWAN, J. (1981). *Human Inquiry: A Sourcebook of New Paradigm Research*. Chichester: John Wiley.

REINHARZ, S. (1985). Feminist distrust: Problems of context and content in sociological work. In D.N. Berg and K.K. Smith (Eds), *Exploring Clinical Methods for Social Research*. Newbury Park, CA: Sage.

ROMEY, W.D. (1972). *Risk-Trust-Love: Learning in a Humane Environment*. Columbus: Charles E. Merrill.

ROWAN, J. (1976a). *Ordinary Ecstasy: Humanistic Psychology in Action*. London: RKP.

ROWAN, J. (1976b). Ethical issues in organizational change. In P. Warr (Ed.), *Personal Goals and Work Design*. London: John Wiley.

ROWAN, J. (1978). *The Structured Crowd*. London: Davis-Poynter.

ROWAN, J. (1983a) *The Reality Game: A Guide to Humanistic Counselling and Therapy*. London: RKP.

ROWAN, J. (1983b). The real self and mystical experiences. *Journal of Humanistic Psychology* **23**(2), 9-27.

ROWAN, J. (1987). *The Horned God: Male Consciousness and Feminism*. London: RKP.

ROWAN, J. (1988). Primal integration. In J. Rowan and W. Dryden (Eds), *Innovative Therapies in Britain*. London: Harper & Row.

SJÖÖ, M. and MOR, B. (1981). *The Ancient Religion of the Great Cosmic Mother of All*. Trondheim, Norway: Rainbow Press.

SMITH, P.B. (1975). Controlled studies of the outcome of sensitivity training. *Psychological Bulletin* **82**, 597–622.

SPRETNAK, C. (Ed.) (1982). *The Politics of Women's Spirituality*. Garden City, NY: Anchor.

STARHAWK (1982). *Dreaming the Dark: Magic, Sex and Politics*. Boston: Beacon.

WHITMONT, E.C. (1983). *Return of the Goddess*. London: RKP.

WILBER, K. (1980). *The Atman Project*. Wheaton, IL: Theosophical Publishing.

WILBER, K. (1983). *Eye to Eye*. Garden City: NY: Anchor.

WILSON, C. (1979). *New Pathways in Psychology*. London: Gollancz.

WOOTON, L.M. (1981). Albert Speer: How to manage an atrocity. *Journal of Humanistic Psychology* **21**(4), 21–38.

Chapter 6
Two Humanistic Psychologies or One?

The Question

I wrote a book in 1975 called *Ordinary Ecstasy: Humanistic Psychology in Action* (Rowan, 1976). It said where humanistic psychology came from, gave details of eight fields where it was used, and suggested directions for the future. I tried to make it the most complete account of humanistic psychology that had appeared up to that time. During revision for a new edition, a very difficult question has emerged.

In the first edition, I was quite clear that there was only one humanistic psychology – the one where we say that there is one great force of growth that pushes forward all the time, and leads us into self-actualisation. We can resist this process because of neurotic or psychotic blocks that we have set up at some point in our lives, or we can be dissuaded from further growth by the pressures of society, but the force is still there and can be resorted to at any time. Personal growth work, counselling and psychotherapy can all be useful in helping us to get in touch again with our own processes of development. This was the view of the two great classics, Maslow and Rogers (and their mentor Kurt Goldstein), and subscribed to in various ways by Perls, Moreno, Assagioli, Schutz, Lowen, Jackins and most of the others I knew at the time. It was also enshrined in the empirical research of people such as Kohlberg (1981) and Loevinger (1976), which seems quite solid, particularly if the work of Gilligan (1982) is included. So far, no problem.

> It should be noted that this basic actualizing tendency is the only motive which is postulated in this theoretical system.
> (Rogers, 1959)

> [For a healthy organism, the primary goal is] the *formation* of a certain level of tension, namely, that which makes possible further ordered activity.
> (Goldstein, 1939)

From J. Rowan (1989). Two humanistic psychologies or one? *Journal of Humanistic Psychology* 29(2), 224–229, with permission.

In the normal development of the normal child, it is now known that *most* of the time, if he is given a really free choice, he will choose what is good for his growth. This he does because it tastes good, feels good, gives pleasure or *delight*.

(Maslow, 1962)

They assume only one basic force in man. Therefore, life is not considered to be a compromise, but rather the process of unfolding of the one force. I have called the position exemplified by these theories the fulfilment model. . . If the force is the tendency to express to an ever greater degree the capabilities, potentialities or talents based in one's genetic constitution, then we are confronted with the actualization version. . . The actualization version is humanistic.   (Maddi, 1976)

But one of the people who has impressed me most over the ten years from 1979 to 1989 was Alvin Mahrer, who seems to me humanistic if anyone ever was, and also a very original and powerful thinker. And he says there is no great force, there is no spiritual path, there is nothing to lead us forward or in any other direction. There is only choice. Because so many of our choices are based on a neurotic (or psychotic) history and a dehumanising social system, most of our choices are more likely to lead us into pain or at least dissatisfaction than any other way – unless and until we take responsibility for them ourselves and own up to the fact that we do not have to make these self-defeating choices if we do not want to. It is up to us. And it seems to me that this is also what May is saying in his own way, and Laing in his.

Potentials for experiencing do not *push* the person into experiencing. They merely stand ready (potential) to experience love or curiosity or whatever. In contrast with concepts such as libido, drive, motivation, energy, need, actualization, growth force, arousal, activation or press, our potentials do not possess any character of shoving, pushing, pulling or driving. They are only potentials, nothing more. . . [Integration of these potentials] involves the commitment to be whatever there is within to be. This is the leap of faith, the tearing of one's self from what one is and the falling into whatever is there within. In this commitment, I am the one to decide, the one who makes or fails to make the commitment. It is my commitment, not my parents' or my group's or my spouse's. I am the responsible director of my own process of internal change.   (Mahrer, 1978)

I see the human being as an organized bundle of potentialities. These potentialities, driven by the daimonic urge, are the source *both* of our constructive and our destructive impulses. If the daimonic urge is integrated into the personality. . . it results in creativity, that is, it is constructive. If the daimonic is not integrated, it can take over the total personality. . . destructive activity is then the result.

(May, 1982)

Personal action can either open out possibilities of enriched experience or it can shut off possibilities. Personal action is either predominantly validating, confirming, encouraging, supportive, enhancing, or it is invalidating, disconfirming, discouraging, undermining and constricting. It can be creative or destructive. In a world where the normal condition is one of alienation, most personal action must be destructive both of one's own experience and of that of the other.

(Laing, 1967)

In history and culture there is no Unseen Hand; there is human action.

(Smith, 1973)

Now here is the problem. If Maslow and Rogers are truly and centrally humanistic (as I am sure they are), and if Mahrer and May are also and equally humanistic – and I would certainly argue very hotly that they are, if anyone doubted it – then how come they differ so much on something so fundamental and basic? The critique of Rogers by May (1982) covers some of the same ground, although focusing more on the question of evil and how to deal with it. I am not really so worried about the question of evil, because I said nothing about it in the first edition, and so there is nothing to revise there.

There may be a way out if we take the ideas of Ken Wilber (1980) seriously. It could be that Maslow and Rogers are basically very broad, and actually are talking about a range of experience reaching from the mental ego (ordinary consciousness) to the subtle self (transpersonal consciousness), while centring on the centaur (existential consciousness), using Wilber's terminology. And it could also then be that Mahrer and May are just concerned with the centaur stage (existential consciousness), and not with the mental ego or the subtle self. This would make them more narrowly and purely humanistic than Maslow and Rogers.

There seems something paradoxical or at any rate strained and unreasonable about saying that those who defined and created humanistic psychology are somehow less pure, less true to the cause, than much less central people who have never been seen as exemplars in the same way.

Yet it is not so unreasonable to suggest that when people start something, they are not so very clear as to what they are starting, and may include a whole mixture of things that are not really necessary; and then by a process of evolution the excrescences are chipped away and the central message is revealed much more clearly by others who come along later. I cannot think of any examples of that, but no doubt there are some somewhere. Usually what the founders feel is just the opposite – that they are offering a whole message, and that people are narrowing it and producing heresies that are clearer but less adequate.

Yet the story I normally tell about humanistic psychology is the Maslow/Rogers one. (For example, I once wrote 'Maslow's theory of human needs and human development says very clearly that there is a normal process of growth which applies to all people'.) To start telling the Mahrer/May story instead seems much more depressing and partial, especially because it seems to exclude the Maslow/Rogers story, in a way that is not equally true the other way round. How do I incorporate the Mahrer/May material without rewriting the whole thing from scratch? It seems so hard to be optimistic and pessimistic at the same time. I would much rather be one or the other. How can I resolve this contradiction? It is driving me crazy.

Postscript

That was my original question to Tom Greening. He pointed me in the direction of some old articles in the *Journal of Humanistic Psychology*, which might throw some light on the question. They only made it harder.

One idea did come up, however; that somehow the idea of paradox might be important. An article by Schneider (1986) suggested something like this. He puts the matter in terms of the finite and the infinite. Some thinkers, he says, emphasise one and some the other, but we have somehow to hold them together, not let them fly to extremes. I suppose here we could put Maslow et al. as standing for the infinite, for the emphasis on freedom and optimism, and May et al. as representing the finite – the emphasis here being on down-to-earth choice in adverse circumstances. Schneider suggests:

> The finite and infinite are seen as polarities rather than absolute contradictions. We do not perceive the world as *totally* finite or *totally* infinite, but as relatively finite or closed and relatively infinite or open. Another way to put this is that the finite is a potentiality when the infinite is emphasized, and the infinite is a potentiality when the finite is emphasized.   (Schneider, 1986)

This would, as it were, allow May to be waiting in the wings when Maslow is on, and Maslow to be waiting in the wings when May is on. This doesn't sound very convincing to me really, now that I look at it. There would still be two humanistic psychologies playing Box and Cox with each other, and this is not satisfying to me.

So the problem remains.

References

GILLIGAN, C. (1982). *In a Different Voice: Psychological Theory and Women's Development*. Cambridge, MA: Harvard University Press.

GOLDSTEIN, K. (1939). *The Organism*. New York: American Book Co.

KOHLBERG, L. (1981). *The Philosophy of Moral Development*. San Francisco: Harper & Row

LAING, R.D. (1967). *The Politics of Experience*. Harmondsworth: Penguin.

LOEVINGER, J. (1976). *Ego Development*. San Francisco: Jossey-Bass.

MADDI, S.R. (1976). *Personality Theories: A Comparative Analysis*, 3rd ed. Homewood, IL: Dorsey.

MAHRER, A.R. (1978). *Experiencing: A Humanistic Theory of Psychology and Psychiatry*. New York: Brunner/Mazel.

MASLOW, A.H. (1962). *Toward a Psychology of Being*. Princeton, NJ: van Nostrand.

MAY, R. (1982). The problem of evil: An open letter to Carl Rogers. *Journal of Humanistic Psychology* 22(3), 10–21.

ROGERS, C.R. (1959). A theory of therapy, personality and interpersonal relationships, as developed in the client-centered framework. In S. Koch (Ed.), *Psychology: A Study of a Science*, Vol. 3. New York: McGraw-Hill.

ROWAN, J. (1976). *Ordinary Ecstasy: Humanistic Psychology in Action*. London: Routledge & Kegan Paul

SCHNEIDER, K.J. (1986). Encountering and integrating Kierkegaard's absolute paradox. *Journal of Humanistic Psychology* 26(3), 62– 80.

SMITH, M.B. (1973). On self-actualization: A transambivalent examination of a focal theme in Maslow's psychology. *Journal of Humanistic Psychology* 13(2), 17–33.

WILBER, K. (1980). *The Atman Project*. Wheaton: Theosophical Publishing House.

Chapter 7
The Self: One or Many

Most people have had the experience of being divided. On the one hand I want to do this, but on the other I would much rather do that, and I am torn between them. It is as if there were two of me, and as if a battle could develop between us. This is not a matter of multiple personality, it is just a normal experience, although sometimes an uncomfortable one.

There are many variations on this theme, and it is a familiar one in literature, as witness for example Hermann Hesse's *Steppenwolf,* where a real conflict breaks out between the man and the wolf of the steppes who lives inside him.

Until recently, however, this has not been recognised in personality theory, at least not since the time of William James. It has not been regarded as a legitimate subject for study.

In recent years the topic of the self has become much more respectable in psychology, and today a number of researchers are working in the field of identity formation and similar topics. We hear of situated identities and role relations, and so on. People, such as John Kihlstrom and Nancy Cantor (e.g. Kihlstrom et al., 1988) have been doing very sophisticated work investigating the discrepancies between different selves of the one person. Yet strangely none of this seems to have percolated through to personality theory. Recently, I have been looking systematically at the way in which personality theory would be affected if some of the new thinking rubbed off on to it, and have completed a book which is to be published later this year.

It is an extraordinary thing that all personality theories assume that there is just one personality. The questions they then ask are: What is the structure of this personality? What are the functions of this personality? What are the origins of this personality? What can we predict about this personality?

From J. Rowan (1989). The Self: one or many. *The Psychologist: Bulletin of the British Psychological Society* 7, 279–281, with permission.

If we give a person a personality test of any kind we assume that there is going to be just one result, one set of figures, one profile. If the results differ from one day to another, we talk about the reliability of the test rather than the variability of the person.

But these assumptions are just assumptions, and they are made largely because it is convenient to do so. Let us not impute any deeper, darker motives such as fear of self-knowledge. Personologists are lazy people, like the rest of us, and do not want the bother of considering that people might be multiple. Other psychologists studying questions, such as the self, identity and so forth, are only too pleased to fall in with this for their own particular purposes.

Subpersonalities

If we ask the awkward question, however, of whether such convenient assumptions are valid, we get a very different answer. Many clinicians and some of the more recent writers in both cognitive and social psychology have been forced to use some concept of multiplicity within the person. Whether with Freud we talk about the ego, the id and the super-ego; whether with Jung we talk about the complexes (or the archetypes); whether with Federn or Berne or John Watkins we talk about ego states; whether with Lewin we talk about subregions of the personality; whether with Perls we talk about the topdog and the underdog (or retro-flection); whether with Klein or Fairbairn or Guntrip we talk about internal objects; whether with Mary Watkins we talk about imaginal objects; whether with McAdams we talk about imagoes; whether with Hilgard we talk about the hidden observer; whether with Denzin we talk about the emotionally divided self; whether with Winnicott or Lake or Janov or Laing we talk about the false or unreal self; whether with Gurdjieff we talk about little I's; whether with Goffman we talk about multiple selfing; whether with Stone and Winkelman we talk about energy patterns; whether with Mahrer we talk about deeper potentials coming to the surface; whether with Mair we talk about a community of self; whether with Ornstein we talk about small minds; whether with Minsky we talk about agents and agencies within the mind; whether with Gergen or Martindale or O'Connor or Shapiro we talk about subselves; whether with Strauss or Rossan we talk about subidentities; whether with Markus we talk about possible selves; whether with Kihlstrom and Cantor we talk about self-schemata; whether with T.B. Rogers we talk about prototypes; whether with Beahrs we talk about alter-personalities; or whether with Assagioli or Redfearn we talk about subpersonalities – all the time we are talking about the same thing – multiplicity of the personality.

My own approach is to talk about subpersonalities, and to say that a given person probably has from four to nine subpersonalities, coming from at least six different origins. My own working definition of a subpersonality is a *semi-permanent and semi-autonomous region of the personality capable of acting as a person.* This definition seems to me specific and usable. It quite clearly cuts out psychiatric cases of multiple personality as being too autonomous altogether, and it cuts out temporary hypnotic states and other altered states of consciousness as being too transient. It cuts out states of spirit possession as being too autonomous and sometimes too transient at once. We are talking all the way through about people who are as normal as you and me.

Up until recently, it would have been necessary, in support of such a view, to use anecdotes (very convincing ones, nonetheless) or clinical experience (very compelling, to be sure) – both sources of information that are somewhat suspect to many psychologists. But over the last ten years there has been more and more work by experimental psychologists who have also found that if we want to make sense of human beings we have to look at this question of their inner multiplicity.

Psychology

The notion of a self-schema is not very old, but it is based on the basic notion of a psychological schema, which goes back to the work of Bartlett in the 1930s. Recently, it has been developed by people, such as Hazel Markus and her colleagues, and it has led to a great deal of interesting work.

For example, Seymour Rosenberg and Michael Gara (1985) did a very interesting experiment where they measured personal identities and the characteristics and feelings associated with each one. From this they derived a matrix which then provided a representation of the person's inner identity structure. This corresponds very well with the definition of subpersonalities used here. They point to the difficulties involved in doing this work, particularly in the area of negative identities; a sense of trust between the researcher and the subject is required in order to deal with them. This whole question of the relationship between the researcher and the subject has of course undergone much scrutiny in recent years, and I have made some contribution to that discussion myself (Reason and Rowan, 1981).

Quite independently, Dan McAdams (1985) was conducting some interesting research involving not only personality tests and questionnaires, but also life stories, divided into chapters. He then extracted what he calls imagoes from these life stories; an imago is the same as what we have been calling a subpersonality. This was not such a tight study as that of Rosenberg and Gara, but it contains some very interesting ideas about methodology.

More recently, Hazel Markus and her colleagues at the University of Michigan have been working on some very interesting ideas in this area.

Markus and Nurius (1987) describe their research on what they call possible selves. These possible selves are actually self-schemata – generalisations about the self derived from past experience that help one integrate and explain one's own behaviour.

Starting from there, these workers went on to carry out several types of studies: survey, experimental and clinical. Subjects are sometimes asked to generate their own list of possible selves, and sometimes asked to choose from a list generated by earlier subjects. One of their main discoveries was that all of the individuals they studied had possible selves, and were willing to describe them and reflect on them, both the positive and the negative. This underlines the point we were making earlier about subpersonalities being normal and not pathological in any way.

Going into more detail as time went on, they began to distinguish between schematics (those who thought their subpersonality-type involvement in a given area was important) and aschematics – those who did not. They found that schematics have many more subpersonalities, both positive and negative, in a given area than aschematics. But the schematics and the aschematics did not differ in number or elaboration of possible selves in domains for which neither group had a schema.

This is very interesting work which throws a lot of light on motivation, particularly for long-term tasks. People in this research created possible selves and then invested quite a lot of energy in them. These possible selves then acted as guides or markers helping to make choices that were consistent with them.

The question arises: If all this work is being done (and there is far more that we could quote) then why do researchers go on ignoring these possibilities? An interesting case in point is the book edited by Terry Honess and Krysia Yardley (1987) dealing with self and identity. The paper quoted above, by Markus and Nurius (1987), comes from another book edited by the same people (different publisher) in the same year, so the editors are not prejudiced or blinkered or ignorant. But every single chapter in this book, written by eminent worthies in the field, organises things in such a way that the concept of a subpersonality cannot emerge. One chapter does use the word 'subidentities', but the concept is not pursued or worked with in any way.

What seems to be the case, therefore, is that people are so used to working with a single self, a single personality, a single identity, that they simply do not notice the work which powerfully suggests that this is not all there is to the matter, and that they had better think again.

Psychotherapy

Now at the same time as this work is going on in psychology, some very interesting new work is coming along in psychotherapy. For many years, the Jungian camp has been interested in complexes and archetypes, and these are very precise equivalents of what we have called subpersonalities. But recently they have shown interest in working with these entities directly in the therapy consulting room using what they call active imagination. For example, Robert Johnson (1986) has produced a handbook giving very precise instructions for working in Jungian psychotherapy with what he variously calls 'inner persons', 'selves', 'figures' and so on. He says that the essential move is to personify some content of the unconscious, emerging in a dream or hypnagogic vision etc. Once this act of personification has taken place, we can have a dialogue with our subpersonality. Of course, this is very much what Assagioli and the psychosynthesis school (Ferrucci, 1982) have been doing for many years now in their own field.

A similar but more elaborately worked-out approach has come from Hal Stone and Sidra Winkelman (1985), who in great detail go into not only how to go into this process of personification, and how to work with the persons once they emerge, but also how to try to classify the personages into groups with similar purposes and natures. This idea of classifying subpersonalities also comes up in Shapiro (1976) and Berne (1961), whose categorisation into parent, adult and child ego states is well known and now becoming increasingly respectable.

On going through the current literature in psychotherapy, I have been surprised to find how widespread the use of subpersonalities is, or the use of some synonym for such. Altogether I have found that this is the case in 16 different schools: Freudian, Jungian, psychosynthesis, psychodrama, gestalt, transactional analysis, Shapiro's ego therapy, Shorr's psycho-imagination therapy, Watkins' ego state therapy, Voice Dialogue, Mahrer's experiential therapy, hypnotherapy, Satir's family therapy, neurolinguistic programming (NLP), Sasportas' astrological therapy, cognitive–behavioural therapy. Some of these are well known, some of them obscure; some are highly respectable, some less so; some use it a lot, others very little; but the fact that so many strange bedfellows exist here suggests that this must be something that has a life of its own, not dependent upon any one framework of thought.

Philosophy

This is not the end of the matter. There has also been a great deal of interest lately in this question in the field of philosophy. Philosophers interested in questions of self and identity have been disturbed by the data emerging, for example, from split-brain experiments (Gazzaniga, 1985), where one hemisphere of the brain is severed from the other by cutting the corpus callosum. Gazzaniga himself believes that his work shows that our brains are organised in terms of independent modules, each capable of action. After reviewing a great deal of this recent philosophical argument, Glover (1988) says:

> It seems that, when the left hemisphere has been removed, the right hemisphere can be associated with consciousness. It is hardly likely that the presence in the same skull of a disconnected left hemisphere changes this. And so it is reasonable to see the disconnected right hemisphere of the split brain patient as a centre of consciousness. If this is right, the experiments do demonstrate divided consciousness. (p. 40)

Once we admit the possibility of divided consciousness in one area, it is harder to hold back on admitting the possibility more generally. For example, after discussing a thought experiment where he had the power to separate the two halves of his brain at will, Parfit (1984) concludes:

> It might be objected that my description ignores 'the necessary unity of consciousness'. But I have not ignored this alleged necessity. I have denied it. What is a fact must be possible. And it is a fact that people with disconnected hemispheres have two separate streams of consciousness – two series of thoughts and experiences, in having each of which they are unaware of having the other. Each of these two streams separately displays unity of consciousness. This may be a surprising fact. But we can understand it. We can come to believe that a person's mental history need not be like a canal, with only one channel, but could be like a river, occasionally having separate streams. I suggest that we can also imagine what it would be like to divide and reunite our minds. (p. 247)

It is perhaps only because so much of this work is so recent that it has still not made much impact on the world of academic psychology. But it seems that this sort of work does make it much more possible to think in terms of multiple subpersonalities rather than just one personality.

Conclusion

Philosophy, too, then, makes us think again about the question of whether there has to be just one personality. I have found the best single summary of all this material in the book which John Beahrs, who is actually a hypnotherapist, brought out in 1982. The way he puts it is to ask these rather different questions:

> *When is it useful or not useful to look upon an individual as a single unit, a 'Cohesive Self'?
> *When is it useful or not useful to look upon any one as being constituted of many parts, each with an identity of its own?
> *When is it more useful to see ourselves as part of a greater whole?
> I use the term 'useful' rather than 'true' since all are true – simultaneously and at all times. (Beahrs 1982, pp. 4–5)

This seems quite a sober statement of the obvious, and I do not see why it has to be particularly threatening to anyone. It just needs us to take it seriously and do something about it. One of the first things we need to do, in my opinion, is to look much more critically at the textbooks of personality: I cannot find a single one that says anything at all about any of the points I have raised in this paper.

References

BEAHRS, J.O. (1982). *Unity and Multiplicity: Multilevel Consciousness of Self in Hypnosis, Psychiatric Disorder and Mental Health*. New York: Brunner/Mazel.

BERNE, E. (1961). *Transactional Analysis in Psychotherapy*. New York: Grove Press.

FERRUCCI, P. (1982). *What We May Be*. Wellingborough: Turnstone Press.

GAZZANIGA, M. (1985). *The Social Brain*. New York: Basic Books.

GLOVER, J. (1988). *I: The Philosophy and Psychology of Personal Identity*. Allen Lane.

HONESS, T. and YARDLEY, K. (Eds) (1987). *Self and Identity: Perspectives across the Lifespan*. London: Routledge.

JOHNSON, R.A. (1986). *Inner Work: Using Dreams and Active Imagination for Personal Growth*. San Francisco: Harper & Row.

KIHLSTROM, J.F., CANTOR, N., ALBRIGHT, J.S., CHEW, B.R., KLEIN, S.B. and NIEDENTHAL, P.M. (1988). Information processing and the study of the self. In *Advances in Experimental Social Psychology*, Vol. 21. New York: Academic Press.

MCADAMS, D.P. (1985). The 'imago': A key narrative component of identity. In P. Shaver (Ed.), *Self, Situations and Social Behavior*. Beverly Hills, CA: Sage.

MARKUS, H. and NURIUS, P. (1987). Possible selves: The interface between motivation and the self-concept. In K. Yardley and T. Honess (Eds), *Self and Identity: Psychosocial Perspectives*. Chichester: John Wiley & Sons.

PARFIT, D. (1984). *Reasons and Persons*. Oxford: Clarendon Press.

REASON, P. and ROWAN, J. (Eds) (1981). *Human Inquiry*. Chichester: John Wiley.

ROSENBERG, S. and GARA, M.A. (1985). The multiplicity of personal identity. In P. Shaver (Ed.), *Self, Situations and Social Behaviour: Review of Personality and Social Psychology*, Vol. 6. Beverly Hills, CA: Sage.

ROWAN, J. (1989). *Subpersonalities: The People Inside Us*. London: Routledge, in press

SHAPIRO, S.B. (1976). *The Selves Inside You*. Berkeley: Explorations Institute.

STONE, H. and WINKELMAN, S. (1985). *Embracing our Selves*. Marina del Rey: Devorss & Co.

Part III
Humanistic
Psychotherapy

The whole of this section takes for granted that there is such a thing as humanistic psychology, which I hope we established in the last section. So we can now move on to consider the way in which these basic ideas are translated into the practical world of therapy.

The first piece in this section – 'The concept of a breakthrough' – is a very basic one, which takes an idea from Ken Wilber and pushes it quite a bit further. I think it helps us to make sense of a very tricky phenomenon, which is quite indisputable but also quite hard to describe accurately.

The next piece – 'Humanistic psychotherapy and psychoanalysis' – is actually part of a correspondence between me and the editor of the *British Journal of Psychotherapy* – Robert Hinshelwood. I think this question of how exactly humanistic psychotherapy relates to psychoanalysis is very important, because the psychoanalysts have a nasty habit of assuming that they are the first and only psychotherapists, and everyone else derives from them.

Then we have a brief squib – 'Against feelings' – designed to counter one of the biggest misconceptions about humanistic psychotherapy, sometimes even held by therapists themselves.

I was asked to contribute a chapter – 'Siding with the client' – to a book called *Key Cases in Psychotherapy*, which was all about cases that had changed our way of working in some way. Later I produced a briefer version of this, shorn of some of the more theoretical material, and it is this version that is included here. It portrays very well, I think, the kind of work that I normally do.

The next article – 'Counselling and the psychology of furniture' – was produced while I was sitting on the accreditation subcommittee of the British Association for Counselling. I think it puts some points quite succinctly. It may amuse readers to learn that the paragraph on the location and height of washbasins in bedrooms was cut by the editor. I have restored it here.

While writing my book on subpersonalities, I came across some fascinating material about the early origins of psychotherapy and the notion of the unconscious. So when *Self and Society* wanted to have a special issue on hypnotherapy, I was happy to write the article 'Hypnotherapy and the humanistic'.

The next article – 'Early traumas: A dialectical approach' – again had a history. The first draft was written for *Changes* magazine, because they had had several articles in the area; however, they said that they had had enough for a while. So I revised it slightly, and sent it in to *Self and Society* which printed it: but later I got a letter from David Boadella asking if he could reprint it in *Energy and Character*, the international journal that goes to body workers all over the world. I think this is a very important area to get clear about, because it is all too easy to go one way or the other – either towards the Freudian view that it is all in the mind, or towards the other extreme, and say that the importance of traumatic events is purely physical.

The final article in this section – 'Encounter groups as a paradigm of integrative psychotherapy' – is based on a chapter in a book on integrative approaches to therapy, but is a bit shorter. It was submitted in this form to the *Journal of Integrative and Eclectic Psychotherapy*, and makes some points which I think have to be considered by anyone who wants to bring the different psychotherapeutic approaches closer together.

Chapter 8
The Concept of a
Breakthrough

> One cold Saturday in February we had an all-day marathon and I had the most profound experience of my life. For on that cold winter day I discovered a whole new world. . . I experienced my own beauty that day, as a woman, as a person. I really felt it on the inside. . . I loved everyone as they were. . . I was seeing differently. . . I went through a door to a place I could only call whole, clear vision.
>
> (Anonymous workshop participant, approximately 1982)

This is the breakthrough in the group – in this case a primal group – which I have spoken of before as one of the most characteristic aspects of personal growth as humanistic psychology sees it.

I have myself experienced this, and called it getting in touch with my real self; I have also seen it happen to many other people, in my own and other people's groups. To me it is familiar territory.

Of course there can be smaller breakthroughs, not so full, not so dramatic perhaps, but still marking an important step forward. In the field of therapy, we often say that each such breakthrough must be followed by a period of working through, to integrate the new material into daily life.

(Before continuing, it seems worth while to dispose of one false obstacle. From a feminist point of view, there may be something suspect about the idea of a breakthrough – it sounds rather masculine and penetrative. But really this is not so – a birth is a breakthrough, and girl babies are just as good at breaking through as boy babies – and need to break through just as much. Feminists need to, and do, break through established conventions more than most people.)

Not long ago I came across a diagram which seems to me to do justice to the idea of a breakthrough. It comes from Ken Wilber's (1977) book *The Spectrum of Consciousness*, and it looks like Figure 8.1.

From J. Rowan (1982). The concept of a breakthrough. *Self and Society* November/December, 281–283, with permission.

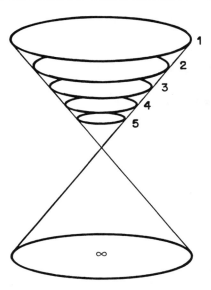

Figure 8.1

What Wilber says – and I am deliberately dropping his labels, because I want to generalise what he is saying – is that we progress in our personal growth, or in our personal or spiritual development, from one number to the next in logical fashion. We extend what we know from 1 to 2, we add more information from 2 to 3, we add new experiences from 3 to 4, we get new feelings and sensations from 4 to 5 – and all these things are interchangeable and additive.

But then we come to the point where the upper and lower cones intersect. This is the point where a complete changeover takes place. Instead of progressing to the next number, we fall through into infinity. All our existing acquisitions become useless at this point, and we cannot use the old approach any more. An entirely new set of rules applies.

This seems to me a very accurate and evocative picture of what happens. Wilber emphasises that the only way we can avoid the logical sequence of regular steps followed by a breakthrough is by refusing to let go. All the way down from 1 to 5, it was a question of acquiring more and more, of getting, even of grabbing, perhaps. But now, at the central point, it is a question of letting go, of abandoning our preconceptions, our identity.

Now Wilber is talking about spiritual development, and the ultimate level of consciousness, whereas I started off this article by talking about personal growth. I am not at all saying that these are the same thing. All I am saying is that they take the same form. There is more than one breakthrough, but all breakthroughs have this same pattern.

This is of course very similar to the idea of the dialectical transformation of quantity into quality. Water gets hotter and hotter until it turns into steam, or colder and colder until it turns into ice. The last straw breaks the camel's back. The caterpillar grows and grows until it turns into a butterfly. Societies change gradually until the revolution comes.

It is also reminiscent of the recent discoveries in catastrophe theory, but I think catastrophe theory is different in that you can always get back to your starting point. With the kind of breakthroughs we are concerned with in personal growth, there is no way of going back.

What I have found in my own experience is that there is one of these double-cones (Wilber's hour-glass figure) below another, so that there is a continual process of learning followed by breakthrough followed by consolidation, followed by new learning, and so on. This is something that has certainly been found in spiritual growth by people, such as Thomas Merton, Evelyn Underhill and James Horne (1978).

So this seems to be common ground between personal growth (the work done in groups and in one-to-one therapy) and spiritual development, the work done in meditation, prayer and ritual. In both cases there is an intellectual element and an experiential element, and in both cases it is the experiential element that is the real heart of the matter, so far as change is concerned.

In both fields this point, where we have to let go of our previous images and self-image, feels very risky and dangerous. But always we find that it is less dangerous and less different than we thought at first. So the message is that all shall be well: and all manner of things shall be well.

References

HORNE, J.R. (1978). *Beyond Mysticism*. Waterloo: Canadian Corporation for Studies in Religion.

WILBER, K. (1977). *The Spectrum of Consciousness*. Wheaton: Theosophical Publishing House.

Chapter 9
Humanistic Psychology and Psychoanalysis:

A Correspondence with Bob Hinshelwood

It started with an editorial in the *British Journal of Psychotherapy* (Vol. 3, No. 2) which said (in part):

> So, it may be important, for a Journal that is aiming to make a small contribution to the integration of the world of psychotherapy, to recognise that there is a very large field of professional activity and practice involving many many people who do not identify with the world of analytical psychotherapy. It has been the assumption of this Journal that the psychoanalytical form of therapy was the first real psychotherapy and remains the core element in psychotherapy today.
>
> However, psychoanalytic theory is not the only framework for thinking about our work, yet it is the only framework that derives from the study of human beings. Psychological learning theory, towards which most non-analytic psychotherapies turn for their conceptual framework, derives from the study of dogs and rats. In my view the animal species giving rise to a psychological theory is of considerable importance, but it is not the only difference we should take note of. The humanism of psychoanalysis, bearing on the subjectivity of the person and the intersubjectivity of his world, takes analytical psychotherapy dangerously, and excitingly, apart from and probably beyond the world of objective science, as I have noted before in these Editorials. Psychological learning theory, in contrast, remains rooted in the deterministic (non-humanistic) tradition of the objective physical sciences; and in a major sense could be unfortunately allied with the medical and pharmacological approach... We need more correspondents willing to jump in with opinions upon the great divide in our profession.

I decided to take the bait, and wrote a letter to the editor (Bob Hinshelwood) which read thus:

I was amazed in the current issue of the Journal to see your editorial statement: '. . .psychoanalytic theory is not the only framework for thinking about our work, yet it is the only framework that derives from the study of human beings.'

From J. Rowan (1986-1987). *British Journal of Psychotherapy* 3(2)-4(2), with permission.

This seems to deny the existence of humanistic psychotherapy. And in the rest of the editorial this denial is repeated, in that there are copious mentions of learning theory, objective science, non-human research, the medical and pharmacological approach and so on, but no mention of humanistic psychology.

Yet you have published a paper by me which was nothing to do with psychoanalysis and was purely humanistic, so you must know that the humanistic approach exists. You mention the Rugby conference, so you must know that the humanistic contingent there is quite active and vocal, and second in size to the psychoanalytic contingent.

Where does humanistic psychology come from? In the early days, one man was the pioneer of this way of looking at the world; Abraham Maslow. Later the movement he had started was joined by others such as Carl Rogers, Charlotte Buhler, Roberto Assagioli, Fritz Perls, Virginia Satir, Kurt Goldstein, Sidney Jourard, Rollo May, Clark Moustakas, Ira Progoff, Alvin Mahrer, Jean Houston, Charles Hampden-Turner, David Boadella.

Carl Rogers does not owe his origins or his theories to psychoanalysis, and neither did Abraham Maslow. Yet these two founding fathers of humanistic psychology have been quoted and analysed and examined in university courses, psychotherapy courses, institutes and centres all over the world, and honoured by many accolades from people in psychology and psychotherapy as having made extremely valuable contributions. For example, they have both been elected President of the American Psychological Association at different times.

Jacob Moreno had nothing to do with psychoanalysis, yet his development of psychodrama contributed one of the most useful ways of working with groups, and his methods are now being approached with great interest by some psychoanalysts. Fritz Perls, the originator of gestalt therapy – a very popular and well-developed discipline – did start out from psychoanalysis, but his main relationship with it was always a negative one, and gestalt therapy does not refer to or depend on psychoanalysis. Alvin Mahrer, who has probably made the biggest contribution to humanistic theory since Maslow, hardly mentions psychoanalytic ideas, and is mainly inspired by existentialist philosophy; his humanistic psychodynamics is both simpler and potentially deeper than the older and more well-known psychoanalytic versions. David Boadella in this country has made a very important contribution in synthesising the various body-work approaches so central to humanistic psychotherapy, and showing how effective this approach can be in actually dealing with people's problems; this work does derive from a psychoanalyst (Wilhelm Reich) but goes beyond it in its devotion to the body. Roberto Assagioli contributed a spiritual aspect to the work which again takes off from an analyst (Carl Jung) but goes further and is perhaps more effective as well as deeper.

This is not to mention the offerings of people like Frank Lake, Stan Grof and Bill Swartley, who took psychoanalytic theory very seriously, and then proceeded to take it further than the psychoanalysts ever intended and certainly further than most of them feel comfortable with. If Klein and the object relations school take experience back to the first months after birth, these people take experience back to birth itself, and life in the womb before birth. We can not only have 'bad breast' experiences – we can also have 'bad womb' experiences too, and they are just as common. The whole field of birth is quite fascinating, and so many data are coming out now from the international conferences on pre- and perinatal psychology, all showing that birth is a consciously experienced process, no one is going to be able to ignore it much longer. And as a review of Grof in the same issue says, those who have taken the trouble to go into this matter for themselves have found that a huge and deeply relevant area of work is opened up when this is done. What the review does not make clear is that psychotherapy naturally goes into this area as soon as clients are permitted to do it, and that LSD or hypnotism are not necessary at all.

This is not the place to argue the various merits and demerits of the humanistic approach, but simply to place on record the fact that it does exist, it does have a great deal to say about psychotherapy, and much of it is not dependent on or derived from psychoanalysis. Please do not try to ignore it, or deny its existence.

After a brief interval, Bob Hinshelwood sent me a letter, which read in part thus:

> My hesitancy in completely retracting the phrase that you complain about is that I am not sure that you are altogether correct in implying such a radical division between psychoanalysis and humanistic psychology.
>
> The act of appropriating the term 'humanistic' for one sector only of psychotherapy is itself a little provocative – it tends to imply that other psychotherapies are inhuman! I don't suppose you really intend to convey that, however, the term 'humanistic psychology' did, I think, grow up in opposition to forms of psychology that were arguably less humane. I write out of ignorance, but my impression is that humanistic psychology arose as a movement in the United States, and in opposition to the psychoanalytic establishment there, which has over the decades been profoundly influenced by the mechanistic forms of psychology, particularly behaviourism. In that context a move towards a more humanistic attitude was entirely appropriate, and to some extent psychoanalysis in the United States has taken the point (the attempt to develop a psychology of the self, for instance; and Bettelheim's *Freud and Man's Soul*). It has seemed to me that this development as an opposition has, typically for oppositional movements, taken much of its character from what it is in opposition to; either by absorption of certain psychoanalytic concepts without really noticing, or the absorption of the opposites of certain other psychoanalytic concepts.
>
> I am therefore of the view, formed in the midst of a considerable ignorance, I admit, that the development of the humanistic psychology movement was exactly fashioned by psychoanalysis.

Now when we come to this country, psychoanalysis as you may know is not at all like psychoanalysis in the United States... With this humanistic style of psychoanalysis in this country, humanistic psychology from the United States is something of an import that is rather out of context...

...It is indeed true that humanistic psychology does embody ideas that do not come from psychoanalysis, nevertheless I am of the impression that such ideas are absorbed into, and thoroughly moulded by, the European psychoanalytic way of thinking.

What would Moreno's psychodrama be now if the ideas of the unconscious, projection, and object-relations etc., had not become part of general psychotherapeutic background thinking? It is even more true of all those psychologies you mention that have clearly derived from psychoanalysts who departed from the main stream – Perls, Reich, Jung – but who were clearly formed in the mould originally.

To which I replied as follows:

Thanks for your letter. I agree with you that psychoanalysis in this country is not as reactionary as it is in the States, but it is still very conservative. You only have to scratch the surface to find that attitudes are quite hard and unshakeable, in spite of a surface appearance of softness and bonhomie. There is still a big contrast, in other words, between humanistic psychology and the psychoanalytic approach, in spite of the greater flexibility of the British schools.

And this difference has to do with the origins of the two orientations. In my encyclopaedia article on humanistic psychology (copy enclosed) I say that it emerged from the confluence of ten different streams: Lewin's group dynamics; Maslow's self-actualisation; Rogers' person-centred approach; Reich's emphasis on the body; existentialism, particularly through Perls and Laing; the experience of mind-expanding drugs; Zen; Taoism; Tantra; and the whole idea of peak experiences as revelatory. Now we could argue about the details of this, but surely it is obvious that these are very different origins from those of the psychoanalytic schools?

Also the practice is very different. I have just brought out a booklet on the humanistic approach, which includes among other things sections on: the person-centred approach; gestalt awareness; encounter; co-counselling; drama approaches; body work; primal integration; transpersonal approaches; dream work; feminist therapy; humanistic education; humanistic management; and humanistic research. Surely you can't maintain that much of this is 'absorbed into, and thoroughly moulded by, the European psychoanalytic way of thinking'?

You ask a rhetorical question as to what Moreno's psychodrama would be now if the ideas of the unconscious, projection, object-relations etc., had not become part of our background thinking. The answer is that it would be just what it always was – an independent invention. In fact, one of the greatest problems for Moreno was that psychoanalysts kept on stealing his ideas and claiming them as their own. It was he, for example, who developed the idea, and the name, of group psychotherapy, which people like Slavson and Foulkes later claimed to have invented.

I don't want to make this reply too long, but I think this is sufficient to show that that humanistic psychology is a genuinely different tradition from psychoanalysis, and does not depend on it to any substantial degree.

The next instalment came in a letter from Bob Hinshelwood which read in part as follows:

> My view about psychoanalysis is that it is not just that it is more flexible in this country than in the United States, but that it is humanistic here, whereas in the United States it is technological. . .
>
> The point is that unconscious determinants of our experiences and actions, transferences to 'mother-figures' and 'father-figures' and many other ideas are now general currency, imported into the common culture and also into humanistic psychology.
>
> Is it not true, incidentally, that the Eastern philosophies have been mined by psychotherapists and psychologists for just those aspects which will fit and express current Western pre-occupations (now suffused in my view with the influence of a century of psychoanalytic ideas)? On the whole there seems to be a cloudy view of what the needs are for a humanistic psychology in the West. To throw out psychoanalytic *thought* because the *people* who practise it appear conservative, is not going to promote clarity of thought about our intellectual inheritance. To import fragments of Eastern philosophies (most of them, incidentally, anti-humanist in original character), merely because they are alien, is not in the best traditions of academic work. It is these emotive and rivalrous aspects of the debate which make me uneasy about stirring up an oppositional view. In fact the differences that exist between psychoanalysis and humanistic psychology, are so embedded in our common roots in Western culture, that we do violence to each of our traditions by pretending to such fervent independence from each other. . .
>
> There is a real problem in this divide, and we should join together to peer over the edge into it.

I duly came back with a further missive, in the course of which I said a few more things:

In your letter you seem to make three main points: one, that psychoanalysis in this country is a humane discipline as distinguished from a technological one, and that therefore it comes into the same bracket as humanistic psychology; two, that Eastern philosophy is not needed and not wanted; and three, that it would be wrong to throw out psychoanalytic thought because the people who practise it appear conservative.

Let us dispose of the third one immediately. I am not contending, and have never contended, that we should throw out psychoanalytic thought. My own book *The Reality Game* has more entries in the index for Freud than for any other person. Obviously Western culture in general, and humanistic psychotherapy in particular, owes a great deal to Freud in terms of a general background understanding of what human beings are like. We can never go back to a pre-Freudian understanding of these matters because the Freudian shift is an historical change which has affected all of us in one way or another. All I am contending for is that some of the most important roots of humanistic psychotherapy are independent of, rather than dependent upon, psychoanalysis, and that much of its content would be disowned by psychoanalysis.

Your second point rather confirms this, because you are contending for a blanket dismissal of all Eastern philosophy. This is just one example of how psychoanalysts may often disown what is important to humanistic psychology. In my book *Ordinary Ecstasy* I describe at some length the contributions of Zen, Tao (or Dao, as we should rather say nowadays) and Tantra, and all three of these seem to have influenced humanistic psychotherapy quite importantly. Whether these things are 'anti-humanist' as you seem to be suggesting seems open to question. Certainly Erich Fromm would not agree with you about Zen, and Tantra has recently been looked upon with some favour by feminists like Barbara Walker. Jung mentions Taoism with approval every now and then, and so does Heidegger on the existentialist side. My view would be that some of this stuff has become just as much a part of the common culture as Freud himself has.

And this brings us back to the first of the points you make. It may well be the case, as you say, that in this country psychoanalysis is not the same as it is in the States. Without knowing too much about it, I would be prepared to grant that the two things are significantly different. But even so, I do not think that puts psychoanalysis and humanistic psychotherapy into the same bracket, so far as this country is concerned. It is sometimes said that 'My enemy's enemy is my friend', but this is not always the case and does not logically have to be the case, certainly. The two things are different in origin, different in spirit and different in practice. Consequently I do not agree that humanistic psychotherapy can be reduced to a version of, or an offshoot from, or a child of psychoanalysis. It is an independent tradition, with its own advantages and disadvantages, its own good points and failings, its own strengths and weaknesses, in all cases different from those of psychoanalysis.

Let me finish by putting this question to you. If we said that the relationship between psychoanalysis and humanistic psychotherapy in this country could be described in terms of a Venn diagram of the logical overlap of sets, how big do you think the overlap would be? My own feeling is that the overlap would be neither tiny nor huge, but quite modest in size. Peculiar to psychoanalysis would be things like the id, the central importance of transference, the abstinence rule, the rule of free association and so on; the overlap would include things like projection, the importance of countertransference, emphasis on the therapeutic alliance, use of therapy for the therapist and so on; and peculiar to humanistic psychotherapy would be things like emphasis on the body, a holistic approach, active interventions, touching the client and so on. If you had to draw a similar diagram, would you really put the humanistic circle inside the psychoanalytic one? That is really what you seemed to be suggesting more than once. What would your diagram look like?

This takes the correspondence up to June 1987. A somewhat different version of this appeared in the *British Journal for Psychotherapy* in the same year.

Chapter 10
Against Feelings

It is often said that humanistic psychotherapy emphasises feelings. There are even Institutes for Feeling Therapy, Centres for Feeling People, and therapists who continually talk about the importance of feelings. I have even met people who concentrate upon just one feeling above all others, so that you are not really getting it right unless you are expressing your anger, or your pain.

As someone who uses primal integration as his main form of therapy, of course I, too, see a lot of deep feelings expressed, and believe that to be a very important part of the whole process in which clients are engaged. But somehow there is a falsity about saying that feeling is more important than sensing, thinking, intuiting, imagining, desiring, and so forth. So why do we concentrate so much upon feelings in therapy? There seem to be two main reasons:

1. Feelings are smaller in number than are thoughts, intuitions etc. This becomes even more true when we get down to deep fundamental feelings. Diffferent people have different lists of basic feelings, but hardly anyone suggests that there are more than eight of them. This then makes it easier to focus on one thing and work with it.
2. Feelings go back further than thoughts in that thoughts seem to need the cortex, whilst feelings can be tied in with much more primitive structures. So we get a longer timespan to deal with, and are able to go back into very early material. The limbic system, in particular, has been shown by Laborit to be particularly adapted to hold long-term memories.

All the other reasons given for working with feelings are, I think, demonstrably inadequate, We are told, for example, that 'What blocks, limits and programmes people are uncontacted and unexpressed feelings.' Not so:

From J. Rowan (1985). Against feelings. *Self and Society* July/August, 189–190, with permission.

anything at all can block, limit or programme somebody – decisions, imagination, desires, what have you – not just feelings. We are told that 'For genuine intimacy to take place, communication on a here-and-now feeling level is essential'. But that is not all, by any means, that is essential. Honesty on a conceptual level, freed energy on an orgasmic level, clear demands on a desire level, all these and other things too are necessary for full intimacy.

The truth of the matter seems to be that in therapy what we are trying to do all the time is to encourage the real person to come out, and this means the whole person. We are trying to help the client get to the point where he or she can put his or her whole self, all of it, behind life and action.

A one-sidedly feeling person would be just as much a monster as a one-sidedly thinking person (or sensing, or intuiting, or imagining, desiring etc.). What we are helping the client towards in therapy is integration, not feelings.

Chapter 11
Siding with the Client

The theoretical orientation to which I mainly hold is primal integration. It follows the work of Bill Swartley, Frank Lake and Stan Grof, and lays the major stress upon early trauma as the basic cause of neurosis. But unlike the somewhat parallel approach of Arthur Janov, it puts great emphasis on the whole person – body, feelings, intellect and spirit. It is a humanistic therapy in the full sense, based on the fundamental belief that the inner core of the client is ultimately healthy, and that it is only the defences that are unhealthy. This is the basic humanistic belief in the real self. This form of therapy makes use of active techniques from a number of sources (body methods, feeling methods, analytical methods, intuitive methods), integrated into a strong theoretical framework, and I am particularly interested in the use of subpersonalities in this work; in fact I am at present writing a major work on this subject. (This was published as *Subpersonalities: The People Inside Us* by Routledge in 1990.) It seems to me that the use of the concept of subpersonalities is very widespread under different names in most forms of psychotherapy. There is a full discussion of the whole theory in my chapter in Rowan and Dryden (1988).

I want to discuss here one session in which I found myself contradicting one of my most basic assumptions. At the time of which I speak my view, expressed in my books, lectures and conversations, was along these lines: that every time I do something for the client, I stop the client doing it. If I really respected and wanted to foster another person's autonomy, I had to do it all along the line. I believed in support and confrontation as the two wings of therapy, but felt that support meant only such things as empathy and resonance – in other words, encouraging people to get in touch with their own resources, their own inner world. A section in one

From J. Rowan (1988). Siding with the client. *Voices* 24(2), 43–49, with permission.
*This article is based on a chapter with the same title which appeared in *Key Cases in Psychotherapy*, edited by Dr Windy Dryden and published by Croom Helm (London and Sydney) in 1987.

of my books had the heading 'The therapist is not a rescuer', and this seemed to me the ultimate wisdom in therapy. 'Every time I take responsibility for the client, I stop the client taking responsibility. Every time I try to help, I get in the client's way.' I was quite dogmatic about this, because it seemed to be so basic. I still think it is very important.

The Client

This is an account of one session with a client I shall call Sarah. This was a woman in her early thirties, recently married, about average height, dark, somewhat overweight. Her main problem seemed to be a sometimes very severe depression, although eating problems were also important at times. The depression had been serious enough to make her attempt suicide by cutting her wrists more than once, but she had never been hospitalised. She had been to a number of therapists before, and was taking a course to become a therapist herself.

Her history was probably the worst I had ever come across. It started before her conception, which took place when her mother was 40 years old. Her mother had just run away with Sarah's father, after an unhappy marriage of 15 years. Her husband was strongly opposed to children, and had made her have an abortion in the early days of the marriage. She had then talked him into having children, but after years of failure had been told she was infertile.

Sarah's father was a man of wide interests and varied talents, and 25 years older than her mother. He looked after her mother, who was in poor health with nervous complaints and poor nutrition. During the pregnancy, she was going through the stress of trying to get a divorce (to which her husband would not agree) and was consuming much black coffee and chain-smoking cigarettes all day.

Having been told that she was infertile, Sarah's mother did not know she was pregnant. As she began to feel a lump in her womb, she assumed it must be a growth of some kind. She was very afraid of doctors, and would not go near them if possible. When the lump grew, she thought it must be cancer, but still did not want to go to a doctor. When it moved, she thought it must be a mobile cancerous growth of a particularly virulent kind. It appears that panic must have got through somehow to the fetus (it is now known that this is possible – see Verny 1982, Ridgway 1987). In reconstruction it seems that the chemical shock of these reactions coming into the fetus every time it moved actually conditioned it to move as little as possible, so that instead of a normally vigorous motion of the fetus in the womb there were just a few rather restricted movements – ironically just the sort of movements to confirm the mother in her beliefs.

Ten days before the birth, Sarah's mother had 'stomach pains' so bad that a doctor had to be called. He told her that she was pregnant. This sent her into a new panic, because she felt she was too old to have a baby, and knew that she had not been eating properly for the past few months.

The birth was prolonged and difficult, and the baby experienced anoxia and extreme paralysing terror as the walls of the uterus closed in and there seemed to be no way out. The mother's hair and nails dropped out after the birth, and she had no milk. The baby had two fingernails not properly developed, and the mother thought she might be mentally deformed or retarded.

Sarah's mother had been brought up very strictly and religiously. She felt extremely guilty at having brought an illegitimate child into the world. As the baby grew, she saw it as fat and ugly and badly behaved. She did not like it. And so it went on, right up to the moment the mother died of cancer when Sarah was 22 years old. Sarah's father had already died when she was 9.

The Therapy

In the early days of the therapy we spent most of the time on Sarah's mother, just following her feelings back into her childhood again and again. We found that her mother kept on turning up in the most extraordinary disguises, in dreams and in fantasies: for example, we spent some time wrestling with a 'death skeleton' which was extremely frightening and threatening, and this turned out in the end to be her mother again. One of the most fearful versions for Sarah was the Black Witch. The Black Witch came up in dreams and fantasies, and actually laid a spell on the child Sarah to strike her dumb. This was a very accurate statement of what happened when Sarah's mother came on the scene: Sarah was dumbstruck.

For a long time it seemed that we were stuck, because Sarah could find no way of facing her mother without being overcome immediately. There seemed to be no strength, no resource, within her that was strong enough to resist.

The event that triggered a change was a lecture which I went to on the work of John Rosen. The lecturer said that one of the problems Rosen had tackled successfully was a client who had an extremely heavy and punitive super-ego. It was as if the super-ego sat on top of the ego and squashed it, with such weight and force that the ego had no chance at all to respond or resist or retaliate in any way. What Rosen did was to line up with the client and throw his own weight against the super-ego as well. This released more energy in the client, by giving explicit permission to answer back, as it were, and also by giving a model of how to do it.

Although in my theory there is no super-ego, and no ego either in the strict Freudian sense, I could see that the super-ego functioned just like a subpersonality. So I could understand what was being said in my own terms, and see the relevance of that to Sarah's case. Sarah also had a heavy and punitive subpersonality sitting on top of her and squashing her, as it were.

But could I use this method? On the one hand it did fit in with my ideas about being imaginative and trying new things, but on the other hand it went right against my ideas about the client being autonomous and self-responsible. So it was as if one voice was saying 'Try it!', whilst another voice was saying 'Don't you dare!'. In the event, my curiosity won out over my conscience. At the next opportunity, I lined up with Sarah against her mother. In my way of working, where Sarah was sitting on one cushion and her mother (in whatever guise) on the other, this was in fact very easy to set up. I simply put another cushion next to Sarah's and sat on it myself, saying things to support Sarah's own statements.

However, this did not work. Sarah's mother (what I would call the bad mother subpersonality) was still too strong for both of us together. Again we had to retire, baffled and frustrated. But something seemed to have shifted slightly, although I was not quite sure what it was. There was a definite movement, such that I felt that here was a promising approach, if only some way could be found of taking it further.

The Session

The next time the opportunity arose, we were both more ready to grab it and use it constructively. What happened was that we were working on a dream about a giant spider. Sarah had done a painting of the dream which I have in front of me as I write (see Figure 11.1). It shows a fetus in the middle of the page, pinkish on a blue background, with a huge purple umbilical cord going out to the left, through the red border of the womb, to a yellow moon hung in a night sky with yellow and silver stars. Below the sky, on the left of the picture, is a blue-green sea with smooth waves.

On the right of the picture, filling the whole space, is a huge black hairy spider, with red eyes and what look like two horns with knobs on the ends. The legs are too big to be contained on the page, and disappear over the edge of the paper to the right, and behind the womb to the left. The background on the right-hand side is red, except at the top, where it becomes red and yellow flames against a violet background. So it looks like a sort of devil-spider. One of the legs curves right over the top of the spider's head, and looks almost like an alternative umbilical cord.

As I often do, I suggested, after going through the dream and finding that the spider represented her mother, that we put the spider on to a cushion and talk to it. Sarah agreed to this, and we set it up, but I could see that she was experiencing some fear. I remembered the previous incident where I had taken her side, and it suddenly occurred to me how we might make it work better this time.

Figure 11.1

This time I said: 'Now there is a magic glass screen just here [I indicated a line] between you and the spider. You can talk to the spider, but the spider can't get through the screen. The spider can still hear and see and talk through the screen, but is completely blocked by the screen. You can get at the spider if you want to, but the spider can't get at you. And the screen will stay there until I take it down again.'

Now I lined up with Sarah as before, and supported her against the spider, shouting back to the spider that she had no right to attack Sarah, that Sarah had seen through her game, that she was not going to stand for it any more, and so on. This time, as we went back and forth between Sarah and the giant spider, the spider diminished in size and paled in colour. It became smaller and smaller and weaker and weaker, until Sarah felt capable of facing it and dealing with it by herself.

For the first time, we had the feeling of victory against her mother. For the first time, her mother respected Sarah. We had broken through, and the positive feeling was tremendous. In talking with Sarah afterwards, she said that the magic screen was like a protection that made her feel safe. It made her feel that she was allowed to communicate. Before this, she had felt no right to communicate, particularly where her mother was concerned (the dumb child motif mentioned earlier).

But of course there were other things going on too. It may be felt that I was perhaps functioning on one level as a bigger magician than the Black

Witch, and beating her on a magical level. At an unconscious level, perhaps I was her father come back to rescue her this time. Perhaps the glass screen was simply a schizoid defence, a temporary neurosis. Sarah's own view, expressed later, was that I was showing her how to talk back to her mother: she had no model or script for it, so did not know how to do it until she saw me do it. Once she had picked up the model, she was able to use it, and this seemed to break the dumbness spell put on the child by the Black Witch.

But as a therapist with the theory outlined above, I was in turmoil. To line up with the client seemed to go against everything I believed. It was taking responsibility away from the client and giving it to the therapist. It was making the client dependent on the therapist. It was not respecting the inner strength of the real self. It should be the client doing it, not the therapist doing it. I could not reconcile what I had done with the theory I held.

The Aftermath

However, my supervisor supported me in lining up with the client, saying that it seemed quite legitimate to him in the particular circumstances at hand here. He reminded me of my old slogan – 'You alone can do it, but you don't have to do it alone'.

What I have moved to now is a belief that what we are talking about here is not therapy, but a preliminary act of clearing the ground so that any therapy can take place at all.

This makes a distinction between doing therapy and doing other things that help the therapy and in this sense are therapeutic. There are many examples of this: some people may have a very poor sense of boundaries and limits in their lives, and finishing the session on time may be therapeutic for such a person, although it is not therapy; one may ask a client to lie down to make fantasy or regression easier, and lying down may be therapeutic in this sense, but it is not therapy; I may ask clients to take off their glasses before going into an active phase of the session, but taking off glasses is not therapy. Similarly here, siding with the client may take some of the pressure off temporarily, long enough to enable the client to muster more resources, but it is not therapy. The therapy is when the client does it on her own and for herself.

There seem to be many instances where the therapist does this kind of activity, clearing the way, or laying foundations, or offering choices which may not have been seen before by the client. They are all part of the therapeutic process, but they are all things the therapist does, rather than things the client does. It is the things the client does that are the real therapy. This has always seemed to me a very important distinction, and now more so than ever with the new example in this case history.

I now consider this episode to have been extremely important as a turning point in the whole process of therapy for Sarah. Without it, I feel as if we would still be stuck with her mother, totally blocking off any other areas we might need to be working on. Her mother did in fact remain an issue for some time after this, but we have found it much more possible to deal with her, and in a recent session Sarah even found herself feeling sorry for her mother.

References

RIDGWAY, R. (1987). *The Unborn Child*. Aldershot, England: Wildwood House.

ROWAN, J. and DRYDEN W. (1988). *Innovative Therapy in Britain*. Milton Keynes: Open University Press.

VERNY, T. (1982). *The Secret Life of the Unborn Child*. London: Sphere.

Chapter 12
Counselling and the
Psychology of Furniture

As a result of some conversations with people on the Accreditation Subcommittee of the British Association of Counselling, it seemed that something needed to be written about the conditions under which counselling was being conducted. It is of course the responsibility of each counsellor to make sure that he or she has a suitable place to conduct the necessary interviews. If he or she is given a totally unsuitable position, such as in a corridor (and this is not unknown), or a room with a window in the door such that passers-by can peer in, or a room with a good deal of intrusion by external sounds, this must be opposed and the relevant people informed that this is unacceptable. But there are some more subtle things too, and it seemed that some counsellors were quite unaware of the implications of the furniture in the rooms where they were counselling: for example, there seemed to be counsellors who did their counselling in their bedrooms and saw nothing odd in this. It seemed, therefore, worth while to put together some observations on furniture more generally.

I first came across the importance of furniture in the early 1970s, when I found that an exercise which worked perfectly well when carried out in a room furnished with cushions did not work at all in a room furnished instead with chairs. I had already come across the essay by Paul Goodman (1962) which struck me as very good, and this reinforced my opinion that here was something of great importance. Later I did a number of workshops on body language and read up most of the available literature on this, and even ran a couple of workshops on 'The psychology of furniture'.

One of the most interesting examples of how useful this approach can be came when I was working with the London Fire Brigade on their new

From J. Rowan (1988). Counselling and the psychology of furniture. *Counselling* 64, 21-24, with permission.

appraisal system for firefighters wanting promotion. The officers in the Fire Brigade struck me as very practical, down-to-earth people, not very much interested in psychology or counselling as such.

In an appraisal interview the ideal is to approach the person in the spirit of 'Let's look together at what you have been doing and see how you have been getting on'. This is much more like counselling than like giving orders or evaluating performance in a one-sided way. But I did not want to explain the whole theory of counselling or give them a complete training in counselling, because this did not seem appropriate or necessary. So what I did was to say that the basic difference between an appraisal interview and the normal kind of interview was that in the normal interview the parties sat opposite each other with a desk between them, whilst in an appraisal interview both parties sat on the same side of the desk, looking at the papers together, and discussing them side by side. This they were able to understand and do immediately, and the whole spirit of the interaction changed automatically with the change of physical position.

The success of this very simple manoeuvre persuaded me that furniture can be very powerful in creating certain expectations at a psychological level, without the parties necessarily being aware of how this is working.

Paul Goodman (1962) contrasts Freudian analysis, Sullivanian therapy, Reichian therapy and gestalt therapy from the point of view of what furniture they employ and how they use it, and shows that each arrangement springs out of the theory of what has gone wrong in the client, and what is needed to put matters right. He goes on to discuss architecture more generally in this light.

Counselling

When it comes to counselling, the standard arrangement that I have most often seen is two chairs, often high-backed chairs with wooden arms, at right angles to each other, and about two feet apart. Often there is a coffee table between the chairs, enabling a box of tissues, a diary or whatever to be placed handily for immediate use. This arrangement is so common because in many ways it is perfect. Let us look at its features one by one.

The angle

If chairs are placed opposite each other, so that counsellor and client are head on, there is a suggestion of opposition or attack. Where chairs are placed like this, there is often a desk or table between, to make the attack less likely. As Goodman points out, the desk or table conceals the genitals and makes the situation safer. It is particularly suitable for schizophrenics or people with extremely weak or immature egos – the desk lends an atmosphere of objectivity and practicality, where we are not going to discuss things such as dreams or fantasies. But with the desk taken away, and the angle adjusted to 90 degrees, counsellor and client can look at each other or look away very easily, and this gives much more flexibility as to what can be talked about.

The chair

The straighter the chair, the greater is the suggestion of rationality. The tubular chairs which I have seen used in the Tavistock clinic are perhaps the limit of this. There is a very strong suggestion with a straight chair that one will not move out of one's chair, and one will not say anything that might cause anyone else to move. Arms to a chair give more support, and make it less likely that the client will sit with arms folded – a closed position which does not make for easy rapport. A softer chair offers a suggestion of more relaxation, and more possibility of being emotional, but still suggests a basic rationality, a need to be sensible rather than silly. Cushions on the floor give much more flexibility and a suggestion that it is all right to be child-like or even childish. A couch or mattress lends itself to fantasy, dreams, deep regression and loss of conscious rational control. All these things are there in the situation, in the furniture, before anyone comes on the scene.

The distance

The studies of proxemics which have now been carried out by many people all over the world, and which are described in books such as that by Pease (1981), tell us that there are four basic zones around a person. There is the intimate zone (6–18 inches), the personal zone (18–48 inches), the social zone (4–12 feet) and the public zone (over 12 feet). Now it seems obvious that counselling is mostly appropriate to the personal zone, because this is the zone for talking to someone we know on a personal level and want to exchange personal information with. However, at certain points in counselling we may need to enter the intimate zone, where a definite emotional closeness can be experienced. So the ideal distance is just beyond the 18-inch limit, but in such a way that one can reach into or lean into the 18-inch zone when this is appropriate. In other words, the counsellor should be within reach of the client. I remember seeing on television a counsellor who sat on one side of his fireplace, whilst the client's chair was on the other side of the fireplace; this seems to me quite wrong on all counts. There is an illusion prevalent among some counsellors that any mistakes, anything that is wrong between counsellor and client, can be counselled away, but this sort of ever-present structural fault cannot be counselled away. It is not a question of interpreting it or dealing with it, it is a question of putting it right.

Equipment

If a box of tissues is prominently displayed, this gives permission, as it were, to the client to cry. It offers a silent witness to the fact that people often cry in this room, and that it is OK to cry. One counsellor told me that a box labelled 'Professional wipes' was remarked on favourably by one client, as presumably superior to Sainsbury's own label. Similarly all the other things that happen to be in the room can tell their own story. A clock can either be available to the client as well as to the counsellor, or turned so that only the counsellor can see it; there seems to be more of a power play about the clock which the client cannot see. It hardly needs to be said that a telephone should not be in the same room where counselling is done, and that if there is no way of eliminating it, it should not be answered during a session. A tape recorder is quite acceptable to the client if it is acceptable to the counsellor (Russell, Crimmings and Lent, 1984).

Premises

Taking all this into account, what are we now to say about the situation where the counsellor does counselling in the bedroom? What are the suggestions there? A bed is unlike a couch, massage table or mattress in that it clearly suggests that someone uses the room for sleeping. If it is a double bed, it also suggests that someone sleeps with someone else. A double bed has the further function of suggesting that this is a room occupied by a conventional heterosexual married couple, and many of the implications of this could be deleterious for a client who was gay or having problems of sexual identity or had feminist insights or feelings. Even if it is a single bed, there is a suggestion that it could be used for sex as well as for sleeping.

Now it is already well known that the very act of getting rapport in counselling is reminiscent of courtship and making friends (Rowan, 1983, Chapter 4). This can bring great difficulties for a new client, who may be overwhelmed by the warmth of this new setting. To bring a bed into such a situation seems likely to exaggerate these possibilities considerably, and to be crossing some invisible boundary. One would expect that there would be a greater number of clients not returning for a second interview in such circumstances. Another thing which could happen would be if the client did continue with the sessions, but also went to another counsellor, or some other form of treatment, at the same time as seeing the first (bedroom) counsellor: the crossing of one boundary (by the counsellor) can lead to the crossing of another boundary (by the client).

One would also expect a greater suppression of sexual feelings and sexual material generally in such a context. Transference matters could

very easily be complicated and made more difficult and intense with a bed
in the room, especially where transference was a central element in the
type of counselling being offered.

Another possible suggestion aroused by a bed is that someone could be
sick or ill. It could arouse memories of sickness or illness.

Van Velden (1984) has suggested that furniture also has important implications for sexual politics. He points out that the average home is designed
to underwrite and facilitate male dominance and female service roles, in a
variety of ways. For example, the kitchen sink and the sink or handbasin
placed in the bedroom are of different heights. They are both intended for
the same purpose – to wash the hands or to wash things with the hands
– so one might expect that they would be of the same height. But the top
of the kitchen sink is always higher than the top of the bedroom sink: why
should this be? It is because the sink in the bedroom is designed for
emergency use as a receptacle into which men may urinate. It has to be
low enough to make this possible. As van Velden says, buildings are
designed and built by men to fulfil male needs and male standards, under
rules and regulations created by men, so none of this should be surprising.

A further point is that a bedroom setting may suggest that other rooms
in the house or flat are being used by other occupants. The client may
even hear other occupants moving around or talking, switching on radios
or vacuum cleaners, and so forth. There may be an issue here about the
counsellor being afraid to be alone with the client. Clients may pick this
up as an avoidance of real one-to-one engagement. More generally, the
issue here is whose interests are paramount – is the counselling setting
for the client's benefit or for the counsellor's benefit? Obviously both sets
of interests must be satisfied; the question is, what is the balance, and
how is this balance seen by the client?

It seems, then, that counsellors would be well advised not to counsel
in their bedrooms. But the same principle applies to other rooms too. The
living room can suggest a whole lifestyle, and therefore a set of expectations which will underlie everything the therapist says or does. Books on
shelves may be particularly revealing about the counsellor and his or her
interests, and books by the counsellor may be especially powerful in
impressing the client with authority problems. There is a moving
paragraph in Ernst and Goodison, (1981) where the author says:

> The oppression lay in *who he was,* the questions *he didn't ask* and the material *I
> didn't present.* It lay in the way I felt when I arrived at his house on my bicycle
> and he drew up in his large car; the sense I had that he must see his wife and
> family and home as normal and my household as a sign of my abnormality. To be
> cured would be to be capable of living like him.

Now obviously there is nothing we can do about some of this sort of thing,
but it is important to be aware of these issues and not to indulge in unnecessary obstacles to understanding. The client is always going to have some

fantasies about the counsellor. The question is – how does our furniture feed those fantasies? Everything in the room is going to say something. And the more disturbed the client, the more important these issues may be. The trouble is that difficulties with the premises very seldom come out directly in the form of objections by the client – all the effects are indirect, although they often come up between the lines, as it were, in the choice of topics to discuss or the emphasis in the way they are talked about. We are very little aware, in most cases, of what our furniture is saying. To the extent that we can be more aware of these matters, it must have an effect on the excellence of our counselling.

References

ERNST, S. and GOODISON, L. (1981). *In Our Own Hands*. London: The Women's Press.

GOODMAN, P. (1962). Seating arrangements. In *Utopian Essays and Practical Proposals*. New York: Vintage Books.

PEASE, A. (1981). *Body Language*. London: Sheldon Press.

ROWAN, J. (1983). *The Reality Game*. London: RKP.

RUSSELL, R.K., CRIMMINGS, A.M. and LENT R.W. (1984). Counsellor training and supervision: Theory and research. In S.D. Brown and R.W. Lent (Eds), *Handbook of Counselling Psychology*. New York: John Wiley & Sons.

VAN VELDEN, F. (1984). *Environment and Sexual Violence*. Eindhoven: Turtle Editions.

Chapter 13
Hypnotherapy and the
Humanistic

At first I thought there was no connection between the various forms of hypnotherapy, on the one hand, and humanistic psychology, on the other. I was quite critical of the way in which hypnotherapy so often seems to offer quick and shallow training and quick and shallow treatment, and I really thought I could dismiss it from my mind. When I made out comparative lists of different forms of psychotherapy, hypnotherapy was not even on the list.

But then I started working on a book on subpersonalities – those inner people who affect our lives in so many ways, for good and ill. I wrote about the parent, adult and child ego states of Eric Berne, and showed that these were subpersonalities; I wrote about the autonomous complexes of Jung and showed that these were subpersonalities; I wrote about the topdog and underdog in the gestalt therapy of Fritz Perls and showed that these, too, were subpersonalities. As I went on, the field seemed to get bigger and bigger; I found no less than 25 different synonyms for subpersonalities. And then I discovered Ellenberger.

Henri Ellenberger, back in 1970, wrote a fat and magisterial book called *The Discovery of the Unconscious*. In this book he gives the whole history of the way in which the unconscious mind was first thought of, and how it was first investigated. It turns out that the history of the modern study of the unconscious, for the first 150 years of its existence, is the history of hypnosis.

Most primitive cultures, both ancient and modern, have been aware of altered states of consciousness and spirit possession, both of which are forerunners of the modern idea of hypnosis. Priests, witchdoctors and shamans have made these ideas a stock in trade since early in the history

From J. Rowan (1989). Hynotherapy and the humanistic. *Self and Society*, January/February, 3-7, with permission.

of the human race. There were 'sleep temples' in ancient Greece and in Egypt where patients were encouraged to go into altered states of consciousness, were actually hypnotised or were talked to during their sleep and given curative suggestions. The Druids, the Celtic priesthood, are supposed to have been experts in the use of these methods. In primitive cultures, these changes have often been brought about through the use of trances, and trance induction has been brought about by means of rhythm, drums, dancing, chanting etc.

More dramatic, of course, is the idea of spirit possession. For centuries this was the only way of explaining how someone could be 'taken over' by another spirit, another personality. In possession, the appearance of the person could change, the voice could change and the whole emotional range of the person would extend. This is just a dramatic illustration of the fact that there are potentials within us which can come out and be personified, and the first people to explore this whole area in detail were the hypnotists, who at first were called mesmerists or magnetizers.

We can even pinpoint a year (1784) when the idea of the unconscious came into the sphere of psychology, through the work of the Comte de Puységur, who lived at the same time as Mesmer (Chertok and de Saussure, 1979). In the nineteenth century the thing grew and grew, and by the end of the century hypnosis had acquired great respectability, being used at the great mental hospitals of the time. All through the 1890s Charcot and Janet and their colleagues were working on the problems of hysteria, and linking them with the phenomena of hypnosis. And of course here came the link with Freud, who learned hypnosis from Charcot and also got from Charcot the idea that sexuality was the important thing to look for in the origins of neurosis.

But around 1910, Ellenberger tells us, the whole thing collapsed. Freud had gone off hypnosis and now said it was not the answer; the rising tide of behaviourism had no use for hypnosis; even the new schools just arising, such as gestalt psychology, had no use for hypnosis. It was said that hypnotists did not understand the transference and were basically just seducing their patients and kidding themselves in one way or another.

Hypnotism went underground, and mainly surfaced in stage demonstrations and the unsung work of a few dentists and doctors who still found it useful as a pain-killer. Otherwise it seemed only to exist in the advertising columns of sleazy magazines, offering miraculous cures to gullible people.

But what I then found was that there is a modern revival of hypnotism which is far from this image. This is partly through the work of a master clinician, Milton Erickson, partly through the work of a very fine researcher, Ernest Hilgard, and partly through the rethinking of a few people such as Lewis Wolberg, John Beahrs and John and Helen Watkins.

Hypnotherapy

When I started on this book, I knew nothing about hypnotherapy. But the more I went into it, the more I found I had to go into hypnotherapy and find out more about it. It turns out, as we saw earlier, that the whole of psychotherapy comes out of the tradition initiated by Mesmer, de Puységur, Liebault, Bernheim, Janet, Charcot and the rest. It also turns out that some of the best and most accurate research on subpersonalities has been done in the hypnotic tradition, as Hilgard (1986) has demonstrated with a wealth of detail. He mentions that a whole issue of the *International Journal of Clinical and Experimental Hypnosis* was devoted to evidence and issues related to the kind of thing we are interested in here (April 1984, Vol. 32, No. 2). And it also turns out that much of the best thinking about subpersonalities comes from hypnotherapy.

The stunning book by Beahrs (1982), which I only discovered recently, gives a practical and also a philosophical rationale for working with subpersonalities, and in it the author gives a great deal of information about other people in the hypnotic tradition who have made interesting and useful contributions in this area. He has himself done a great deal of work with subpersonalities, and agrees with others that:

> Our goal is not to be 'rid' of a psychological process, but to shift it from the harmful or maladaptive ('pathological') dimension to where it is useful in its effect, so that what was once a symptom can truly become a skill.   (p. 82)

He takes the same position as we have already mentioned above, that mood changes, altered states of consciousness, subpersonalities and multiple personality are points on a continuum of dissociation, with the boundaries becoming thicker and more marked as we go along that line. He also agrees with another of our positions:

> I consider dissociation to be essential for healthy functioning; in addition, I believe that it is a creative act. Kohut (1971) has taken the same position regarding vertical splitting, which I use almost synonymously with dissociation. Everyday examples of creative dissociating are dreams and fantasies, roles and specific skills, imaginary playmates, projection of both positive and negative aspects of the self on to others, selective amnesia for stimuli, and virtually any defence function. In each, an aspect of overall mental function is put in relief by dissociation in a way that enhances one's powers for action.   (p. 85)

Another point that was new to me comes from the work of Allison (Allison and Schwartz, 1980), who classifies subpersonalities into three categories: persecutors, rescuers and internal self-helpers. The first two of these are relatively familiar, but the internal self-helpers were new to me. According to Allison, they have characteristics differing from pathological subpersonalities and are a great potential resource in treatment.

In his [Allison's] view, they differ in having (1) no identifiable time and reason for their formation; (2) no defensive function; and (3) far more accuracy of perception, to the point of being 'incapable of transference' and able to tell a therapist all his mistakes.   (Beahrs, 1982, p. 109)

This is fascinating if true, and certainly something worth looking out for and exploring in more detail. It reminds me of the important idea of Langs (1982) that the unconscious of the patient is often very accurate about the unconscious of the therapist.

More recently, Karle and Boys (1987) have given an interesting example of one way in which early child abuse can be handled. This is of course just the kind of trauma which has been found to be implicated in many cases of multiple personality. The client was a middle-aged woman who had been sexually abused by her father:

She was asked to return in hypnosis to the time her father had molested her sexually, and simultaneously to observe the scene as her adult self. The scene was played out without the therapist intervening, up to the moment at which the child was ordered to her room. At this moment, the therapist asked the patient to enter the scene in her adult self, meet her child self on the stairs, pick her up, comfort and reassure her, and generally to act as she would to any child in such a situation. She was to continue in this fashion until the child was wholly reassured and at peace, and then to return to the present day. The patient reported successful performance of the task in terms of the child's restored equanimity. Perhaps more important was the feeling that she could recognize in her adult self that her child self. . . was in fact innocent. . .   (pp. 250–251)

Whether the client needed to be hypnotised to do this work is a moot point, and I personally would not take it for granted that this would be so. But certainly it is an approach that fits very well with the hypnotic tradition.

In general, work with subpersonalities is no more common in hypnotherapy than it is in other modalities. But John and Helen Watkins are two people who have taken this approach a very long way, and have developed a whole therapy, which they call ego-state therapy, that is becoming quite popular and well known. As with the work of Berne and Shapiro, it is based on the theorising of Paul Federn (1952), and shares the same terminology. Their definition of an ego state runs as follows:

An ego state is an organized system of behaviour and experience whose elements are bound together by some common principle but which is separated from other such states by boundaries that are more or less permeable.
                                                      (Watkins and Watkins, 1986, p. 145)

They make many of the same points that others have also made in this field, but add some interesting ideas such as the thought that working with ego states is like a kind of family therapy. This is, I feel, a very fruitful thought, and it seems worth while to look at the way they put it:

> Ego-state therapy is the utilization of family and group treatment techniques for the resolution of conflicts between the different ego states that constitute a 'family of self' within a single individual.   (Watkins and Watkins, 1986, p. 149)

They give the example of a student who could not study successfully. A strong ego state close to consciousness wanted him to study and was very upset when he could not do so. However, another ego state, identified as a 4-year-old child, wanted more play and less study, and refused to let the student study unless he was treated better. The therapist made friends with the child, and persuaded him to play at night, thus permitting the student to study during the day.

> A week later Ed returned in great delight reporting that he had studied well during the past week and had gotten an A on his foreign language examination. He wondered, though, why he was having such vivid dreams and 'in technicolor' every night.   (Watkins and Watkins, 1986, p. 150)

It turned out that the child had kept his agreement and was playing at night. The student was not aware of this ego state until the therapist informed him about it afterwards.

So this is very interesting work, and I have acquired a new respect for at least some aspects of hypnotherapy since coming across it.

References

ALLISON, R. and SCHWARTZ, T. (1980). *Minds in Many Pieces*. Wade: Rawson.

BEAHRS, J.O. (1982). *Unity and Multiplicity: Multilevel Consciousness of Self in Hypnosis, Psychiatric Disorder and Mental Health*. New York: Brunner/Mazel.

CHERTOK, L. and DE SAUSSURE, R. (1979). *The Therapeutic Revolution: From Mesmer to Freud*. New York: Brunner/Mazel.

ELLENBERGER, H. (1970). *The Discovery of the Unconscious*. New York: Basic Books.

FEDERN, P. (1952). In E. Weiss (Ed.), *Ego Psychology and the Psychoses*. New York: Basic Books.

HILGARD, E.R. (1986). *Divided Consciousness: Multiple Controls in Human Thought and Action*, expanded edition. New York: John Wiley.

KARLE, H.W.A. and BOYS, J.H. (1987). *Hypnotherapy: A Practical Handbook*. London: Free Association Books.

KOHUT, H. (1971). *The Analysis of the Self*. New York: International Universities Press.

LANGS, R. (1982). *Psychotherapy: A Basic Text*. New York: Jason Aronson.

WATKINS, J.G. and WATKINS, H.H. (1986). Hypnosis, multiple personality and ego states as altered states of consciousnes. In B.B. Wolman and M. Ullman (Eds), *Handbook of States of Consciousness*. New York: Van Nostrand Reinhold.

Chapter 14
Early Traumas: A Dialectical Approach

In a recent issue of *Changes* (Vol. 5, No. 1), Zaida Hall raises the question of what she calls 'soul murder'. She makes it clear that the early regime of children may be so oppressive and so hard to escape that the person can only be regarded as a victim. Of course this has a great deal to do with the question of whether early traumas are best regarded as real or as fantasies. More recently again, Helen Sheldon (*Changes*, Vol. 5, No. 2) raises the issue, and again comes to the conclusion that the main problem is the way in which therapists can ignore the truth of sexual abuse, and push the whole question back into the mind of the victim.

Janet Malcolm (1986) has shown how important this controversy has become within psychoanalysis. According to her account, it is rather like a battle in which one side says that early trauma explains everything (what is outside the person causes the neurosis), and the other side says that it is the responsibility of the patient that explains everything (what is inside the person causes the neurosis). Perhaps it would make more sense to take up a dialectical approach, where we see that each of these positions is a moment in a process, such that each of them is inadequate without the other.

The example which comes to mind is the case of Sybil (Schreiber, 1975) which was made into a vivid film, shown more than once on television. Here is a case in which both moments in the dialectic come out with great clarity. The child was innocent, abused and maltreated, both sexually and otherwise, by a psychotic mother, supported by a passive father. The defence she chose was splitting, in the form of disso- ciated personality. Over a period of time she developed and showed 16 distinct personalities. So this was her form of defence, in response to a very real attack. The very fact that we call these things defences leaves

From J. Rowan (1990). Early traumas: A dialectical approach. *Energy and Character* **21**(1), 37–42, with permission.

the way open to the consideration that the attack might come from inside or from outside.

Alice Miller

Of course this is very much Alice Miller territory. It was Alice Miller (1985) who raised so acutely the need to deal with the suffering of the hurt child, and not to dismiss it as fantasy. She puts in a moving way the need to pay attention to the poisonous pedagogy of the majority of parents. Most parents, she says, deal with children in a way that suits them but offends against the integrity of the child, and this produces ill-effects in the unfortunate child. The child is then prevented from complaining, because the parents have to be right – that is the system. She is, as it were, on the side of the injured child. This has made a big impact on the psychoanalytic world, because it seems to argue counter to the Freudian theory of repression – what Miller calls the drive theory. Shengold (1975) makes some very similar points, as Hall says in the article referred to above, but I do not think he makes the point that Alice Miller does: she argues that a great deal of what psychoanalysts do is another form of the same poisonous pedagogy that the patient suffered from in the first place. Analysts, too, prevent the child from complaining, by turning it all back on to the patient, and having to be right.

The Secret Psychotic

The most recent and spirited expression of this sort of view is to be found in the first issue of the *Journal of the Institute of Self-Analysis*. Here John Southgate and Liz Whiting (1987) have brought together a number of papers all centred in this area. One discusses the process of Freud's self-analysis, and brings out the way in which he hides from himself all those things that might threaten his opinion of his own father.

One of the most interesting papers reviews a book by Robert Fliess. Robert Fliess was the son of Wilhelm Fliess, Freud's correspondent and friend. At the very time when Freud was conducting his self-analysis and writing about the theory of sexual abuse (which he called by the rather gentler name of seduction) in childhood, Fliess was sexually abusing his own son. As a result of discovering this in his own analysis (Robert Fliess became a psychoanalyst himself), he put forward the following three contentions (Fliess, 1973):

1. The neurotic seriously in need of analysis is apt to have at least one psychotic parent. [He explains that this can be an 'ambulatory' or 'secret' or 'unknown' psychosis, which is undiagnosed and not spoken about, and which often never comes to light, because it is in no one's interest to disclose it.]
2. He has been victimised by the bizarre sexuality of this parent.

3. He has suffered the (largely defused) aggression of which this parent has made him the object.

How can these parents (it can be either the mother or the father who is involved here) behave in this atrocious way? Fliess says that they see nothing wrong in what they are doing, because they do not see the child as a person. So they do not feel guilt at what they are doing. Instead, says Fliess, it is as though the child takes over all of the feelings of guilt over incest that the parent should have had, but being psychotic, did not. So the unfortunate victim has the pain of the assault, and the guilt about it, both at the same time.

Fliess makes the interesting point that when faced with this sort of material from a patient, many therapists run out of empathy – they cannot feel themselves into the situation, because it is too bizarre; it is beyond their experience. And he says at this point that the therapist just has to listen, and to trust the patient and admit that empathy does not get you everywhere in this business.

Another difficulty for the therapist is that transference can get very heavy indeed if the therapist is seen as a repetition of the parental abuser. The therapist is quite likely to be seen in this way if he or she treats the client in a parental manner, giving advice, having to be right, confronting the client in an aggressive manner, and so on. One patient of Fliess said: 'You do not listen to me; you interrupt me; you do not let me talk; you even speak like my father; you even use the same words.'

This is a very powerful paper, giving details of material which is not easily come across – the book is not published or distributed in this country, and it had to be obtained by order from the USA.

Levels of Trauma

There are several other papers in this Journal, all worth reading. They all seem to add up to the same thing – namely, that early trauma, particularly in the way of sexual abuse, is usually important for any long-standing and important neurosis; and that the therapist has somehow to get on the side of the innocent and abused victim and speak from there.

Now Janov has always said much the same thing. In his 1970 book he was already making the point that the traumatised child not only has the pain, as Fliess says, not only has the guilt, as Fliess says, but also has the pain of not being believed or listened to. In his 1977 book he is very clear that trauma really is important, and he too is on the side of the child. In general, most of the humanistic psychotherapists go with the idea that infantile trauma is real and has to be worked with as such.

Frank Lake (1980) argued that there are four levels of trauma, and what happens inside the individual depends very much on exactly what level of trauma is involved. He made no distinction between sexual and any other type of trauma. The first level is pain free, and is the ideal state. The second level has to do with coping, and is where the stimulation is bearable and even perhaps strengthening, because it evokes effective and mostly non-neurotic defences. The third level involves opposition to the pain, but it is so strong that it cannot be coped with, and repression takes place. If the trauma happens in infancy or earlier, the defence will be splitting rather than repression. The fourth level Lake calls transmarginal stress, and it is so powerful or so early, or both, that the person cuts off completely and may even turn against the self, wanting to die. Some recent work by Southgate and others suggests that many child accidents are in fact unconscious attempts at suicide, based on this fourth level of trauma. And if the trauma was actually a case of sexual or other abuse, and if the abuse is repeated or recreated somehow in later life, a real adult suicide may result, again possibly disguised as an accident. This has been coming up recently in a number of cases.

Grof (1985) is very clear that early trauma can be very real and very important, and relates it particularly to the process of birth. He distinguishes four stages of birth, and says that adult neurosis is very frequently based upon traumas suffered at one or other of these stages. Lake (1980), in one of his charts, brings out the way in which his four levels of trauma can be related to Grof's four stages of birth to make a matrix of sixteen cells which account between them for many of the origins of many of the neuroses. And again, of course, many of the drastic things which happen in the lives of adults may result from repetitions of the original trauma in some direct or disguised form.

Innocence

But perhaps the key point where the dialectic becomes so important is on the question of innocence. There is a statement which comes at the very head of a list that Alice Miller has produced to summarise her contentions: 'The child is always innocent.'

Let me say at once that I think this statement is for the most part true. The dictionary says that the word means 'Doing no harm; producing no ill effect or result; not injurious; harmless, innocuous'. It would depend exactly on where we drew the line for the word 'child' here, because there have been murderers as young as 6 years old, but over a very wide range of the youngest children we would certainly have to agree that this was a true statement.

But what is obvious to me is that this language is one-sided and non-dialectical. I do not agree that this is the language of psychotherapy. I cannot believe that therapy is about deciding on guilt and innocence, still less about deciding in advance about guilt or innocence. Certainly children can have harmful wishes and fantasies at very early ages – everyone who has worked with early life has agreed on that, because it emerges so unmistakably. All the work of Klein, Fairbairn, Guntrip, Winnicott, Lake, Grof, Laing, Swartley, Verny, Ridgeway, Farrant and others working in this area implies that children are certainly not innocent in their hearts or minds, although they will almost certainly be so in their actions.

The dialectic goes like this: if someone is injured, that is a one-sided action, and it is only the one doing the injuring who could legitimately feel guilty; but if the injured party tries to get revenge, that is also a one-sided action in response. If the revenge is successful, we may feel either happy because poetic (or some other) justice has been done, or sad because the evil has been perpetuated. It is only when reparation and restitution is made that the action is completed and the pattern made up.

But to say that 'The child is always innocent' would presumably be to deny that. At least I do not really understand it if that is not what it means.

Mahrer in his research has found, as most of us have, that even where the client reports the most violent abuse, they also very often report a sort of excitement about it too, which may sometimes make them feel guilty or implicated afterwards. But the therapist who took the position 'The child is always innocent' would presumably have to tell them not to be so silly, not to blame themselves, not to have any truck with guilt. But this is not to work through the guilt nor to take it seriously – is it not fairly close to some kind of pedagogy?

I do not believe therapy is ever about telling people what happened or what to think or feel about it. If it is anything defensible, it is a process of discovery and self-discovery, where whatever comes up has to be taken seriously and worked through properly. The moment the therapist tries to know better than the client we have an abandonment of the most central feature of psychotherapy – the way in which it takes the client seriously, even when the client is clearly wrong, mistaken, in error or otherwise off the wall. This is one area in which I think that Masson (1986) is quite right.

Now I happen to think that it is OK to teach things to the client in the process of psychotherapy. We had a very interesting third-year seminar on this at the Institute where I work, which went so well that we presented it at a plenary meeting of the whole Institute. There are all sorts of occasions when the client just has not thought of some possibility, or does not have a certain position on the mental map, and it is then OK in my book to tell them about such possibilities or positions, so that they can take them into account instead of leaving them out.

What is not OK is to tell the client that they are not feeling what they are feeling, that that they are not having the experience that they are having, that they are innocent when they feel guilty.

But worst of all is to lay all the emphasis on what was done to the child and none on what the child's response was then and can be now –

because to do this is to take responsibility and power away from the client who is being worked with in the present. In Charles Hampden-Turner's (1976) moving book *Sane Asylum* he tells of the work of the Delancey Street Foundation, which is a therapeutic community of ex-criminals. One of the main statements which he quotes from John Maher, who started the venture, is: 'The system made you what you are, but if you want to change the system, you have to accept the responsibility for what you let the system do to you.' Those who did accept this, made it; those who didn't, didn't. To take that responsibility away from people is to rob them of the one thing they need in order to take their own power. It is the essence of being human that we have choice, that we are not pawns or puppets, that we respond to events rather than reacting to them – and the whole weight of prenatal research (Verny, 1982; Ridgway, 1987) goes now to show that we do not start being human at 7 years old, or at 4 years old, or at 2 years old or at birth – we are human right from the start.

Conclusions

As always, we have to make the point that when we use the word trauma we do not necessarily mean a single event. It may be a situation of some duration which is apparently coped with and even accepted by the victim. Nor is it the case that early traumas cannot be overcome. Even the earliest traumas – and Lake traced some of them back to the first 3 months in the womb – can be reached and dealt with by suitable psychotherapy. Grof (1985) makes the point that going into such deep matters may in many cases bring us closer to the spiritual. I have gone into this in much more detail in a book (Rowan and Dryden, 1987) where there is probably not one contributor who would practise poisonous pedagogy in the therapy session – that is, taking up a parental position, siding with the parents or having to be right.

But it also needs to be said that therapy does not stop with anger against the parents. Sybil (Schreiber, 1975) eventually got down to the anger, but then when her symptoms had disappeared she was able to forgive her mother, and forgive herself, and see her mother as a psychotic sufferer, and feel sorry for her. If you can let go of your symptoms, you can let go of your hate too. You can take responsibility for your part in the events, without it turning into self-blame. You can complete the dialectic and come full circle.

This does not mean that everyone has won, and everyone must have prizes. It means that we have to beware of overlooking poisonous pedagogy, whether perpetrated by parents or by therapists. It means that we have to go with the client into the client's world, and see it through the client's eyes, before doing anything else, and maybe instead of doing anything else.

Someone else who has taken up this position, but for different reasons, is Alvin Mahrer. In his latest book (Mahrer, 1986)* he shows how early traumas can be very complex, with more than one thing going on at the same time, and how the therapist may need to get right inside the experience to make any really adequate sense of it.

In fact, I think he is the only person who actually tells us how to get on the side of the child, how to get inside the child's world and see things from there. He gives full instructions as to how to line up with the client instead of trying to have a relationship over against the client.

Of course, some therapies do not give much importance to early trauma, and for them this whole controversy must be rather lacking in interest. To them we can only say that an awareness of these matters is very valuable, simply because many clients will bring it up in some form or other, whether they are supposed to or not. It is even true, apparently, that a student of Zen meditation came up to the *roshi* and said 'I expected to get enlightenment, but all I am getting is all this childhood stuff'.

References

FLIESS, R. (1973). *Symbol, Dream and Psychosis*. New York: International Universities Press.

GROF, S. (1985). *Beyond the Brain*. New York: SUNY.

HAMPDEN-TURNER, C. (1976). *Sane Asylum*. New York: William Morrow.

JANOV, A. (1970). *The Primal Scream*. London: Abacus.

JANOV, A. (1977). *The Feeling Child*. London: Abacus.

LAKE, F. (1980). *Studies in Constricted Confusion*. Oxford: CTA.

MAHRER, A.R. (1986). *Therapeutic Experiencing*. New York: W.W. Norton.

MALCOLM, J. (1986). *In the Freud Archives*. London: Flamingo.

MILLER, A. (1985). *Thou Shalt not be Aware*. London: Pluto Press.

RIDGWAY, R. (1987). *The Unborn Child*. Aldershot: Wildwood House.

ROWAN, J. and DRYDEN, W. (1987). *Innovative Therapy in Britain*. Milton Keynes: Open University Press.

SCHREIBER, F.R. (1975). *Sybil*. Harmondsworth: Penguin.

SHENGOLD, L. (1975). An attempt at soul murder: Rudyard Kipling's early life and work. *Psychoanalytic Study of the Child*. New York: International University Press.

SOUTHGATE, J. and WHITING, L. (Eds) (1987). *Journal of the Institute for Self-analysis* 1(1).

VERNY, T. (1982). *The Secret Life of the Unborn Child*. London: Sphere.

---

*Mahrer has, of course, now written several more books [1991].

Chapter 15
Encounter Groups as a Paradigm of Integrative Psychotherapy

It seems to me that encounter is by its very nature integrative but it may be as well to spell this out in some detail, because there are several different versions of encounter, some more and some less integrative.*

The great authoritative text on groups by Shaffer and Galinsky says that the encounter group proper is 'an outgrowth and compendium of all the group models that preceded it' (Shaffer and Galinsky, 1989, p. 201).

This kind of group originated in the 1960s and reached its most classic development in the 1970s. It is now the most general type of group, and someone who has learned how to lead this type of group will find any other type of group relatively easy. But it does require a great deal of skill from the group leader.

It is of course a humanistic group, and shares with other humanistic approaches a belief that the person is basically OK. Consequently it refuses to call people 'patients', and calls them instead participants or group members.

It is also a holistic group, and shares with other holistic approaches the motto 'Go where the energy is'. This energy can be expressed on the physical level, on the emotional level, on the intellectual level or on the spiritual level. The basic rule for the leader of an encounter group is to look for the signs of some kind of energy ready to come out.

My own belief is that the main line of development of ideas about encounter, as worked out in the 1960s and early 1970s, runs through the work of Will Schutz, Jim Elliott and Elizabeth Mintz, and it is their work

---

From J. Rowan (1991). Integrative encounter. *Journal of Integrative and Eclectic Psychotherapy* **10**(2), 150–163, with permission.
*For example, Rogers (1970) has talked about 'basic encounter', which is not very integrative; Schutz (1973) has talked about 'open encounter', which is fully integrative; Mintz (1972) has talked about 'marathon encounter', which is also fully integrative; and Yablonsky (1965) has talked about 'Synanon encounter', which is not fully integrative.

which lies at the heart of this paper, although some updating material is needed and will be added.

Theory

There are many definitions of what we mean by the term 'integrative', as Mahrer (1989) has pointed out in his magisterial book, and some are more adequate than others.

What I think is meant by the fullest and most appropriate use of this term is any approach that unifies the three basic legs on which psychotherapy stands: the regressive, the existential and the transpersonal. This is a wholehearted definition which implies a wholehearted approach.

By *regressive* I mean the whole business of delving back into the past, and into the personal unconscious, to find out what went wrong there, and how it can be put right. Certain approaches specialise in this, as, for example, classical psychoanalysis, Kleinian analysis, the body therapies such as bioenergetics and postural integration, and directly regressive approaches such as primal integration and primal therapy. It seems to me that no therapy can really ignore this area. Even approaches which appear at first to ignore it do actually have to cover it, as we can see from any reasonably extended case history (e.g. Kutash and Wolf, 1986; Dryden, 1987).

Laing (1983) makes the point that we must also talk about recession, by which he means a move from the outer to the inner world. Going back is no use unless at the same time we are going deeper into our own experience. Regression without recession is of little use or interest.

By *existential* I mean any approach that emphasises the here-and-now at the expense of the past and the future, although of course all approaches have to deal perforce with past, present and future-oriented material. Also, of course, virtually all therapies work their most effective magic by bringing the past into the present in some way. But I am speaking here mainly of an approach that says that the most important thing to pay attention to is whatever is going on right now, either inside the client or between the present participants. Approaches that specialise in this aspect include group analysis, personal construct therapy, cognitive–behavioural therapy, neurolinguistic programming (NLP), existential analysis, person-centred therapy and gestalt therapy. Again all therapists do very often enter this area in one way or another.

By *transpersonal* I mean the way in which some approaches emphasise the future: the direction of the person, the higher potentials of the person, the deeper perspective given by a spiritual insight. In the terms that Assagioli (Ferrucci, 1982) introduced many years ago, it has to do with the higher unconscious as distinct from the lower unconscious. These approaches emphasise the intuition and creativity of both therapist and client, and the way in which the boundary separating therapist from client can sometimes disappear, with advantage. Such approaches include Jungian analysis (Zurich and archetypal versions), psychosynthesis and transpersonal psychotherapy. In recent years there has been some very good work published in this area (e.g. Vaughan, 1985; Wilber, Engler and Brown, 1986; Grof, 1988). Some forms of psychotherapy contrive to ignore this area, but at their peril.

A truly integrative approach, in my opinion, would deal with all three of these areas and be able to handle them, and in this way be able to cope with the whole person who comes into the consulting room or the group space.

Practice

Many of the humanistic groups manage to deal with all three of these areas, but the most coherent version is the encounter group, as developed by people such as Will Schutz, Jim Elliott and Elizabeth Mintz. The encounter group manages it very naturally and with little difficulty. Let us look at each of these areas in turn.

Regression

Will Schutz has probably given the most adequate account of encounter in its full form. His book *Elements of Encounter* (Schutz, 1973) gives a succinct account of the history of the development of the encounter group, and also of the principles that emerged from that history. And in his book *Joy: Twenty Years Later* he says:

> I still regard encounter as the queen of the human potential methods; the best method to experience before any other training, so that the person is clear, aware, self-determining, and ready to profit much more from any other training.
>
> (Schutz, 1989, p. 161)

What happens in an encounter group is that the group produces an issue of some kind through one or more of its members, and the leader finds a way of dramatising that issue so that it can be worked through for the benefit of the individuals who raise the issue, and the group as a whole.

There is an assumption here that this may well lead into something to do with the past, and may also lead the person deeper into their inner world. This is because of the concept of the energy cycle. This is something that gets fairly close to the gestalt notion of a cycle of aware-ness (Clarkson, 1989). As a need begins to be felt, energy is mobilised to deal with it, and this rises to a peak when the challenge is met; after this there is a relaxation period, when the person winds down. If, however, the challenge is never met, then the tension of mobilised energy is held in the body, and chronic body structuring may be set up in the worst cases. So in his groups, Schutz looks for the signs of held tension, and seeks to enable the person to complete the energy cycle, by dealing with the real life events that need to be dealt with.

For example, a tension between two men may lead to them both carrying out an exercise suggested by the leader, and this may lead to one of them getting in touch with feelings about his father (e.g. Shaffer and Galinsky, 1989, p. 207).

Jim Elliott (1976) has given us what is perhaps the most thorough examination of what is actually done in an encounter group, and again made clear that this is a coherent and principled approach, not in any sense a ragbag of different techniques. Its emphases are on interpersonal communication in the here and now; contacting, exploring and expressing feelings; and moving towards self-directedness and self-actualisation.

Elliott says that growth is a three-stage process: first destructuring; secondly the emergence of noetic material (mental contents such as thoughts, feelings, desires and so forth); and thirdly integration of this material.

Elliott regards feelings as very important in this. Feelings, he says, are the royal road to the noetic world (the world of mental contents). Feelings are like icebergs, with the most socially acceptable aspects visible, and the more powerful, more primitive aspects submerged out of sight.

> Part of my strategy in working with feelings is to help people get deeper into the feeling iceberg. What I find when I start with a tiny 'insignificant' surface feeling is that it leads to other feelings, deeper down, that seem to occur in layers. The full expression of one layer leaves noetic space for the next layer to emerge. Growth, then, involves work on oneself in the form of uncovering layer after layer of feeling, until one gets to what have been called primal feelings, such as deep rage and pain. That's where the very earliest blocks are released and the most energy becomes liberated.   (Elliott, 1976, p. 95)

He goes on to say that it is important in such cases to elicit the complete configuration rather than have a dissociated feeling. This includes the somatic component, the imagery component and the belief component, as well as the feelings themselves. This enables the further processing to take place which leads to real integration with the rest of the person's life.

It can be seen here how regression and recession are very important, but they are not the end of the road. Work still needs to be done on integrating the insights into the person's ordinary everyday world.

A good example of this kind of work in action is to be found in Gerald Haigh's (1968) article, too long to quote here, where a woman goes into her feelings about her mother and resolves something very important once and for all. So again the regressive content can be very central.

Elizabeth Mintz (1972) has told us particularly about the marathon group, which is in a way the most complete expression of what the encounter group has to offer.

She makes the point that the power of the encounter group is related to its simultaneous functioning as a reality experience and as a symbolic experience. This is more implicit in the work of the other two people we have examined, but of course equally true of their work.

She is also clear that an encounter group is not only a growth group but a therapy group. She denies that there is any real distinction between the two, as if the healthy were healthy and the sick were sick, and a neat line could be drawn between the two. In an encounter group we go down into the neurotic and even psychotic material which we all have within us. This often means regression into the past, and recession into the inner world.

In these ways the Mintz account is complementary to the two accounts already given.

Existential

Let us come now on to how encounter deals with the here-and-now aspects of the matter. Schutz himself lays particular stress upon the existential issue of openness and honesty:

> Honesty and openness are the key to your evolutionary growth. Being honest allows your bodymind to become a clear channel for taking in all the energy of the universe, both inside and outside your body, and to use it profitably.
>
> (Schutz, 1973, p. 16)

This is really the classic existential approach of the encounter group, but it is interesting to see that Schutz says that it only really happens once the other issues are out of the way. In this it is perhaps reminiscent of the point which psychoanalysts sometimes make, that when the client can really free-associate the therapy is over.

Mintz has some points to make about the way the group should be run. At the beginning of the group she lays down certain requirements:

> that the group must function as a group at all times, without one-to-one relationships or subgrouping; that social chatter and history taking are not useful; that after the ending of the group any personal data which have been revealed are to be treated confidentially; and that any reaction which one group member has to another is to be expressed openly and directly.   (Mintz, 1972, p. 17)

She goes into the question of what the norms actually are in an encounter group. Her list is so similar to those of Schutz and Elliott that I have taken the liberty of making up my own list which is based on all three (Table 15.1).

Table 15.1 Integrative encounter groups: basic practice

Awareness of the body	Your body is you. It expresses your feelings, if you will let it. You can learn how you feel by going into your own body and noticing what you find there. If you suppress your own body, you will probably be willing to suppress other people – and they may pick this up. In groups like this we often get rid of chairs and tables so that interaction may take place physically as well as verbally
The here and now	Talk about what you are aware of in this group at this moment. If you want to talk about the past, or about events outside the group, find ways of making them present to the group members. This can often be done by action or role-playing
Feelings	Let reality have an emotional impact on you, especially the reality of the other group members. Let yourself feel various emotions – but if they are blocked, be aware of that too. Feel what it is like to experience whatever is happening at an emotional level
Self-disclosure	Be open about your feelings or lack of them. Let people into your world. If you are anxious, let people know about it; if you are bored, it is OK to say so. Be as honest as you can bear to
Taking responsibility	Take responsibility for yourself – do what you want and need to do, not what you think the group wants you to do. If the leader suggests something, it is still your decision whether to go along with it. Be aware of what you are doing to other people by what you say and do, and take responsibility for that. Be aware of the 'I and thou' in each statement. You are not an impartial observer
Risk taking	If you are torn between expressing something and not expressing it, try taking a risk. Doing the thing you are most afraid of is usually a good idea in this group. You can reduce the danger of hostile statements by saying them non-evaluatively: instead of saying 'You are a cold person', say 'I feel frozen when you talk like that'. This is more likely to be true, and it makes you more real to the others.
Listening	Listening to others lets us in to their worlds. But listening is not just about words – it means being aware of expressions, gestures, body positions, breathing. Allow intuition. Really be there with the other people in the group
Bridging distances	As relationships in the group become clearer, there may be one or two members you feel very distant from – or want to be distant from. By expressing this, a quite new kind of relationship may begin to appear. Opposition and distance are just as likely to lead to growth as closeness and support
Distress	When someone in the group is distressed, encourage them to stay with that feeling until the distress is fully worked through, or turns into some other emotion. There is a 'Red Cross nurse' in all of us who wants to stop people feeling distressed, and usually jumps in too soon. A person learns most by staying with the feeling, and going with it to its natural end, which is often a very good place
Support and confrontation	It is good to support someone who is doing some self-disclosure, some risk-taking, some bridging of distances. It is good to confront someone who is not being honest, who is avoiding all risk-taking, who is diverting energy away from the group's real work. It is possible to do both these things with love and care
Avoidance	Don't ask questions – make the statement which lies behind the question. Address people directly, saying 'I' rather than 'it' or 'you'. Don't say 'I feel' when you mean 'I think'. Ask yourself 'What am I avoiding at this moment?'
The saver	Don't take any of these rules too seriously. Any set of rules can be used to put someone down – perhaps yourself

I sometimes use this as a one-page handout to give to naïve groups, especially if they are likely to be rather rigid and intellectual: I first used it with a group of engineering students, who found the whole idea of psychology very difficult, but found these rules quite understandable.

Schutz is particularly keen to emphasise the centrality of the body in all this. Non-verbal methods are used consistently, and body movements and postures are referred to constantly. Stuck feelings are usually held in the body in some quite noticeable way, and it often makes sense to exaggerate some physical action until it reveals what was behind it. Encounter agrees with the body therapies, and with gestalt, that my body is a map of my experience and my being. Schutz says:

> You are a unified organism. You are at the same time physical, psychological and spiritual. These levels are all manifestations of the same essence. You function best when these aspects are integrated and when you are self-aware.
>
> (Schutz, 1973, p. 16)

This is a good statement of one of the basic beliefs of the humanistic approach which is so fundamentally committed to integration.

Elliott emphasises more the existential interactions of the group members. He points out that the tangles they get into with each other represent here-and-now material for the leader to work with and untangle: the members then also learn how to deal with such tangles in their everyday lives.

> By using such a format, the encounter group leader can: 1) encourage interpersonal interactions among group members in the here-and-now; 2) elicit the feelings that accompany such interactions; 3) encourage the individual to get deeper into the feelings; 4) help the group deal with the norm-setting attempts that inevitably occur as a reaction to the expression of feelings; 5) help the group create an appropriate climate in which intensive work may be done; 6) train people in more effective ways of communicating and relating; and 7) help people grow by showing them how to disengage themselves from whatever they have become attached to and, from that new, freer position, become involved with whatever aspects of human existence they wish.   (Elliott, 1976, p. 32)

So Elliott is stressing here the value of members of the group working with each other, and we shall see later that this is a theme that has become more important as the years have gone by.

There are differences, then, as well as great similarities between different exponents of encounter. Let us see how these work out when we come to the next category we are examining.

Transpersonal

This is a category of working where, as Stan Grof has said, we are involved with 'experiences involving an expansion or extension of consciousness beyond the usual ego boundaries and beyond the limitations of time and/or space' (Grof, 1975, p. 155). We feel we are getting information from we know not where. At first this sounds very unfamiliar and unusual, until we realise that virtually all therapists, counsellors and group leaders rely on their *intuition* a great deal.

Now according to the psychosynthesis school, which has done a lot of work in this area, intuition is one of the faculties of the higher unconscious. This higher unconscious, or superconscious, is a natural feature of the human mind, which does go beyond the usual ego boundaries. By giving it its proper name, we are able to work with it better and understand it more fully. Intuition, then, takes us into the realm of the transpersonal.

Let us move on to take up another, similar, point about imagination. Encounter group leaders use *imagery and fantasy,* and these too are part of the transpersonal realm. When we ask a participant to bring to mind an image of his or her inner conflict, or suggest that they imagine what their opponent might turn into, or invite them to bring to mind a certain scene, we are invoking the imaginal world, which is the realm of the transpersonal.

So when Schutz tells the story of a British woman in one of his groups who was asked to become very small and go inside her own body (Shaffer and Galinsky, 1989, p. 218), he was working in a transpersonal way. We can see from this that imagery very often involves playing with the normal limitations of time and space. (In his more recent work, Schutz (1981) explicitly uses meditation, prayer, chanting and Arican spiritual exercises.)

Elliott does not say as much as Schutz about the spiritual aspects of his work, but he does say that human beings are not just physical objects but are best characterised by such words as freedom, choice, growth, autonomy and mystery. He also refers to *creativity* and liberation (Elliott, 1976, p. 58).

Another phenomenon noted by Elliott is the fusion experience, which often happens after primals and similar cathartic experiences. The whole person is involved, and seems often to be taken outside his or her ordinary world. 'Looking back on the experience, [one has] the feeling that one was outside time and space. Typical comments are "The world fell away"...' (Elliott, 1976, p. 198).

Mintz does not say much about spirituality in her 1972 book, but makes up for it in a later book which is all about it. In this book she gives an example where a young man's impotence was cured, not by the usual process of therapy, but by a group ritual in which he symbolically castrated each of the other men in the group. This arose quite spontaneously in the group, and she says of the event: 'It was an enactment of a mythic ritual, a primitive ceremony, which tapped the deep levels of the collective unconscious; it was a transpersonal experience' (Mintz, 1983, pp. 153–157).

In the same book, Mintz talks of countertransference of such a kind that the group leader actually feels inside her own body the next thing that needs to happen for the participant. This links directly with the research on countertransference mentioned by Samuels (1989) in his recent book, which again links this with the transpersonal, and with the Jungian idea of the imaginal world.

It is my strong impression that the climate has changed considerably in recent years, in the direction of more open acknowledgement of the importance of the transpersonal. It was always important in encounter, but it is only more recently that people have said so very much.

In an encounter group it is possible to catch a glimpse of spiritual realities which go beyond ordinary consciousness. In a recent book Anthony, Ecker and Wilber (1987) have suggested that these glimpses are extremely important in opening up a sense of spiritual possibilities. They can show briefly what is possible more permanently if spiritual development is continued. The gibe which is sometimes hurled at encounter groups – that the sense of wonder they engender is temporary and therefore false – is seen to be a crass misunderstanding of the real meaning of the experience. The breakthroughs and peak experiences that come through these means – what Perls calls the mini-Satori – are not illusory, even though they are temporary. They represent what I have argued at length elsewhere are mystical experiences (Rowan, 1990).

Some Updating Material

A good description of the encounter group is given by Shaffer and Galinsky (1989), who put it in the context of other approaches to group work and again make clear that it is a coherent and expressive form of group work, which can stand with any of its competitors in a sturdy and respectable way. They also see Schutz as central in the development of the encounter group model, and some of the comments made on him above are based on their account.

Also quite recently, Mike Wibberley (1988) has given a stimulating outline of how encounter is progressing in Britain today. During the 1980s, the general tone of the encounter group became more equalitarian. Now it was not a question (as it was in the 1970s) of a few revolutionaries raising awkward issues, but rather of the ethos of the group as a whole. Leaders found they had to become more like members of the group, rather than keeping to the more formal and therapist-like role which they had formerly adopted. This is not a simple matter, however. As Wibberley points out:

> There is often ambivalence in the group, with some people wanting the leader to be 'one of us', and at the same time resenting him or her for not being the mythical, perfect authority who knows all the answers and is able to solve all their problems and lead them to Nirvana.   (Wibberley, 1988, p. 72)

But certainly my experience is that groups in recent years are much less likely to allow the leader to be very distinct and separate than they used to be.

I think this is a permanent change, and that the old group scene can never now return. I feel quite a pang about this, because the old methods, dominant though they often were, did work and did liberate a lot of people. The new ethos seems to me slower and less effective in the short run, although no doubt healthier in the long run.

Case Example

My own work in encounter started in 1970, when I went to groups at the biggest growth centre at the time – Quaesitor – which at that time was located at Avenue Road in St Johns Wood. It was there that I actually went to a weekend workshop led by Will Schutz, who impressed me very much. Later I also attended groups led by Jim Elliott and Elizabeth Mintz, and met Will Schutz many times in different contexts.

What I like about encounter is the way in which it allows the practitioner to use the whole range of his or her talents, and to explore the gamut of the group's capacity for healing and discovery. I find that I can stretch my capacities to the full in following the energy of the client who is focal at a given moment.

In my own work this has happened several times, as, for example, where a young woman was working on her fear of men. This was in a group held in a well-organised therapy centre where I knew there were resources for dealing with anyone who might become distressed or disturbed more than usual. Also there were several experienced leaders in the group.

This woman was quite clearly distressed and ready to work. The previous episode in the group's life had triggered off her own response, a memory of her own rape in terrible circumstances.

I pointed out that I was a man, and encouraged her to see in me the person she was afraid of. First of all she simply experienced her fear, trembling and crying, but quite quickly it changed into anger. She now had in front of her, as it were, the source of the fear and the support to do something about it.

So she took the opportunity to attack me. I held a big cushion in front of myself, and she punched and tore at it. She put a great deal of energy into this, and it seemed to go on for a long time; in reality it was not that long, but it did go on for several minutes. She punched me from the middle of the large room well into one corner. She carried on, with the encouragement of me and the rest of the group, until she could go on no longer.

When she collapsed exhausted, I encouraged the women in the group to gather round her and support her. They held her and spoke softly to her and made much of her, demonstrating that they accepted and appreciated her, and generally enabled her to return. So far this is pure regression work, encouraging the person to go back into the past and relive an episode from it with full emotional recall, at the same time transforming it by ensuring that safety is present.

While the women were working together, I was working with the men, who gathered round to find out what their role was to be. I suggested that they line up in a row along one end of the room, and whispered to them that they should accommodate whatever happened, in the manner outlined by Alfred Pesso (1973) in his work. This meant going with whatever the woman did, and exaggerating its effect. They each held a big cushion in front of them, as I had. The object of an encounter group is to allow action and feelings to be expressed and explored in a therapeutic way, not for people to get physically hurt or take unnecessary risks.

When she had recovered somewhat, the women encouraged her to attack the row of men, one by one. As she beat on each one, he screamed and threw up his hands and staggered into a corner and collapsed, until one side of the room was completely covered with a row of prostrate male bodies. So far this is pure existential work, bringing an activity into the here and now which takes forward the insights and feelings released by the earlier regression work. The strength released by the recession into her inner feelings was now enabled to come out and to be expressed publicly.

She looked around, and seemed to feel that it was not quite finished. Then she took the ritual into her own hands (or in this case feet), and trampled all over the men, feeling more and more triumphant over them. It should perhaps be said, for those who are not familiar with encounter groups, that it is normal for people to take off their shoes in such a group, and to sit on cushions bare-foot or in socks.

The protagonist then sat down between two sympathetic women, who held her while she relaxed and came back to herself.

In the discussion afterwards, she said how powerful she had felt during this episode, and the other women in the group said they had been quite inspired too. The men were quite shaken, but were impressed by what had happened and wanted to understand it for themselves.

Now to those who are familiar with Eastern mythology, the last part of this episode forcibly brings to mind the words of Arthur Avalon as he talks about the relationship between the male and female polarities in Tantric religion:

> The fully Real, therefore, has two aspects: one called Śiva, the static aspect of Consciousness, and the other called Śakti, the kinetic aspect of the same. Kāli Śakti, dark as a thundercloud, is represented standing and moving on the white inert body of Śiva. He is white as Illumination (Prakāśa). He is inert, for Pure Consciousness is without action and at rest. It is She, His Power, who moves. Dark is She here

because, as Kāli, She dissolves all in darkness, that is vacuity of existence, which is the Light of Being Itself.   (Avalon, 1978, p. 42)

What we had here, in effect, was a re-enactment of a very ancient ritual, expressing the way in which female energy is sacred and has to be respected and treated correctly by the male. We had gone right outside the boundaries of the group room, and had been in touch with archetypal forces. I do not think it is right to identify the archetypal with the transpersonal, but it is through the transpersonal that we most readily get in touch with the archetypal. Assagioli (1975) says that the collective unconscious is much more complex and broad than the higher unconscious or superconscious, and I think he was the first to make this distinction clear. In any case, in this example we had moved instantly and irreversibly into the transpersonal.

The next phase of the group was all around male–female relationships, and brought out some deep here-and-now material affecting several people in the group who had problems in this area. Here we had moved back into the existential mode once again.

This ritual affected everyone in the group very strongly, and it seems to be a fact that the transpersonal does come across with great power when this is allowed and encouraged.

Conclusion

The advantage of the integrative approach is that it enables the practitioner to do what is appropriate in a given situation, rather than sticking to some previously worked out theory. It enables, in particular, the regressive, the existential and the transpersonal all to be given their due weight. In this way theory and practice are in a dialectical relationship, each informing the other. The theory gives rise to the practice, and the practice in turn enables the theory to be further developed.

References

ANTHONY, R., ECKER, B. and WILBER, K. (Eds) (1987). *Spiritual Choices: The Problem of Recognising Authentic Paths to Inner Transformation*. New York: Paragon House.

ASSAGIOLI, R. (1975). *Psychosynthesis*. London: Turnstone Books.

AVALON, A. (1978). *Shakti and Shakta*. New York: Dover.

CLARKSON, P. (1989). *Gestalt Counselling in Action*. London: Sage.

DRYDEN, W. (Ed.) (1987). *Key Cases in Psychotherapy*. London: Croom Helm.

ELLIOTT, J. (1976). *The Theory and Practice of Encounter Group Leadership*. Berkeley: Explorations Institute.

FERRUCCI, P. (1982). *What We May Be*. Wellingborough: Turnstone Press.

GROF, S. (1975). *Realms of the Human Unconscious*. New York: Viking Press.

GROF, S. (1988). *The Adventure of Self-discovery*. Albany: State University of New York Press.

HAIGH, G. (1968). The residential basic encounter group. In H.A. Otto and J. Mann (Eds), *Ways of Growth*. New York: Grossman.

KUTASH, I.L. and WOLF, A. (Eds)(1986). *Psychotherapists' Casebook*. San Francisco: Jossey-Bass.

LAING, R.D. (1983). *The Voice of Experience*. Harmondsworth: Penguin.

MAHRER, A.R. (1989). *The Integration of Psychotherapies*. New York: Human Sciences Press.

MINTZ, E.E. (1972). *Marathon Groups: Reality and Symbol*. New York: Avon.

MINTZ, E.E. (1983). *The Psychic Thread: Paranormal and Transpersonal Aspects of Psychotherapy*. New York: Human Sciences Press.

PESSO, A. (1973). *Experience in Action: A Psychomotor Psychology*. New York: New York University Press.

ROGERS, C. (1970). *On Encounter*. Harmondsworth: Penguin.

ROWAN, J. (1990). Spiritual experiences in counselling. *British Journal of Guidance and Counselling*, **18**, 233–249.

SAMUELS, A. (1989). *The Plural Psyche*. London: Routledge.

SCHUTZ, W. (1973). *Elements of Encounter*. Big Sur: Joy Press.

SCHUTZ, W. (1981). Holistic education. In R. Corsini (Ed.), *Innovative Psychotherapies*. New York: John Wiley.

SCHUTZ, W. (1989). *Joy: 20 Years Later*. Berkeley: Ten Speed Press.

SHAFFER, J.B.P. and GALINSKY, M.D. (1989). *Models of Group Therapy*. Englewood Cliffs: Prentice-Hall.

VAUGHAN, F. (1985). *The Inward Arc*. Boston: New Science Library.

WIBBERLEY, M. (1988). Encounter. In J.Rowan and W. Dryden (Eds), *Innovative Therapy in Britain*. Milton Keynes: Open University Press.

WILBER, K., ENGLER, J. and BROWN, D.P. (1986). *Transformations of Consciousness*. Boston: New Science Library.

YABLONSKY, L. (1965). *Synanon: The Tunnel Back*. London: Macmillan.

Part IV
Transpersonal Psychotherapy

The first article in this section, 'The real self and mystical experiences', represents a very exciting voyage of discovery which I made in the early 1980s. It is hard now to recapture the unfamiliarity of this material, but almost every word represents a discovery and a new thought.

The article on 'Holistic listening' is a slight improvement on an article I wrote for the *British Journal of Psychotherapy*, entitled 'Listening as a four-level activity'. This too was very exciting to write, and put together some ideas which made more sense that way than they did apart.

The third article I feel is particularly important, as it adds a dimension to the discussion of meditation which is very often left out of account. 'Meditation and therapy: A quadrant approach' attempts to show not only that meditation has a similar structure to many other human activities, but also that psychotherapy itself can sometimes be regarded as one type of meditation. I think this is a real contribution.

The next piece, entitled 'A growth episode', is again very personal, and some people have said that it reveals too much. But my own view is that unless people do reveal this sort of thing, no one is ever going to know much about the real changes which go on in psychotherapy, or what sorts of results can be obtained. After all, Freud revealed a great deal of himself in his book *The Interpretation of Dreams,* and I personally respect him for that.

The article 'Spiritual aspects of primal integration' was again an improved version of an earlier paper, published in the *British Journal of Guidance and Counselling*. It was delivered as the keynote address at the annual conference of the International Primal Association in New Jersey, and represented the furthest I had gone at that time in relating spirituality to psychotherapy.

The article 'Four hills of vision: Groupwork in men's consciousness' brings together and summarises several years of work with men in groups devoted to examining the role of men in relation to feminism. This is work which I think is terribly important, and which I would like to have done much more of. It is close to the more intellectual work I do in relation to the magazine *Achilles' Heel,* which has now reached its eleventh issue, and which is the most consistent and effective voice in the anti-sexist men's movement in this country.

'The downward path to wholeness in transpersonal psychotherapy' comes from a presentation at the second conference of the European Transpersonal Association (EUROTAS) in Strasbourg. It puts forward my thinking on the issue of paganism as a force that has to be taken into account in understanding transpersonal psychology. It links in with the work of Hillman in the Jungian tradition, who has done so much to point out the importance of polytheism. I don't think even he, however, does enough justice to the chthonic gods – the gods of the earth. I believe that it is only the real understanding of female power that is going to save the planet from the depredations of male power. This is going to require a much greater respect for the downward direction, for the underworld that underlies all our conscious resolves. So here we link in with the Green movement and the ecological consciousness that goes with it.

Chapter 16
The Real Self and Mystical Experiences

Introduction

One of the central concepts in humanistic psychology is also one of the most ambiguous. It is the notion of self-actualisation. What exactly is this self which is to be actualised? This is a hard question to answer, and I began to wonder why. Then I went through a sequence of experiences that enabled me to question everything I had thought up to then about the self, and came up at the end with these findings. Let me take you through them.

Self-actualisation

We get the idea of self-actualisation from Maslow, of course, and here is what he says about it:

> Self-actualization is defined in various ways but a solid core of agreement is percep-
> tible. All definitions accept or imply (a) acceptance and expression of the inner
> core of self, i.e. actualization of these latent capacities, and potentialities, 'full
> functioning', availability of the human and personal essence. (b) They all imply
> minimal presence of ill health, neurosis, psychosis, of loss or diminution of the
> basic human and personal capacities.   (Maslow, 1962, p. 184)

This clearly suggests that there is just one inner core, which just has to be accepted and expressed. But what exactly is this inner core or self? Maslow became more and more convinced that the concept of Being would help to elucidate this:

> This state of Being, rather than of striving, is suspected to be synonymous with
> selfhood, with being 'authentic', with being a person, with being fully human.
>   (Maslow, 1962, p. 188)

From J. Rowan (1983). The real self and mystical experiences. *Journal of Humanistic Psychology* **23**(2), 9–27, with permission.

He went on to show that it was in peak experiences that people most readily entered into the realm of Being, and therefore obtained a sense of selfhood in this way:

> Of course, being in a state of Being needs no future, because it is already *there*. Then Becoming ceases for the moment and its promissory notes are cashed in the form of the ultimate rewards, i.e. the peak experiences, in which time disappears and hopes are fulfilled.   (Maslow, 1962, p. 200)

This then starts to sound like a fully fledged mystical experience, an experience of enlightenment. And indeed as early as Maslow's first book, he was explicitly making this connection:

> Those subjective expressions that have been called the mystic experience and described so well by William James are a fairly common experience for our subjects . . . It is quite important to dissociate this experience from any theological or super- natural reference, even though for thousands of years they have been linked. . . Because this experience is a natural experience, well within the jurisdiction of science, it is probably better to use Freud's term for it, e.g. the oceanic feeling.
> (Maslow, 1954, p. 216)

In his later books, he makes it very plain that peak experiences are both examples of mystical experience and exemplars of what the self is or could be. It is equally clear that he thinks that there is just one mystical experience, which is the same the world over:

> It has begun to appear strongly that this phenomenon (the peak experience) is a diluted, more secular, more frequent version of the mystical experience that has been described so often as to have become what Huxley called *The Perennial Philosophy*. In various cultures and in various eras it takes on somewhat different coloration – and yet its essence is always recognizable – it is the same.
> (Maslow, 1973, p. 64)

The sequence now seems clear. If we want to know what self-actualisa- tion is, go to the peak experience, go to the experience of Being. When we do this, we discover the same kind of unity as that of the mystics down the ages. And this, Maslow tells us, is transcendence:

> Transcendence can mean to live in the realm of Being, speaking the language of Being, B-cognising, plateau living. It can mean the serene B-cognition as well as the climactic peak-experience kind of B-cognition. After the insight or the great conver- sion, or the great mystic experience or the great illumination, or the great full awakening, one can calm down as the novelty disappears, and as one gets used to good things or even great things, live casually in heaven and be on easy terms with the eternal and infinite.   (Maslow, 1973, p. 287)

The map now appears to be complete. In the process of self-actualisation, which Maslow says is a natural process inherent in the very meaning of what it is to be a human being, we occasionally have a peak experience. If we can rise to that occasion and live it and own it, we can get the experience of Being, and let it change our lives; and the experience of transcendence can become a plateau experience, which can, with practice, stay with us. The self we are then talking about is the mystical self, the actualised self.

In a paper called 'Theory Z' (Maslow, 1973, pp. 293–311) Maslow distinguishes between non-peaking self-actualisation and peaking self-actualisation, suggesting that the former is a lower state than the latter. This would mean a two-stage process, whereby contact with the 'real self' comes first, through a process of integration, rather in the manner that Mahrer (1978) has outlined, and then the further state of transcendence comes later.

At first, then, Maslow thought that self-actualisation and transcendence were one and the same, and then later he thought that the latter succeeded the former. But either way, the process ends with a mystical unity with the All. And since Maslow (and Bucke and Huxley) there have been many humanistic and transpersonal writers all taking it for granted that this is the whole story. Havens (1982) says: 'The cosmic-consciousness state has been experienced by people throughout the world over many centuries and under a variety of different labels, including samadhi, satori, moksha, atma-bodhi, enlightenment, revelations, rapture, rebirth, peak experiences and transcendental consciousness, to name but a few.' Keutzer (1982) says: 'Though the terms listed above are obviously not precisely synonymous with one another, all are agreed in calling it [cosmic consciousness] (1) the highest state of consciousness; (2) a self-transforming perception of one's total union with the infinite; and (3) an experience beyond time and space – an experience of the timelessness which is eternity, or unlimited unity with all creation.'

This idea that there is just one thing called 'the unitive consciousness of the mystic' or 'cosmic consciousness' or 'transcendence' seems to me now a fundamental error and a classic mistake.

Mystical Experiences

It so happens that there is an enormous literature on mystical experiences – they have been very thoroughly investigated. and a lot is known about them. But it appears that Maslow – in company with numerous others in humanistic and transpersonal psychology – never read the relevant literature. He assumed that all peak experiences were like all mystical experiences, and that they were about the same thing. 'I take the generalized peak experience to be that which is common to all places and times' (Maslow, 1970, 1973). They might arise out of different circumstances, but in all essentials they were similar. What this does is to confuse the beginning with the middle and the end of mystical experience. *The beginning is an experience of ecstasy and cosmic unity; the middle is another experience of ecstasy and cosmic unity; the end is an experience again of ecstasy and cosmic unity; but these are three quite different kinds of ecstasy and three quite different perceptions of cosmic unity.*

There are, in fact, at least seven quite separable and distinguishable experiences, once we learn to attend to them in sufficient detail. Let us look at each of them in turn.

The peak experience

This is the unpredictable occurrence of ecstatic experiences, most often triggered by nature, music or sex, where I feel one with the Whole. This is a common experience: Wuthnow (1978) did a survey on a representative sample of 1000 people, and found that

> one person in two has experienced contact with the holy or sacred, more than eight in ten have been moved deeply by the beauty of nature, and close to four in ten have experienced being in harmony with the universe. Of these, more than half in each case have had peak experiences which have had deep and lasting effects on their lives [Survey conducted in 1973 in the San Francisco–Oakland Standard Metropolitan Statistical Area].

Other investigations include a Gallup survey (Back and Bourque, 1970) that showed 41 per cent in 1967 claimed to have had a religious or mystical experience; a Gallup opinion index published in 1978 showed 35 per cent answering 'yes' to a similar question. A parallel piece of research, using representative samples of the whole population in the UK, found 31 per cent to 35 per cent answering 'yes' to similar questions. In Britain, of those who had had such an experience, 74 per cent said it was very important to them (Hay, 1982). This sort of experience can also be triggered off by LSD, mescaline and the like. Horne (1978) calls it casual extraverted mysticism. The vast majority of the experiences quoted by Maslow come into this category.

This phenomenon of the peak experience is deeply ambiguous. Because it tends to come so suddenly and unexpectedly, it can be treated in many different ways. It can be deliberately pushed away; it can be welcomed; it can be touched with fear and trembling. To the extent that it is felt as specifically religious, it can become infused with what Otto (1950) calls the numinous – the uncanny, the holy – with strong feelings of awe, dread or terror. It seems to depend on one's assumptions about what the experience means. If a peak experience is reached through the process of self-development, and occurs as a sort of crown to the process, it will be experienced in a very positive, transcendent way, as Maslow suggests; but if it comes to an unprepared person, the effect may be quite different. The work of the Religious Experience Unit in Oxford, which has been collecting accounts of these things for some years now (Cohen and Phipps, 1979; Hay, 1982) shows how variable this event can be.

Pure energy

This is the sense of being in touch with energy or power as such. This may take no particular shape, but may rather be experienced as a surge or flow, which can easily be linked with other forms of energy of a more universal kind. This often comes about in meditation or in energy groups, but it can come in other ways too – from sport, for example (Gallwey, 1974; Spino, 1976; Leonard, 1977; Murphy, 1978). There may again be this mystical feeling of being in touch with the Whole, the All, the Ultimate, as Somendra (1980) has described in some detail. As with all of these experiences, there may be intense fear at the beginning of the phase – it may seem as if the ultimate risk is being taken, as if all there was to do was to fall through the floor to the ultimate scary place. There can be a feeling of letting go, which may amount to something like a trance state in some cases. As with the breakthroughs, there may be an intense experience of light.

This again, as with the first, can be very ambiguous, because it can come so suddenly and unexpectedly. More mapping needs to be done in this area, because it seems to me that this is not the same thing as the sudden surges of energy we get sometimes in bioenergetics and other Reichian forms of therapy. What we are talking about here is a subtle form of energy that is spiritual in nature. Again, it is not the same thing as what people in biofeedback try to study, with brain waves and all that. It seems obvious to me that two people could have the same brain waves and be having importantly differential spiritual experiences which can not be reduced to one another. The Yoga people have been very discriminating in this area (Chaudhuri, 1975) and pay a lot of attention to different qualities of energy flow. So this stage of pure energy may be either casual (unprepared) or serious (induced) depending on what leads up to the experience itself.

Real self

This is the feeling of getting in touch with my own centre, my identity, my true self – the self that lies behind or beyond all self-images or self-concepts. This often happens in growth groups, but it can also happen in many other ways. It is a developmental step, principally discontinuous, involving step-jump rather than gradual form (Pedler and Boydell, 1981). Again, this is often experienced as an ecstatic breakthrough. But it is essentially something that has its feet on the ground. For example, Maslow (1973, Chapter 3) said that self-actualisation involved the conscious experience of choice – learning to be a good chooser. He said that, faced with a decision, one should make an inner hush; listen to the impulse voices; look to the 'Supreme Court' inside ourselves, and let the self emerge. He said that each time one takes responsibility, owns up, is honest about oneself, this is an actualising of the self. He said that to listen to one's own self is to be courageous rather than afraid. He said that self-actualisation means working to do well the things that one wants to do. He said that it means the giving up of one's defences. All these seem to refer mainly to this third experience, which Wilber (1980) calls the 'centaur' stage, the stage of the existential self.

This is an experience of authenticity that consists of self-respect and self enactment. In this experience 'mind and body are both experiences of an integrated self' as has been brought out in research studies (Loevinger, 1976). We have healed the splits of intellect/emotion, left brain/right brain, masculine/feminine, shadow/persona, and so on, and are whole persons, what Rogers (1961) has often called the fully functioning person. I love this stage, and I think it is very important for spiritual development, because it is at this stage that we make the basic mystical move of saying 'I must have this experience for myself; I can't get it from anyone else'. This is the basic attitude of the mystic in all religious traditions – to get inside one's own experience, to commit oneself to one's own experience, to trust one's own experience. I may take religious advice and instruction, and most mystics do (Moss, 1981), but even so, I have to decide which instruction and advice to take and which to follow, and there is no way I can put the responsi- bility for this outside myself. Even if I say that it is a voice inside me, I still have the responsibility for which voice to listen to. I am 'free and alone, without assistance and without excuse' as Sartre (1959) puts it. The paradox of putting this atheistic sentiment at the base of mystical experience of a religious kind is something that needs to be appreciated.

Higher self

This is the sense of being in touch with my higher self, or inner teacher. This often comes about in transpersonal or psychosynthesis groups, but again it can happen in many other ways. It may be seen as a guardian angel, a spirit guide, a high archetype, a guru, a Jesus-figure, a *Yidam*, an *Ishtadeva*, a god or goddess. At first it appears to be outside of us, and may even have a three-dimensional reality, but essentially it has a touch of the divine – it is a symbolic representation of the sacred. It may be very specialised in some cases, very general in others.

If we take it seriously and try to get closer to it over a period of time, getting to know it better and fulfilling its demands upon us, we may be encouraged to put our own identity into it. It becomes us; we become it. 'Not me, but Christ in me' is one version of this. Sometimes an actual voice may be heard, or actual visions be seen, but much more common is a very much accentuated ability to use symbolic forms. Guided fantasy (Assagioli, 1975) and active imagination (Jung) originate from this state of being, as a by-product of development, and to help others to take the next step. Oftentimes the use of symbols can give us special powers or abili- ties, which again seem outside us at first and inside us in the end, if we persevere. The pagans and neo-pagans described by Adler (1979) make it clear that this is essentially a polytheistic phase, where we recognise the existence of many spiritual beings, even though we may relate to one in particular. The end of this stage comes when we have the courage, as Wilber (1980) puts it, to recognise that the higher being was projection – that it was us all the time. There is no putdown in saying this, because we are projecting from the superconscious, not from the personal unconscious. This breakthrough often produces an experience of ecstasy. We have now admitted that the sacredness is inside ourselves – it is we ourselves who are holy.

Another way of putting this is to say, as Hixon (1978) does, that we are not projecting the higher self – rather it is projecting us. Or to put it in his own words (an ishtadeva is a high-archetypal deity-form):

> We are not projecting the ishtadeva. The primal radiance which assumes the form of the ishtadeva is actually projecting us and all the phenomena which we call the universe.   (Hixon, 1978)

This is a more monotheistic view, which really belongs to the next stage.

Deity as substance

This is the sense of being in touch with the Deity, considered as the power behind or beyond the universe – the creator and sustainer of all life and being. This is here seen as the One without a second, the pure substance of spirit. This sense can only be developed through worship and commitment to some particular notion of the Deity, which may be personal, symbolic, or abstract. Here we have to come into the realm of theology, because it becomes very important to know what we are committing ourselves to so totally. The Christian tradition is to offer a person, God the Father. Islam offers Allah, Judaism Jehovah. All the main traditions warn against idolatry at this point: the symbols which were so useful in the previous experience lose their power at this level, and become highly questionable. The Buddhist tradition is the most abstract of all – so much so that it is often said that there is no God in Buddhism. Some of the Hindu ideas about Brahman are also very abstract and very fine. Meditation and prayer become much closer together at this point. We do not pray for gifts or goodies, we just open ourselves up to the Deity. 'I abandon myself to the God whose inspiration I feel at work in the depths of myself' (LeRoy, 1977). But again, the ecstatic end of this process is to give up once again our existing sense of identity – our sense of self has to change once again, and this feels like death and rebirth.

This stage is a great leap forward. At all the previous levels we could have a feeling, after the initial terror or ecstacy, that we were in a swimming pool where it was possible to touch bottom occasionally. But here we are out in the ocean – this is the big league of spirituality. At all these mystical stages, words are inadequate to grasp the experience, but here the sense of verbal inadequacy is increased much further. The language of paradox is resorted to more and more, making it clear that we are transverbal rather than preverbal, using Wilber's (1982) useful distinction. The possibilities for deception and self-deception are also much greater; the dangers have been very well spelt out by William McNamara (1975). We feel the need for a church or *sangha* to resort to for support and guidance, and our cultural background may play a great part in what we choose.

One very difficult area here is the spiritual culture in which we have been brought up. At very deep levels, we assume somehow the maleness of the Deity, and also the skyward direction. It seems important at this point in history to question both of these assumptions, and to give much more recognition to the femaleness of the Deity, and to her downward direction. The marvelous book by Monica Sjöö and Barbara Mor (1987) makes it clear how much has been suppressed here, and how brutally. And Wilber's *Up From Eden* (1981) makes a clear distinction between the Great Mother (the earlier and more primitive version, corresponding to stage four in our schema here) and the Great Goddess, a monotheistic creator deity. Christianity has been wrestling with these ideas recently, and Dart (1982) has a good summary of some of these controversies. June Singer (1977) has written about androgynous monotheism: I am not sure that this is the answer, but at least it is pointing to the problematic area.

Deity as process

This is the sense of being in touch with the Deity as process, rather than as subject or object, no matter how fine or abstract. This is not the same as pure energy, because there is a definite focus, and a definite notion of Deity. It is also not the same as Deity as substance transforming itself into a multitude of shapes. It entails a real sense of otherness as well as oneness: and this other is not subordinate or an illusion. So it requires a process of going out, meeting this other, recognising and doing justice to this, entering into it and being it, and returning enriched precisely because of the genuineness of the otherness. This is a process known variously as spirit, as love, as reason, and as will – none of which is at all adequate for what is really being referred to.

The only version of this I am at all familiar with is the Holy Trinity of Christianity, as described by Hegel (1895) in a fine but little-read work. More up-to-date and accessible accounts of it are given in Moltmann (1981) in an intellectually satisfying way, and by Maloney (1979) in a more personal and rhapsodic fashion.

This again needs commitment and worship if it is to be developed, and it can probably only be done effectively in the company of other believers

– all the mystics at this level warn against trying to go it alone. This is even more difficult to hang on to and talk about than the previous experiences, which does not seem to prevent mystics from trying to share their vision with others. But it seems important to say that the end of this experience does not seem to be unity in the same way as it does for the others. The idea of love comes to the fore here very strongly, and love implies at least two, as Johnston (1978) has urged. In fact, the whole strength of this process version of the Deity is that it does justice to the other as well as to the one. Instead of excluding the inadequate or bad aspects of people and the world in general, it includes them. And this means that the concept of evil gets radically transformed here. At the higher self level of development there is a systematic confusion about evil, and evil often gets personified and symbolised in the form of demons and devils, elementals, and so on. At the Deity as substance level there can be (at the symbolic end) even more powerful images of the devil, the ultimate power of evil, the ruler of hell; or (at the abstract end) the notion of evil as illusion, as a mistake, as an error of interpretation. But at this Deity as process level evil becomes fully taken up into the self-movement of Deity itself.

> The contradiction is already implicitly solved; evil is known as something which in the Spirit is virtually and absolutely overcome, and in virtue of the fact of its being thus overcome the subject has only to make its will good, and evil, the evil action, disappears. (Hegel, 1895, vol. 3. p. 130)

Obviously it is impossible here to do justice to all this, and the interested reader will have to go to the references cited for the full story. What does come out clearly, however, is that at this stage the intellectual content of what is believed becomes more important than ever before. We have much greater choice over what to believe, and these choices must be informed choices; so we have to go into questions of theology whether we like it or not. It may well be that we do ultimately have to give up all that we have learned in theology, but this sort of thing is true at every stage. We always start by trying to understand what is happening, and we always finish by giving up that kind of external understanding. But at each stage what we have to understand is more difficult, and at each stage giving it up becomes harder.

The ultimate

This is the sense of having fallen into the Void, into the Ultimate, of being everything and nothing at the same time. I do not intend to describe it here, because it has been described so well by others – Wilber (1977) has pages and pages all about it. This is the most difficult and final stage of all, where one is left without anything solid to hang on to. But it does seem to me that the actual experience of this appears to be extremely similar to the experience of breakthrough found at each of the previous stages. It is therefore open to doubt whether this stage exists at all – it is a kind of logical terminus or asymptote, which is of course very tempting and seductive, but whether anyone has actually been there is open to doubt. It seems clear that in someone this is an ideal – every one of the previous stages prefigures it in some way – but it may be no more than an ideal. Of course it is highly heretical in mystical circles to say this, because all the greatest mystics seem committed to some such notion.

In a way the void was my starting point in all this (and what follows is not a chatty interpolation – it tells you where I am coming from, and I wish more mystical writers would do this). Back in 1950 I met Harold Walsby, a student of Hegel and an original dialectial thinker in his own right (Walsby, 1947), who demolished all my most fundamental assumptions, and left me with nothing. He then explained that nothing was the dynamic beginning of everything, along the lines of Sedlak (1919). This was purely at an intellectual level. But when I came later to mystical experience, I found that this concept of the dynamic nothing (creative, powerful, orginating, energetic) became concrete and real for me. For a long time I thought that this was the Void that the mystics talked about, and found this very confusing, because it seemed obvious to me that I had not really gone very far along the mystical path. But then I realised that every time I had a deep or important breakthrough in my spiritual development, this experience of losing everything that was most important, of having to let go completely, was repeated, and I was falling down into the nothing all over again. This is what makes me suspicious of the Void. But it obviously has to go on the list, and in the last place. There is nowhere further to go – or at least, so it seems. Wilber (1980) has a useful warning, I think, when he says that the individual ultimately has to surrender his or her 'exclusive love affair with the Void' – even this has to go.

Meditation

These are the seven (at least) different, importantly different, distinguishable experiences. At each stage, we see the experience first of all as 'out there', as objective, as relatable to; and each stage closes with an experience of unity, of becoming that which we relate to. This is always the basic mystical move – from separateness to unity – but the unity feels different and is different in each case. I know that there are at least these seven, because I have experienced them myself. The only one I am not sure of is the last one, for the reason that I have put forward.

One thing that emerges very strongly from this is that anyone who reduces all mystical experience to the first one of these, the peak experience, is probably not very reliable. For example, Pahnke (1970) lays down nine characteristics of 'the mystical state of consciousness', all of which refer to the peak experience. (Many of the other papers in White, 1972, do the same thing.) We find this in Maslow, when he mixes things up as in the following quote:

> Resacralizing means being willing, once again, to see a person 'under the aspect of eternity,' as Spinoza says, or to see him in the medieval-Christian unitive perception, that is, being able to see the sacred, the eternal, the symbolic.
>
> (Maslow, 1973, p. 52)

In terms of the distinctions that I have been drawing in this presentation, 'the medieval-Christian unitive perception' had to do with Deity as substance or Deity as process, and required a great deal of work, which Underhill (1961) describes very well in her classic on mysticism. Spinoza is something else again, but is probably closer to Deity as substance than to anything else. 'The symbolic' refers primarily to the higher self level, although it can extend to other levels too. To run all these things together is misleading.

Another matter that is clarified by our analysis is meditation. Most of what passes for meditation has nothing much to do with mystical experiences at all – it is just the achievement of a very calm state. But it is possible to get small or large peak experiences through meditation, and if these are very impressive, they may amount to the *pseudonirvana* described by Goleman (1978). It is possible to get into pure energy through meditation, particularly in the more abstract types of meditation. It is possible to get into higher self-states through meditation of the symbolic type. It is possible to get into Deity as substance states through meditation, but here there are important choices to be made the object of meditation, which cannot be evaded. These choices become even more important at the Deity as process stage. At the ultimate stage we are back again to no choice, it seems.

It can be seen from this brief account that meditation is almost tailor-made for massive self-deception. By being vague enough about the focus of one's meditation, one can be at stage 1 and fool oneself that one is at any subsequent stage, including stage 7. Even the advanced meditator may find it easy to kid himself or herself that stage 7 has been reached, when it is only a particularly abstract version of stage 5. If I read Hegel correctly, this is exactly what he says always happens: stage 6 is in fact the final stage of all.

One of the phrases that have come to me recently is, 'A lot of this spiritual stuff is just people puffing themselves up to be more important than they really are'. As soon as you have a set of mystical grades – which is really what it comes to, as far as I can see – people want to promote themselves into the highest grade, or else to cast doubt on the highest grade. I can see this in myself, not only in other people. But it seems that it can only do good to be more aware of this.

The Spiritual Path

It needs to be said that there is a spiritual path, and that mystical experience in any true sense must go along it to the end. The end may be very much like the beginning, so far as attempts to describe it go, but it is not the beginning:

> The path is not as yet the goal, and Spirit does not reach the goal without having traversed the path. It is not originally at the goal; even what is most perfect must traverse the path to the goal in order to attain it.   (Hegel, 1895, vol. 1, p. 75)

If the nature of the path is consistently obscured by our teachers, we are likely to get confused. I am not maintaining that my sevenfold phenomenology of mystical experiences is fully accurate or the end of the story; what I am contending for is that this is a researchable area, and that it has in fact been researched to some degree. I have found Horne's (1978) book particularly helpful, with its careful distinctions between casual or serious experiences; extravertive or introvertive experiences; induced or spontaneous experiences; and pantheistic, dualistic, or monistic experiences. He says that casual, extravertive, spontaneous experiences are very common, and calls this 'nature mysticism', remarking that Underhill (1961) calls it an 'illuminated vision of the world' that can be had on occasion by people who are not mystics at all. This is the peak experience, and it comes early on the spiritual path. It gives us a genuine whiff of the holy. If we then try to get it back deliberately, and succeed, this then becomes induced rather than spontaneous, and perhaps serious rather than casual. It may still remain extraverted, as happened in the case of Bucke (1974), or it may become introverted, in which case we have started upon the mystical path proper. It then starts to become a question of our focus – pantheistic, dualistic or monistic. Horne (1978) does not seem to provide for a higher self stage at all, which seems strange, nor for a Deity as process stage, which seems even stranger. But this just demonstrates that it is very difficult to draw maps in this area. Even the latest and best attempts known to me, such as those of von Eckartsberg (1981) and Wilber (1980) seem incomplete or one-sided.

The concept of a breakthrough seems to me very important. I think Wilber (1980) is right when he says that each breakthrough on the spiritual path gives us a new sense of self, a great change in our idea of who we are. Each breakthrough gives us something apparently more risky to hang on to; something less concrete, less publicly acknowledged, less socially acceptable than the last. I am very impressed by Marlan's (1981) argument that it is incorrect to talk about the dissolution of the ego or losing the ego; he says that it is the ego-image that is transcended, not the ego as such.

But of course – and we know this very well in the case of therapy – each breakthrough needs a period of time so that it can be worked through. This process of working through a sharp change in our self-concept is something that cannot be rushed – it has to be given its due time. This means that the spiritual path is a long and slow one – it involves our whole being, and not just part of ourselves. It is all too easy for the intellect to zoom on to the next breakthrough, and the next, and the next, and soon to convince itself that it is there at the end of the road already, up there with Meister Eckhart and Hakuin and Krishnamurti.

It is all too easy to cover all this up with ambiguity, so that we do not know where we really are, and we do not let anyone else know where we really are, either. I remember a couple of years ago I did a talk on the self, and someone came up to me afterwards and said, 'When you talked about the self, it sounded to me as if you were really talking about God'. And indeed I was vague about that, because I had not really sorted it out in my own experience then. The real self is indeed a bit like the Deity, in the sense that it is a step on the spiritual path that may one day lead to the Deity. But it is only a *bit* like the Deity; it is also a bit like the mental ego that it has just left behind, and a bit like the higher self, and a bit like everything else on the path. It is essentially an integration of all the bits and opposites – mind and body, emotion and intellect, left and right – and an actualisation of a great many potentials (Mahrer, 1978). It is a very important staging post, which gives an authentic meaning to our lives (Bugental, 1965). But it still leaves us as separate individuals, still leaves us locked inside our own shells.

Jung saw this, and talked about the collective unconscious as a rich realm full of symbolic, archetypal good things capable of taking us out of our separate shells and participating in a wider awareness. But because his mental image of the collective unconscious was essentially of a sea on which everything else floated, he could not see that what he was talking about was the higher self stage and nothing more. This is another instance of how limiting maps can be. Whatever we define as ultimate prevents us from going any further.

Real Self as Safe Gateway

If this analysis is anywhere near true (and it wouldn't surprise me to find that a lot of the details were missing or wrong) the real self of humanistic psychology is a crucial and amazing invention or discovery. It is the missing link between the psychological and the spiritual. It offers a safe way into the difficult and apparently dangerous realms of mysticism.

Why it is so useful and so safe is because of the vast number of usable and effective techniques developed within humanistic psychology for encouraging people to work through their neurotic or psychotic fantasies and myths. In the past, people often embarked upon the spiritual path without having done this work, and promptly fell prey to demons, devils, elementals and so forth – most of which were projections of their own shadow, their own nastiness. By going the therapy way, we dispose of all these misunderstandings and confusions before we start; and hence, when we meet a demon, we know exactly how to handle it and how to speak to it, without giving it a status it does not deserve.

We can go along the spiritual path much faster if we have spent 10 years or so getting in touch with our real self, and working through all the implications of that. It turns out that a lot of the unpleasant and long-drawn-out experiences of the mystics are all about working through terrible rubbish about shoulds and oughts and have tos. We have done all that already, and don't need to spend more time on it.

For the first time, we can have a clean mysticism, not cluttered up with womb stuff, birth stuff, oral stuff, anal stuff, oedipal stuff, shadow stuff, anima stuff, parent–adult–child stuff, character armour and all the rest of it. For the first time we can relate to the Deity without wondering and worrying whether what we are relating to is just a projection of our parents.

It has been put to me that this is my generation speaking – the generation that got into this stuff mainly in the early 1970s. The young, I am told, are galloping through all this stuff really fast, and are finding ways of working on a number of levels simultaneously. I am only advocating the slower way, I am told, because it is what worked for me. There may well be some truth in this, but certainly it seems to me that clarification of what the different levels are, and the dangers of each, can only be helpful. I like very much, for example, Wilber's (1979) clarity in distinguishing between working on the mental ego, working on the real self and working on the higher self. He is in full agreement that the shadow and the persona need to be dealt with, even before we work seriously on the real self. At least it seems clear that anyone working on more than one level at the same time needs to be aware of the pitfalls on the path.

By doing the proper work on each level, it seems as though a real religion might be possible – a religion that puts right the distortions of the past, coming from unaware psychology. By dealing with our shadow, we shall not need demons or devils. By dealing with our parent complexes, we shall not need heavenly fathers or mothers. By dealing with our patripsych we shall not have to make the Deity male, or upward, nor have patriarchal relations in our religious groups and organisations. (*Patripsych:* internalised structure within the mind of each person brought up in a patriarchal system, which keeps the system in place. Its deepest roots are unconscious; Southgate and Randall, 1978.) By dealing with our internal conflicts, we shall not need to project them into the world and other people. By dealing with our sexuality, we shall not need to put down other people's. By dealing with our guilt, we shall not need to look for figures to exploit or forgive us. We can proceed on our voyage without all this unnecessary impedimenta cluttering the decks.

Through therapy or personal growth, we lean how to open up to our own inner process. Through mysticism, we learn how to carry on with that same process, into the deepest depths of all.

References

ADLER, M. (1979). *Drawing Down the Moon*. New York: Viking Press.

ASSAGIOLI, R. (1975). *Psychosynthesis*. London: Turnstone.

BACK, K. and BOURQUE, L.B. (1970). Can feelings be enumerated? *Behavioral Science*, **15**, 487–496.

BUCKE, R. (1974). *Cosmic Consciousness*. New York: Causeway Books.

BUGENTAL, J. (1965). *The Search for Authenticity*. New York: Holt, Rinehart & Winston.

CHAUDHURI, H. (1975). Yoga psychology. In C.T. Tart (Ed.), *Transpersonal Psychologies*. London: Routledge & Kegan Paul.

COHEN, J.M. and PHIPPS, J-F. (1979). *The Common Experience*.

DART, J. (1982). 'New' concepts in Christianity revive ancient ideas: Is Holy Spirit best seen as female? *Los Angeles Times*, April 10.

GALLWEY, W. (1974). *The Inner Game of Tennis*. London: Jonathan Cape.

GOLEMAN, D. (1978). *The Varieties of the Meditative Experience*. London: Rider.

HAVENS, R.A. (1982). Approaching cosmic consciousness via hypnosis. *Journal of Humanistic Psychology* **22**(1), 105–116.

HAY, D. (1982). *Exploring Inner Space*. Harmondsworth: Penguin.

HEGEL, G.W.F. (1895). *Lectures on the Philosophy of Religion* (3 vols.). London: Kegan Paul, Trench, Trubner.

HIXON, L. (1978). *Coming Home*. Garden City, NY: Anchor.

HORNE, J.R. (1978). *Beyond Mysticism*. Waterloo: Canadian Corporation for Studies in Religion.

HUXLEY, A. (1946). *The Perennial Philosophy*. London: Chatto & Windus.

JOHNSTON, W. (1978). *The Inner Eye of Love*. London: Collins.

KEUTZER, C.S. (1982). Physics and consciousness. *Journal of Humanistic Psychology* **22**(2), 74–90.

LEONARD, G. (1977). *The Ultimate Athlete*. New York: Avon.

LEROY, E. (1977). Le probleme de Dieu. In D.B. Phillips et al. (Eds), *The Choice is always Ours*. Wheaton, IL: Theosophical Publishing.

LOEVINGER, J. (1976). *Ego Development*. San Francisco: Jossey-Bass.

MCNAMARA, W. (1975). Psychology and the Christian mystical tradition. In C.T. Tart (Ed.), *Transpersonal Psychologies*. London: Routledge & Kegan Paul.

MAHRER, A. (1978). *Experiencing*. New York: Brunner/Mazel.

MALONEY, G.A. (1979). *Invaded by God: Mysticism and the indwelling Trinity*. Denville, NJ: Dimension Books.

MARLAN, S. (1981). Depth consciousness. In R.S. Valle and R. von Eckartsberg (Eds), *The Metaphors of Consciousness*. New York: Plenum Press.

MASLOW, A.H. (1954). *Motivation and Personality*. New York: Harper & Row.

MASLOW, A.H. (1962). *Toward a Psychology of Being*. Princeton, NJ: Van Nostrand.

MASLOW, A.H. (1970). *Religious Values and Peak-experiences*. New York: Viking Press.

MASLOW, A.H. (1973). *The Farther Reaches of Human Nature*. Harmondsworth: Penguin.

MOLTMANN, J. (1981). *The Trinity and the Kingdom of God.* London: SCM Press.

MOSS, D.M. (1981). Transformation of self and world in Johannes Tauler's Mysticism. In R.S. Valle and R. von Eckartsberg (Eds), *The Metaphors of Consciousness.* New York: Plenum Press.

MURPHY, M. (1978). *The Psychic Side of Sports.* Reading, MA: Addison-Wesley.

OTTO, R. (1950). *The Idea of the Holy,* 2nd edn. Oxford: Oxford University Press.

PAHNKE, W.N. (1970). Drugs and mysticism. In B. Aaronson and H. Osmond (Eds), *Psychedelics: The Uses and Implications of Hallucinogenic Drugs.* Garden City, NY: Anchor Books.

PEDLER, M. and BOYDELL, T. (1981). What is self-development? In T. Boydell and M. Pedler (Eds), *Management Self-development.* Farnborough: Gower.

ROGERS, C.R. (1961). *On Becoming a Person.* London: Constable.

SARTRE, J-P. (1959). *The Age of Reason.* New York: Bantam.

SEDLAK, F. (1919). *Pure Thought.* London: George Allen Unwin.

SINGER, J. (1977). *Androgyny.* London: Routledge & Kegan Paul.

SJÖÖ, M. and MOR, B. (1987). *The Great Cosmic Mother: Rediscovering the Religion of the Earth.* San Francisco: Harper & Row.

SOMENDRA. (1980). *Energy and Transformation.* London: Alchemy International.

SOUTHGATE, J. and RANDALL, R. (1978). *The Barefoot Psychoanalyst,* 2nd edn. London: AKHPC.

SPINO, M. (1976). *Beyond Jogging.* Berkeley, CA: Celestial Arts.

UNDERHILL, E. (1961). *Mysticism.* New York: E.P. Dutton.

VON ECKARTSBERG, R. (1981). Maps of the mind: The cartography of consciousness. In R.S. Valle and R. von Eckartsberg (Eds), *The Metaphors of Consciousness.* New York: Plenum Press.

WALSBY, H. (1947). *The Domain of Ideologies.* Glasgow: Maclelland.

WHITE, J. (Ed.) (1972). *The Highest State of Consciousness.* Garden City, NY: Anchor Books.

WILBER, K. (1977). *The Spectrum of Consciousness.* Wheaton, IL: Theosophical Publishing.

WILBER, K. (1979). *No Boundary.* Boulder, CO: Shambhala.

WILBER, K. (1980). *The Atman Project.* Wheaton, IL: Theosophical Publishing.

WILBER, K. (1981). *Up from Eden.* Garden City, NY: Anchor Doubleday.

WILBER, K. (1982). The pre/trans fallacy. *Journal of Humanistic Psychology* **22**(2), 5–43.

WUTHNOW, R. (1978). Peak experiences: Some empirical tests. *Journal of Humanistic Psychology* **18**(3), 59–76.

Chapter 17
Holistic Listening

Counselling is a discipline that depends heavily upon listening. Whether we talk about 'free-floating attention' (Freud), 'empathy' (Rogers), 'diagnostic listening' (Wolpe) or 'construct elicitation' (Kelly), we are always needing to refer to the necessity of making contact with the world as the client experiences it. Unless we can hear what the client is saying, we cannot even begin to start any rationally defensible form of psychotherapy or counselling, which in this respect are the same.

However, there is more than one kind of listening. For example, Rice (1980) notes that it is possible to listen for liveliness: 'There is a kind of voice quality that seems to indicate an inner focus on something that is being seen or felt freshly.' And she gives some indications of how to look out for this. She then says that something else to listen for is 'a point at which the therapist truly doesn't understand the client', and that has a real and particular importance. She goes on to point out that listening is a response, and one can deliberately play with it: for example, turning a client statement outside-in. There seems to be, she says, a kind of 'inner listening' that can be consciously developed in this way.

This is just one example of something the recurs again and again in the literature of counselling and psychotherapy. The counsellor, analyst, therapist or whatever comes up with some new twist on the listening process and perhaps names it as 'listening with the third ear', or 'active listening', or whatever seems appropriate, or perhaps does not name it at all.

It seems possible to codify these odd isolated insights by using a structured model. In this article I will try to do this, using a model derived from Wilber (1980) and von Eckartsberg (1981), although these writers have not suggested any of the detailed applications advanced here. The model says that human beings operate on four levels: body, feelings,

From J. Rowan (1986) Holistic listening. *Journal of Humanistic Psychology* **26**(1), 83-102, with permission.

intellect, and soul or spirit. Both of these authors say that the soul level is different from that of spirit (one depending heavily on symbols and archetypes and the other doing without them), but for our present purpose it seems appropriate to merge these two levels into one.

In human interactions it is common for people to approach one another at first in terms of the intellect, and of course this is what is encouraged through our education system. We may then get to a feeling level of communication and, if increasing intimacy develops, to a body level. We can communicate at the level of soul/spirit to the extent that we believe such a thing to be possible.

The unconscious mind, if we believe in that, can also be thought of in the same way. We can attempt to contact or investigate it at the level of intellectual analysis, or at the level of feelings, or at the body level, or at the soul/spirit level. So these four levels operate irrespective of whether we are referring to the conscious or to the unconscious mind.

For the purposes of this article, it will be convenient to give to each of these levels a letter: I for intellect, F for feelings, B for body, and S for soul/spirit. We can now produce a diagram that illustrates an interaction between one who talks and one who listens (Figure 17.1).

In Figure 17.1 it can be seen that the two intellects are next to each other, which means that they are in a position to interact with each other. The other levels are held out of the interaction, and are not permitted to be recognised.

This is listening to the intellectual content of what is being said by the talker. As described in the textbooks, such as Egan (1975), the essence of it is being able to play back to the talker what he or she said, in such a way that the talker recognises that that is indeed what he or she did say. As the Guerney (1977) AOS scale has it: 'A paraphrasing of content that is in accord with the main thrust of the other's meaning. Accurate, acceptant, but not stating any feelings of the other.' This is all that is required for a good rating on accurate empathy.

But it is harder than it sounds. Rachel Pinney (1981) advocates for the accurate listener 'total switching off his own views for the duration of the listen'. That may be impossible to do totally, but unless we try we may find ourselves getting angry with the talker, directing the talker, getting

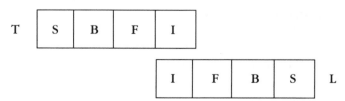

Figure 17.1   Basic accurate empathy

scared of the talker, competing with the talker, getting confused by the talker, and generally distorting what the talker is saying or trying to say.

This is why it is so important for psychotherapists to work on themselves, even at this most basic level of listening. If we don't, we are much more likely to get hooked by the client's material, or to project our own material onto the client, and in either case to respond to something that is not really there, or that is seriously distorted in some way. The extraordinary thing is that some therapies ignore this crushingly obvious point, and assume that somehow therapists can get by without any attempt to change their own consciousness.

This is of course doubly important if we are trying to work at an unconscious level, but those who do such work usually recognise the importance of their own responses and the difficulties involved in being clear about them. What Figure 17.1 makes clear is that even if we do work with the unconscious, it is still possible to leave out a great deal.

A key point to make here is that there is a tendency to ignore the political content of what is being said in favour of listening to the personal content. This can easily result in the putting down of women, blacks, homosexuals, the working class and handicapped people. (There is a full account of the issues raised here in Chapter 10 of my book *The Reality Game* (1983), so it will not be dealt with further here.) The same point arises at each of the succeeding stages, and must never be forgotten.

In Figure 17.2 we are listening to the emotional overtones and undertones of what is being said, and being able to play it back in such a way that the client feels accepted and understood. This is what is most often taught in courses on empathy, as Egan (1975) has again spelled out. It should be remembered, however, that Jacobs (1981) has shown that most training in empathy is actually quite ineffectual in producing people who are even minimally empathic.

Empathy is obviously important in listening, and Hogan (1979) has accumulated evidence to show that it is the most important ingredient in psychotherapy. It is at the heart of the whole Rogerian approach, and psychoanalysts recognise it too, as, for example, in Reik's (1948) idea of 'listening with the third ear'. This corresponds with the two highest positions on the Guerney (1977) AOS scale:

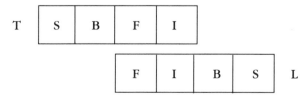

Figure 17.2 Advanced accurate empathy

(7) Recognising feelings with full attention to mood, but not conveying sensitivity to level of intensity, or not responding fully to the significant feelings. Also, content, if any, in accord with the main thrust of the other's meaning.

(8) Verbally reflects (states) the deepest feelings expressed by the other. Also, content, if any, accurately reflects the main thrust of the other's meaning. A highly empathic response.

It is of course important to emphasise the other listener qualities, such as congruence (genuineness) and non-possessive warmth (validation, unconditional positive regard); it is never a question of empathy alone.

At this stage a number of techniques can come into operation, such as repetition, contradiction, role-playing, acting into an emotion, and so on. This can amplify the emotional material and make it easier to hear.

Now extraordinary as it may seem, this is as far as many courses go. Yet even the most orthodox research reveals that the body has much to offer in the way of communication. Gladstein (1974), Haase and Tepper (1979), and others have shown how crucial the body language both of the client and of the therapist can be.

In awareness we listen to the body–feeling–thinking whole that is the talker in such a way as to pick up what is being said and be able to play it back in such a way that the talker is surprised at having said so much (Figure 17.3). Gestalt therapy has emphasised this, as have the body-oriented therapies described so well by Dreyfuss and Feinstein (1977).

An example from my own work would be a situation in which the talker uses a certain movement of the hand at some point:

L: What is your hand saying?
T: I want to hold on.
L: Hold onto what?
T: Hold onto my teddybear.
L: What is the feeling about the teddybear?
T: I love him – I don't want to let him go.
L: If you could say something now to your teddybear, what do you say?

As soon as we start noticing the talker's posture, gestures, eye movements, breathing, voice tones, and the whole range of non-verbal communication we are opening up something important for counselling, something that is underused.

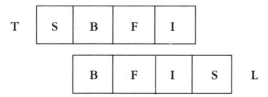

Figure 17.3 Awareness

For example, one of the first things we notice is how the client is sitting. No real work can be done in counselling or psychotherapy until the person 'opens up'. Like so many phrases, this can be interpreted literally as well as figuratively. If the client is sitting in a closed-up position, this is probably quite accurate in expressing what is going on. Closedness can be expressed in many ways – not only crossed arms, crossed legs and hunched-up positions, but buttons done up, handbag clutched, body pointing away or leaning back, hand in front of mouth and so on. As long as the client is closed-up, not much counselling or therapy can be carried out. So the first step is always to encourage the client to abandon these positions, and people such as Scheflen (1974) have described how this is done. Bandler and Grinder (1979) have some useful ideas on how to build a rapport with a client on a body level, completely non-verbally.

The counsellor or therapist who can use body awareness can be more effective than one who cannot. The sheer positioning of furniture can make a difference to listening. Putting a desk or table between counsellor and client immediately cuts down the amount of emotional material that is likely to come out. Upright chairs are more inhibiting than soft armchairs, which are more inhibiting than cushions on the floor. So by arranging the furniture, we have already determined the kind of thing we will be listening to (see Chapter 12).

One specific thing here is the question of sitting up or lying down. Sitting up gives a conversational set and is good when we want to explore current experience and everyday life. Lying down is much better for regression to childhood or earlier, and for unconscious fantasies. So again what we can listen to is very much influenced by body positioning. We are controlling the whole interaction by furniture in more ways than we usually care to consider, and Pease (1984) has a good discussion of this.

This is not the place to discuss the whole question of touch, which I have written about at length elsewhere (Rowan, 1983), or the whole vexed question of dependency, affiliation and courtship (Frankland, 1981), because they are not so directly connected to the issues around listening with which we are concerned here.

Coming back to the question of non-verbal communication, however, it is important to point out that we notice microgestures and microexpressions (Ekman and Friesen, 1975; Kendon, 1975) and respond to them automatically, without necessarily noticing how we do it. It is a question now of using this kind of awareness. Of course we do this all the time without even noticing it, as part of our normal everyday behaviour, but by becoming conscious of it we can use it much better. A good example of this is found in Stevens (1975), who advocates encouraging the client to pay attention to internal feelings of the body. Gendlin (1981) has also advocated this kind of self-listening as a valuable adjunct or grounding for any form of therapy.

Any psychotherapy involving regression to childhood, infancy and such is going to work at the three levels involved here, and Janov and Holden (1977) have a good discussion of how this works in terms of brain physiology, distinguishing between first-line, second-line and third-line primals. Tom Verny (1982) has a fascinating discussion of how we are now forced, by the increasing weight of research evidence, to admit that personal experience goes all the way back through infancy and birth to the womb and fetal life. Also Lake (1980), Grof (1980) and Laing (1983) have spelled out the implications of this for deep work in psychotherapy.

So the importance of the body is now being seen from a number of different angles, and it seems that it must increasingly be given its due. But let us now go on to more controversial ground, where we shall have to tread very carefully.

In Figure 17.4 we include the soul/spirit aspects as well, and do not leave them out of the picture. Richard Schuster (1979) has a good account of this type of listening, in which he refers to Maslow's (1986) concept of the realm of Being. Instead of grasping and grabbing the world, we find ourselves allowing the world to come in to us, so that we can then flow out and become that world, losing our usual boundaries. Instead of focused perception, we have what Krishnamurti (1969) called choiceless awareness. Schuster suggests that this kind of awareness can be cultivated by the practice of meditation, particularly those types that emphasise mindfulness and witnessing. We can then suspend thinking and be aware of our experience in the ever-flowing present. This could be called holistic listening.

But this is not all. If we can listen in this full way, our own psychic faculties can come into the picture. We can use our intuition in making remarkable leaps, leading to striking insights. We can use symbol and fantasy instead of words. We can tune in to the mythic aspects of what is being said. A recent book by Elizabeth Mintz (1983) goes into this in some detail. She gives one example in which a young man's impotence was cured, not by the usual process of therapy, but by a group ritual in which he (symbolically) castrated each of the men in the group. This arose quite spontaneously in the group, and she says of the event: 'It was an enactment of a mythic ritual, a primitive ceremony, which tapped the deep levels of the collective unconscious; it was a transpersonal experience.'

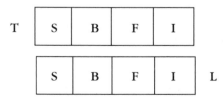

Figure 17.4　Advanced awareness

The term 'transpersonal' is often used for work in the area of soul or spirit, and it is hard to come across a good definition of this word. The best succinct account is from Grof (1975), who says it is concerned essentially with 'experiences involving an expansion or extension of consciousness beyond the usual ego boundaries and beyond the limitations of time and/or space'. There is always some sense of what Otto (1950) called 'the holy' about it. An example from my own work that has to do with this area comes when a client got stuck in a problem:

Therapist: Who would know the answer to this problem – anyone, fact or fiction, from the past, present or future?

Client: I think Aldous Huxley would know. I've always admired him.

Therapist: All right, here is Aldous Huxley sitting on this cushion. Talk to him about it.

Client: Which house should I buy, out of these two I like?

Therapist: Now move over to the other cushion, and be Aldous Huxley, and answer back.

Client: (As Huxley) Don't assume it's going to be either of them, and keep looking.

In this example the person did in fact keep looking, and eventually bought a quite different house. This is work at the symbolic level; in this case the symbol of the greater self was Aldous Huxley, but it could just as well have been the guru, the saint, Jesus, the Goddess, the inner teacher, the guardian angel, or any other suitable symbolic figure, depending on the belief system of the person involved,

Hoffman (1979) makes the point that if the client sees an image of the greater self as a guide of some kind, it is good practice to ask the client to check out the genuineness of the guide:

Walk up to your guide as if removing a mask. A true guide will not object. If the face comes off, you have encountered an imposter. Mentally tell the imposter to leave . . . and repeat . . . until you get a guide who *cannot* be unmasked. When you have your real guide, ask his or her name.

This guide can then be used in future work as an important ally and resource at the transpersonal level.

But of course other symbols can also be used at this level, and Emmons (1978) has pointed out that light is an important symbol, too. He quotes an example of this from a therapy session with a 20-year-old woman:

It was as if there were a bright light encompassing my whole body. My body seemed to inflate and balloon out and 'I', the 'me-ness' of my body, seemed to be filled and carried with this light. . . The light then narrowed into a stream of an intensity I would imagine a laser beam to have and focused deep down somewhere, no place physical that I can point to, just deep in my 'me-ness.' . . . After awhile the light seemed to be focused on the lump in my throat where I'd tried to hold down my tears. . . .The lump in my throat dissolved. . . .I feel great.

This symbol of the laser-beam light was used in later sessions as a guide, helping to awaken the client's psychic potential. Emmons has quite a lot to say about light in other forms too.

Another symbol that can be very powerful is water. Perls (1976) has an example of this in a recorded session called 'Madeline's Dream'. This again is a young woman talking, this time about water pouring out of a vase held by a statue in the middle of a lake. Perls asks her to be the water:

> I don't know much about myself. [Pause, begins to cry] I come. I don't know how I come but I know I'm good, that's all I know. I would like you to drink me because I know I'm good . . .[Crying and sniffing]. . .I'm there and I'm white and pure, and if you ask me where I come from I can't tell you. But it's a miracle, I always come out, just for you to drink me. . . .[Crying].

This was quite clearly a peak experience, what Perls sometimes used to call the 'mini-Satori'. And it is clearly work at the symbolic level.

Working at the level of spirit is different again, and no example will be given of this. Just a word of warning: Not everything that calls itself the spirit actually is the spirit; more often it is just another version of the symbolic level.

This seems at first like the end of the road. Having brought all four or five levels into the picture, what more is there? By the way, I should emphasise that the unconscious can come in at any of these stages of listening. Wilber (1980) points out that there are at least five levels of the unconscious. But to go into the unconscious here would take us too far away from the main aim of this article. Suffice it to say that the more we are aware of our own unconscious processes, the more we can take into account this aspect of the matter when we are doing our listening at all levels.

The next thing we do have to bring in, however, is countertransference. This term from psychoanalysis refers to the way in which unresolved conflicts in the therapist are stirred up by the patient. The patient may remind the analyst of someone in the past, and the analyst may react to the patient in terms of the past rather than the present. At first this was looked on as a fault, but nowadays 'rather than being considered a sign of instability in the analyst and therefore a therapeutic obstacle to be overcome as soon as possible, such reactions are considered by analysts as being potentially useful for analytic resolution, and with some patients, an indispensable ally' (Giovacchini, 1975). Let us set this up in Figure 17.5.

In Figure 17.5 the listener is aware of his or her own internal body/feeling/thinking responses to what the client is saying and doing, in such a way as to be able to feed back to the talker the effects of his or her own actions. This means that we as listeners use our own subjectivity – even our own neurosis – rather than simply trying to get rid of it. Devereux (1967) has shown that this is important not only in

Figure 17.5 Countertransference

psychotherapy but also in social science research. It means, he says, treating as a basic source of information phenomena coming from one's own unconscious mind. The listener allows the talker 'to reach – and to reach into – him. He allows a disturbance to be created within himself and then studies this disturbance even more carefully than he studies the (talker's) utterances'.

Similarly, Racker (1957) says that the emotional response of the listener is often a more accurate clue to the psychological state of the talker than is the listener's conscious judgement. So this can be an important kind of listening. The next kind follows on from it very directly.

In Figure 17.6 we are doing just the same thing as before, only now bringing in the level of soul/spirit, rather than leaving it out of the picture. It is still a case of listening to our inner responses, whether conscious or unconscious, but this time not only what Wilber (1980) calls the submergent unconscious and the embedded unconscious, but also the archaic unconscious and the emergent unconscious. To put it in terms made familiar by Assagioli (1975), we are now listening to our own superconscious and paying attention to that. As before, we are allowing the talker to reach, and to reach into, our own subjectivity, but this time we are not excluding the transpersonal.

The issues involved in moving from the previous stage to this are well outlined in Chapter 9 of Wilber's *No Boundary* (1979) and in Walsh and Vaughan (1980). By tuning into our own superconscious, with all its symbolic and psychic powers, and allowing the talker's superconscious to overlap and interpenetrate with that, we can become aware of an extra dimension of relatedness. Again, Mintz (1983) has something to say about this.

She gives an example in which she was working in a group, and had to take the role of Jack's mother. He asked her, 'Mom, did you ever want to kill me?'

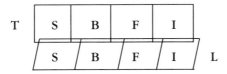

Figure 17.6 Advanced countertransference

> I literally could not answer. My voice was blocked. Only odd noises came forth,
> pig grunts. . . .I was in no physical discomfort, but when I tried to speak, I choked
> and could say nothing.

Jack went into a cathartic experience at this, because when his mother
used to beat him up, he said, she could not talk. She grunted like a pig.

> The question remains as to why I *behaved* like the Pig Mother instead of helping
> Jack reconstruct his memory in verbal terms, which as a therapeutic stratagem
> would have been less effective. My conjecture is that when I role-played the Pig
> Mother I was unconsciously in touch with the two great archetypes of mother-
> hood, the Evil Mother (which I acted out) and the good Great Mother (providing
> empathy for this tragically deprived man).

Apparently Jack's mother had actually been psychotic, and in uncontrol-
lable rages threatened the life of her little boy. This was confirmed by the
records of the social agency that had placed Jack. She had committed
suicide a few years after turning Jack over to the agency. But all this only
came out later.

Here again, we seem to be in touch with the transpersonal. This would
be another form of holistic listening.

In advanced countertransference we are admitting the whole of the
archetypal, symbolic, and even psychic aspects of ourselves, and paying
attention to these. Many examples of countertransference on the level of
psi are given by Eisenbud (1970). Here is one of them:

> it illustrates what can sometimes be done with the merest fragment of a dream.
> 'All I can remember is something about some small animals in an attic or garret'
> . . . the patient admitted to suicidal fantasies. . .he felt that he was imposing on
> my time. . .
> At the time of the dream 'small animals in an attic' happened to be in the forefront
> of my thoughts and feelings. . . .[He had many squirrels in his attic, and had called
> in the exterminators.] But the men showed up, on the morning of the patient's
> dream, armed with rifles and immediately started shooting the squirrels out of the
> trees. . . .I watched in horror as the man walked over to where the wounded animal
> lay frantically wriggling and calmly stomped it out of existence. . . .
> In his dream. . . the patient may be construed to be identifying with the squir-
> rels who were first fed and then disposed of by me. This is experienced by him,
> apparently, as a repetition of what happened at the hands, or rather, at the breast
> of his mother. . . . Her death has been expected for some time. The patient's suici-
> dal fantasies. . .represented an ambivalent identification with her, and a way of
> following her to a place where she could not get rid of him as I, in what he uncon-
> sciously [on a psi basis] experienced as a repetition of the original situation, was
> trying to do.

Whether we are attracted to or convinced by this example will have a
lot to do with whether we are attracted to or convinced by psychoanalytical thinking in general, because it is precisely parallel to many
examples that are considered by analysts (e.g. Giovacchini, 1975) to be
perfectly orthodox.

Eisenbud (1970) points out that countertransference that extends to the therapist's dreams and events in the therapist's life are usually not noticed or counted. Brookes (1980) suggests that Jung was aware of this sort of thing, and linked it to his principle of synchronicity. 'For Jung, dreams, fantasy, and indeed most aspects of phenomenal (psychic) experience are better understood from a synchronistic point of view than a causal point of view.'

There is still another way of listening that I have not mentioned yet.

In Figure 17.7 the listener sets up a model of the talker inside the listener. The listener, in the terms of Berne (1972), sets up an ego state corresponding to the client and puts energy into that. In that way the listener can be with the talker from the inside and share the talker's subjectivity. So resonance, according to Watkins (1978), is that inner experience within the listener during which we co-feel (co-enjoy, co-suffer, co-experience) and co-understand with the talker, although in mini-form. This is rather like putting two pianos side by side. If we hit the A key on one piano, the A string on the other piano will vibrate in sympathy. Watkins points out that this kind of listening is different from empathy:

> Rogers says that empathy means the *understanding* of the feelings of another. He holds that the therapist does not necessarily himself experience the feelings. If he did, according to Rogers, that would be identification, and this is not the same as empathy. Resonance *is* a type of identification which is temporary.

Similarly he argues that resonance is not the same as countertransference.

Mahrer (1983) calls his own approach experiential listening rather than resonance, but it seems to come to much the same thing. The listener shares and attends to the talker's attentional centre, and allows that centre to shift to inside the listener:

> It is remarkable how similar the constructed attentional center in the passive therapist is to that occurring in the patient. When several therapists take this position and listen in this way, it is remarkable how similar are their constructed attentional centers, both to one another and also to that which is occurring in the patient.

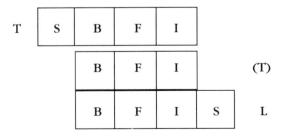

Figure 17.7 Resonance

When the talker says 'I' the reference is shared by both talker and listener; the listener shares the talker's phenomenal world, and has experiencings that are also occurring in the talker.

This is a remarkable way of working, but it is really only a continuation of the general process, usually recommended in the education of therapists, of getting inside the world of the client or 'assuming the internal frame of reference' (Brammer and Shostrom, 1982). It simply takes down the barriers further than most. But suppose we take down the barriers still further?

Figure 17.8 demonstrates an approach that is theoretically possible but that I have not seen written up anywhere. It would presumably be much like resonance, except that instead of leaving out the soul/spirit aspects of the person, they would be included. Little can be said about this approach until more data are in, and I am sure this will not be long in arriving. It would presumably entail the listener sharing the same archetypes as the talker, and knowing them better than the talker does. And this could be fed back to the talker in such a way as to lead closer to individuation, very much the Jungian aim. Perhaps it would even be possible to diagram it another way, to suggest that the barriers are more permeable (Figure 17.9).

I would guess that this would fit with the experience of some of the people working in the transpersonal field, but enquiries I have made so far have not turned up any examples of it. This would presumably be the fullest form of holistic listening.

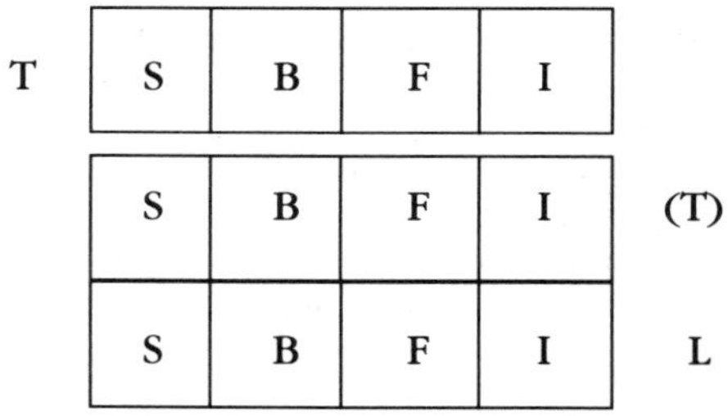

T	S	B	F	I	
	S	B	F	I	(T)
	S	B	F	I	L

Figure 17.8   Advanced resonance

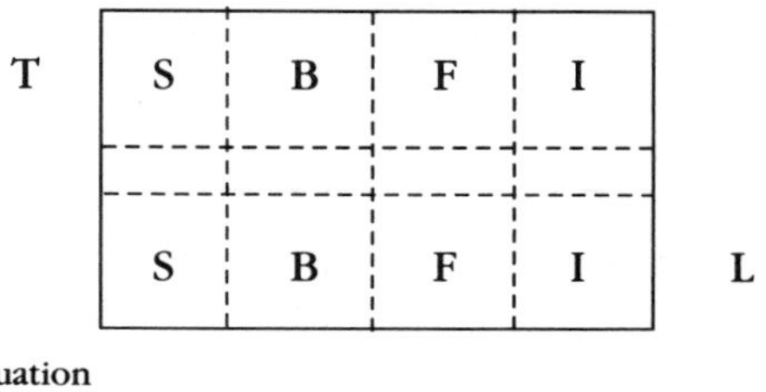

T	S	B	F	I	
	S	B	F	I	L

Figure 17.9   Individuation

Discussion

It is important to remember, as Wilber emphasises, that this kind of transpersonal communication, which is the closest yet to holistic listening, is not to be confused with the symbiosis between mother and baby. This latter kind of merging, in which the baby is not sure where it ends and mother begins, is prepersonal. The kind of dropping of barriers we are now reaching, however, is transpersonal. The one does not yet know what it is to be personal; the other does, but goes beyond it. Similarly, it is different from the dropping of identity that happens in crowds: this is essentially a regression to a prepersonal state, whereas what we are now learning about is a progression to a transpersonal state. This is an extremely important point, as Wilber (1983) spells out:

> *Since* development moves from prepersonal to personal to transpersonal, and *since* both prepersonal and transpersonal are, in their own ways, nonpersonal, *then* prepersonal and transpersonal tend to appear similar, even identical, to the untutored eye. In other words, people tend to confuse prepersonal and transpersonal dimensions – and there is the heart of the pre/trans fallacy.

If this is understood, we do not need to fear falling into a regressed stage by working in this final way, but instead look forward to an increase in deep insight and energy.

With this point reached, let us now look back at the example we began with. The listening out for the voice quality would be an example of work at the level of *awareness*. Voice quality is a non-verbal, bodily quality, and hence must be to do with a recognition of the importance of the body. The listening out for lack of understanding is an example of work at the level of *countertransference*, because it is looking for something inside the listener. An example of *resonance* is the kind of inner listening in which we really get inside the world of the talker by setting up within us a subpersonality (ego state, internal object, complex, attentional centre etc.) corresponding to the talker. So we are now able to locate the incidental discoveries and observations of an experienced psychotherapist within a framework that does justice to them and shows how they relate to other experiences within psychotherapy.

If what we have been dealing with here has any validity, then it has a number of implications for training in psychotherapy. No longer will it be sufficient to talk in terms of two levels of empathy and leave it at that. Incomplete listening will come to seem less and less adequate and less and less defensible. To leave out body and soul will come to seem absurd.

It also has implications for research in psychotherapy. To do research on listening and the relevance of listening for process or outcome without taking note of body language (of client *and* therapist) and without taking note of the transpersonal side of the interaction will again come to seem partial, incomplete and inadequate.

It has implications, too, for the selection of therapists by clients: a client will probably feel that he or she does not want to see a therapist who is not going to listen in the way that will be most helpful.

But the fact that the implications may be far-reaching does not give us the right to ignore the considerations that are raised here. It seems that any approach to psychotherapy, training, or research that pushes aside these questions is going to be more and more questionable as time passes and these ideas become more widely accepted. I think that they are widely accepted already, they are just not talked about much, except in rather vague and informal ways. This article tries to put into words what many of us have been saying, thinking and doing already, not to introduce anything new.

References

ASSAGIOLI, R. (1975). *Psychosynthesis*. London: Turnstone.

BANDLER, R. and GRINDER, J. (1979). *Frogs into Princes: Neuro Linguistic Programming*. Moab: Real People Press.

BERNE, E. (1972). *What Do you Say after you Say Hello?* New York: Grove.

BRAMMER, L.M. and SHOSTROM, E.L. (1982). *Therapeutic Psychology*, 4th edn, Englewood Cliffs, NJ: Prentice-Hall.

BROOKES, C.E. (1980). A Jungian view of transpersonal events in psychotherapy. In S. Boorstein (Ed.), *Transpersonal Psychotherapy*. Palo Alto, CA: Science and Behavior Books.

DEVEREUX, G. (1967). *From Anxiety to Method in the Behavioural Sciences*. The Hague: Mouton.

DREYFUSS, A. and FEINSTEIN, A.D. (1977). My body is me: Body-based approaches to personal enrichment. In B. McWaters (Ed.), *Humanistic Perspectives*. Monterey, CA: Brooks/Cole.

EGAN, G. (1975). *The Skilled Helper*. Monterey, CA: Brooks/Cole.

EISENBUD, J. (1970). *Psi and Psychoanalysis*. New York: Grune & Stratton.

EKMAN, P. and FRIESEN, W. (1975). *Unmasking the Face*. London: Prentice-Hall.

EMMONS, M. (1978). *The Inner Source*. San Luis Obispo, CA: Impact.

FRANKLAND, A. (1981). Mistaken seduction. *New Forum* 7(4).

GENDLIN, E. (1981). *Focusing*, rev. edn. New York: Bantam.

GIOVACCHINI, P.L. (Ed.) (1975). Preface. In *Tactics and Techniques in Psychoanalytical Therapy: Countertransference*. New York: Jason Aronson.

GLADSTEIN, G.A. (1974). Nonverbal communication and counselling/psychotherapy: A review. *Counselling Psychologist* 4(3), 34–57.

GROF, S. (1975). *Realms of the Human Unconscious*. London: Souvenir.

GROF, S. (1980). *Psychotherapy*. Pomona, CA: Hunter House.

GUERNEY, B.G. (1977). *Relationship Enhancement*. San Francisco: Jossey-Bass.

HAASE, R.F. and TEPPER, D.T. (1979). Nonverbal components of empathic communication. *Journal of Counselling Psychology* 19, 417–424.

HOFFMAN, B. (1979). *No One is to Blame*. Palo Alto, CA: Science and Behavior Books.

HOGAN, D. (1979). *The Regulation of Psychotherapists*. Cambridge, MA: Ballinger.

JACOBS, D. (1981). Successful empathy training. *Journal of Humanistic Psychology* 21(4), 39–56.

JANOV, A. and HOLDEN, M. (1977). *Primal Man*. London: Abacus.

KENDON, A. (1975). *Organization of Behaviour in Face-to-face Interaction*. The Hague: Mouton.

KRISHNAMURTI, J. (1969). *Freedom from the Known*. London: Gollancz.

LAING, R.D. (1983). *The Voice of Experience*. Harmondsworth: Penguin.

LAKE, F. (1980). *Studies in Constricted Confusion: Exploration of a Pre- and Perinatal Paradigm*. Oxford: Clinical Theology Association.

MAHRER, A.R. (1983). *Experiential Psychotherapy: Basic Practices*. New York: Brunner/Mazel.

MASLOW, A.H. (1968). *Toward a Psychology of Being*. New York: Van Nostrand Reinhold.

MINTZ, E. (1983). *The Psychic Thread: Paranormal and Transpersonal Aspects of Psychotherapy*. New York: Human Sciences Press.

OTTO, R. (1950). *The Idea of the Holy*. London: Oxford University Press.

PEASE, A. (1984). *Body Language*. London: Sheldon.

PERLS, F.S. (1976). *The Gestalt Approach* and *Eyewitness to Therapy*. New York: Bantam.

PINNEY, R. (1981). *Creative Listening*, 3rd edn. London: R. Pinney.

RACKER, H. (1957). The meaning and uses of countertransference. *Psychoanalytic Quarterly* 26, 303–357.

REIK, T. (1948). *Listening with the Third Ear*. New York: Farrar Straus Giroux.

RICE, L.N. (1980). A client-centered approach to the supervision of psychotherapy. In A.K. Hess (Ed.), *Psychotherapy Supervision*. New York: John Wiley.

ROWAN, J. (1983). *The Reality Game: A Guide to Humanistic Counselling and Therapy*. London: Routledge & Kegan Paul.

SCHEFLEN, A.E. (1974). *How behavior Means*. Garden City, NY: Doubleday.

SCHUSTER, R. (1979). Empathy and mindfulness. *Journal of Humanistic Psychology*, 19(1), 71–77.

STEVENS, B. (1975). Body work. In J.O. Stevens (Ed.), *Gestalt Is*. Moab: Real People Press.

VERNY, T. (1982). *The Secret Life of the Child*. London: Sphere.

VON ECKARTSBERG, R. (1981). Maps of the mind: The cartography of consciousness. In R.S. Valle and R. von Eckartsberg (Eds), *The Metaphors of Consciousness*. London: Plenum.

WALSH, R.N. and VAUGHAN, F. (Eds) (1980). A comparison of psychotherapies. In *Beyond Ego: Transpersonal Dimensions in Psychology*. Los Angeles: Tarcher.

WATKINS, J. (1978). *The Therapeutic Self*. New York: Human Sciences Press.

WILBER, K. (1979). *No Boundary*. Los Angeles: Center Publications (now RKP).

WILBER, K. (1980). *The Atman Project*. Wheaton, IL: Theosophical Publishing.

WILBER, K. (1983). *Eye to Eye: The Quest for the New Paradigm*. Garden City, NY: Doubleday.

Chapter 18
Meditation and Therapy:
A Quadrant Approach

The triangle model of meditation presented in Naranjo and Ornstein's book (1976) is well known, and I have used it for years. It says that there are three types of meditation: the way of forms, the expressive way and the negative way.

Through working with the developmental model of Ken Wilber (1983), however, I have come to see not only that there is a very important fourth type, but that the actual relationships between all four are very much clarified. The work of John Southgate (1983) is also very relevant to this.

Wilber says that in understanding the process of psychospiritual development, we have to use at least two dimensions, both of which, in quite different ways, could be called *eros* versus *thanatos* (love versus death). The horizontal dimension we could call preserve (eros) against release (thanatos). When we preserve something or somebody, we hang on to them, we want to keep them, we want to be near them, we want to be involved with them, we want to know what they are doing – all of these involve some kind of desire, as Southgate has underlined.

Conversely, at the other pole of this dimension, we are willing to let go, willing to be separate, willing to be independent or autonomous, willing to be alone, willing to be free, willing to finish with something or somebody. These again are in the realm of desire.

The vertical dimensions we could label ascend (eros) versus descend (thanatos). When we ascend we push towards creativity, we go towards love, we move towards orgasm, we thrust towards satisfaction – all these, as Southgate has remarked, have the nature of *drives*. Again if we look at the opposite pole, we push towards destruction, we go towards hate, we move towards violence, we thrust towards depression. This again is seen as an active drive: as Wilber puts it 'Not a fear of death, but a drive towards it'.

From J. Rowan (1986). Meditation and therapy: A quadrant approach. *Self and Society* January/February, 2–5, with permission.

Now we can come back to the types of meditation outlined by Naranjo and Ornstein, and see where they fit in.

The way of forms, otherwise known as concentrative or absorptive meditation, is any way of working that involves a definite object which is held to. This object may be a mantra (word or phrase), a yantra (symbolic design), a mudra (movement of the hands), a bija (seed affirmation), a kasina (plain object or colour), a symbol (such as cross, lotus, heart, sun etc.) or something else. In the meditation we focus on this object, and if we find ourselves drifting away from it, we bring ourselves back to it. This is an Apollonian, outer-directed form of meditation, which fits very well into the 'ascend–preserve' quadrant of our model. Very often the symbols chosen represent some form of aspiration, as in Bhakti yoga.

The expressive way is more Dionysian, and may include possession by gods, spirits or energies. A very familiar version of it is dynamic meditation, which involves heavy breathing, fast movement, loud chanting and so on. In this form we take the things that distract us, and which in other forms of meditation are often the enemy, so to speak, and make them the very centre of the meditation. Some of the shamanic forms, such as the sweat-lodge, use this approach, and Sufi dancing works in this way. 'Speaking in tongues', as in the Charismatic Church, can also be regarded as an example of this way of apporaching the divine. But because it also includes the martial arts, we put this way into the 'descend–preserve' quadrant. We actually focus on the opponent, so to speak, as the thing we need to keep in front of our gaze.

The negative way is where we try to eliminate all forms, all expression. The yoga meditation of Patanjali is a good example of this. The Zen practice of shikantaza is another. The phrase neti-neti, loosely translated

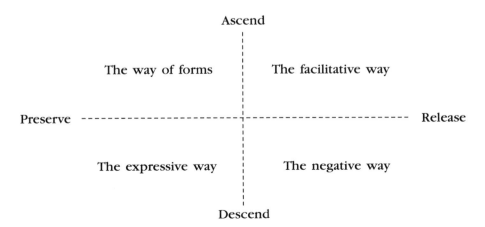

Figure 18.1   Four quadrants of meditation

'not this, not that', is appropriate too. The work is done by letting go, but in a way which merely empties the mind. Clarke has written at length about this, in a book which came out recently, how we can progress by attending more and more intensely to fewer and fewer things, until the zero point is reached. Because this is a kind of deprivation, we place it appropriately in the 'descend–release' quadrant of our diagram.

This now leaves the facilitative way, which simply opens awareness to what is there. These are the forms of meditation that are all about witnessing whatever takes place. Whereas most forms of meditation focus on one thing, this form flows with whatever is being experienced, following it and allowing it. In Vipassana, Mahavipassana and Satipatthana meditation, we are mindful of whatever passes. This mindfulness can be extended in every direction: 'If any further comment, judgement or reflection arises in the meditator's mind, these are themselves made the focus of bare attention' (Goleman, 1977). So this fits in to the 'ascend–release' quadrant, because it is friendly to everything, and enables fresh movement to take place.

The advantage of putting matters in this way is to see that there are real differences in the various forms of meditation, depending on where they fall in the structure. The way of forms and the expressive way are both seen to be quite conservative, in the sense that they tend to hold on to what is. This is quite easy to see in the case of the classic, Apollonian, way of forms, which so often is attached to an orthodox religious structure of discipline, but it is much harder to accept in the case of the apparently Dionysian and romantic expressive way. Certainly the followers of the expressive way often see it as radical or challenging. But the proof of the pudding is in the eating. The followers of the expressive way seem in practice to be as strongly attached to a firm structure of firm leadership as any of those following the way of forms. They are in fact very orthodox in their adherence to a guru or other head. So, in social terms, things stay as they are.

In the case of the negative way, social impotence is the result. Because good is no better than bad, because all distinctions ebb away, there is no impulse to do anything in the world.

But in the facilitative way – and if we are correct in our location of these forms in our fourfold structure – both Wilber and Southgate say that it is here that real change and development can take place. And we can now see the connection and similarity between this way and the best in therapy. As Levin (1981) puts it:

> Health, radically understood, is simply a question of staying with the situated experiential process just as it presents itself, and letting the spontaneous play of energies flow freely, not separated by conflict into subject and object, inner and outer, myself and others, nor myself (here) and the situation (there). The wholesome flow, or creative interplay, of the process is what principally matters.

He is talking here about Tibetan Buddhist therapy, which seems very close to what we try to do as humanistic practitioners. The results of therapy can be very dynamic in changing the lives of people and the people around them. Furthermore, because the facilitative way of meditation is so similar to good therapy, it can be used along with such therapy as a valuable preparation and follow-up, taking the person further along the path, and encouraging the same mindfulness to be extended to other people and their interdependence.

References

GOLEMAN, D. (1977). *The Varieties of the Meditative Experience*. London: Rider.

LEVIN, D.M. (1981). Approaches to psychotherapy: Freud, Jung and Tibetan Buddhism. In R.S. Valle and R. von Eckartsberg (Eds), *The Metaphors of Consciousness*. New York: Plenum.

NARANJO, C. and ORNSTEIN, R.E (1976). *On the Psychology of Meditation*. Harmondsworth: Penguin.

SOUTHGATE, J. (1983). *Inner and Outer Group Dynamics*. London: Polytechnic of North London.

WILBER, K. (1983). *Eye to Eye*. Garden City, NY: Anchor Books.

Chapter 19
A Growth Episode

One of the most difficult things in the whole growth business is explaining what it is all about. Even the best accounts of episodes in groups, such as the one by Gerry Haigh (1971), leave one wondering about how the person went on afterwards; and even the best accounts of what happened afterwards, such as the one by Carl Rogers (1973), leave one wondering what it felt like from the inside.

What I would like to do here is to piece together a 'complete' episode, from the moment when a problem appeared to the moment when it felt settled. This is presented from the inside; it would be up to someone else to describe it from the outside, because this is what happened to me. I make use of notes, tape transcripts, letters and whatever is available. Short linking passages are inserted whenever it seems to be necessary, in italics. Extracts have been shortened for relevance, and different people might make different decisions as to what is relevant. I feel quite nervous about presenting this, because it is quite personal, but I want to do it anyway.

Notes Made in Early 1972

My experience in the Marty Fromm group. I discovered the heavily controlling self who tightens my throat when I am nervous in certain ways. The person he is controlling is a passive-compliant and very weak self, whose only defence is to say 'I wasn't going to do anything awful anyway, so I don't know what you were worried about'. The controlling self stays aloof, and only steps in when the weak self looks like stepping out of line.

From J. Rowan (1990). A Growth episode. *Self and Society* **18**(5), 24–31, with permission.
This article was first published in *Self and Society* in 1975. It is being reprinted now because we believe that the good accounts of what happens in psychotherapy are as rare and hard to find now as they were then.

The most dramatic bit came when Marty asked me (as the controlling self) to pick up the cushion representing the weak self. I became very flushed, embarrassed, laughing nervously, excited, and couldn't bring the cushion nearer than arms' length. I didn't want it to come too close – I wanted to keep it at a safe distance from me. That real disturbance was a new insight for me.

It seems now that my controlling self is very gentle with my weak self because it has little respect or trust for it. So it only gives it credit for what it has proved conclusively that it can do. One step at a time. Very safe and sound. And maybe this is why I steer clear of the weak, the ill, the handicapped etc. Because they remind me of the weak self I don't want to see or recognise. I only want to talk about my successful self – my strong self. It can be the male strong self, or the female strong self, but it is still the strong self.

But in the confrontation between the strangling self and the strangled self, I was much more into the strangled self – the strangled self was much more me. And I wanted some of that power I saw in the controlling self.

Is this about wanting to get closer to my father, and my father not wanting to get closer to me? And maybe Big Granny comes into it somewhere too?

Later in 1972 I took a trip one small part of which, right at the end, was about my wife's face. The lower half of it was soft and sympathetic like the young servant girl in my childhood dream, and I loved it; but the upper half was hard and accusing, like a hawk or a wolf, and I hated it. Then early in 1973 I took another trip.

The St Valentine's Day Tape

Not all that again, please! I couldn't stand all that again. All that flapdoodle. All that ended by turning Neil into caramel custard. And that's only the bottom of her face. It isn't doing justice at all to the top half of her face. It's the top half of her face I don't like, you see. I can't take the top half of her face. It's all too wolfish, those eyes and teeth and all that – I can't stand all that. But when you come down to that drawsfiddle teacups and the draw-me-down old flopsy and all that, that's just great – but that's the bottom half of her face, you see. And it's only half. I wish I could have half a person. [Crying] I'd get on great with just half of Nellie. We could have a lovely time. We'd just cuddle up soft and we'd be ever so frumley and frapdoodle to each other. We'd be all tucked up comfy and warm anyway. [Pause] Why do I want that so much?

[Later] But definite feeling earlier in session that my heavy controlling person is a woman. Not my grandmother, but something to do with my grandmother. It seems to be this woman who hates Neil.

April 1973

The subpersonality which I call Big Granny should really be called Mr Putdown, or Pure Hate. It is made up of the controlling person I met in the Marty Fromm group, plus a full set of snob knowledge, plus a general desire to harm people and reject them. Its method of operation is largely in terms of avoiding or withdrawing or being silent, rather than any kind of positive action.

On the 1 April 1973 I went to my regular co-counselling group, and got into a big thing about getting rid of Big Granny. Punching the cushion didn't seem very effective, so I started kicking it around the room, more and more vigorously. That seemed very satisfying, and at the end of the evening I felt I had done some damage to Big Granny, and reduced her power considerably. The next morning I got off a bus at the Archway, slipped on the wet pavement, fell and broke my hip. As I was keeling over, I just had time to notice that I was not breaking my fall. Breaking one's hip is unusual for men of my age, but quite common with old ladies.

Big Granny is a bit like Eric Berne's critical parent. . . And it seems that maybe, just maybe, I don't let the child out because he is too scared and weak. And I feel more and more that I need to get to know my child, and fight Big Granny and my father and make it up with mum as a child, and not as an adult, as I've been doing.

May 1973: The Hate Bit

It has been a real torment and a real lot of pain going through the realisation of how much hate there is in me. To realise that I hated Neil was shattering to me.

I found that I hated virtually all the boys at school. Everybody I met I had to put down in some way. But recently I have been getting into the nastiest one of all – self-hate. The taste of my own throat turned into the taste of evil. My whole head disappeared, and became a raw open throat pointing upwards to the sky. I turned into a cat, and a snake. And the cat was Set or Bubastis – an evil cat, full of hate, like in horror stories by Bram Stoker and others which I read long ago. No wonder Freud believed in the bad-animal theory. I must have started hating early. And I think that breaking my hip was an expression of self-hate. But that sudden release of real energy seems to have done something drastic to the self-hate system. It has got smaller, more in proportion. It has become a small part of the background.

June 1973

At last I got into my child self. Two positive directions from co-counselling sessions:

[To my five-year-old self] You're OK – you're actually OK. Don't let them do it to you. You don't have to give up loving them. You can fight them, with love. Because you are strong enough.

[To my father] I gave you that impossible huge fascinating strength which reduced me to two inches high – that all came from me – but I don't want that strength – I just want my own real strength.

December 1973

Dracula and the evil Natasha – I took the evil into my own life – nobody put it there.

6 February 1974: Trip Tape

At the beginning of 1974 I decided to take a trip specifically designed to ask the same eleven questions of all six of my subpersonalities as I saw them at the time. These are the answers of Mr Putdown:

Question 7: What are your blocks to full functioning?
Answer: Well, of course, the fact that I've got to stay hidden, that's very important. I mean, you can't break your cover, you know – I don't want to break my cover. So that everything I do has to be disguised as good humour, or sex, or intelligent conversation, or point-scoring, or ego-boosting – all those safely accepted things that everybody understands and knows about. But like underneath the coat, behind the little swashbuckling epaulettes and all that –

Very difficult. You nearly tempted me out then. You nearly tempted me out. By asking what were my blocks to full functioning. That was clever. I grant you that was clever. You nearly caught me out for a moment.

Question 9: What is your approach to the world?
Answer: Mr Putdown's approach to the world is to try to blow it out. And if you can't blow it out, piss on it. If you can't piss on it, cut it off with scissors. If you can't cut it off with scissors, put an old sock round it.

[Later] It comes back to what I said somewhere along the line. The only way I can avoid Mr Putdown is to be born again. So what is this about being born again? It comes from this wish to be new. But that's one of Mr Putdown's things – everything being the latest, everything being new. How can I cope with Mr Putdown? Mr Putdown is more me than any of them. When I sit down with him it just feels like sitting down with me. How awful. How awful that is. What a thing to say! What a thing to say! Oh, God! Somehow there's got to be a human being in all this. There's got to be a human being in there somewhere.

27 October 1974

In the last co-counselling session with Ruth, had a very powerful experience. Some very early period with my mother. I knew what real love was – picture of baby at breast. But now she was making all sorts of demands – if I did this I would get her love, if I did that I would get it, and so on. But I never actually got it – I got some substitute instead. Here I had a powerful hallucination – my chewing gum suddenly tasted exactly like a rubber teat, and I could even hear the typical squeaky noise that a teat makes when you chew it. I was a really good boy, I did all the right things, but I never got that real love I wanted.

And so I made two resolves. One was that I would destroy my mother. I wasn't strong enough to do it myself, so I would invent a monster who would frighten her to death – it was black and vague and huge, and on top it had a really ugly frightening face, and it could move as fast as the wind. That would deal with her.

The other resolve was that I would do what she wanted now, while I was weak, but when I grew up, I would do just the opposite, and see how she liked that. I would do everything she didn't want and didn't like, when I grew up.

These two resolves explain so much. That frightening black monster, that I called Big Granny at first, and which scared me so much – I believe that was my monster, that I created!

Letter 19 December 1974

I'm still very much into co-counselling, and getting a lot out of it. I'm just amazed at how weak I always thought my child self was, and how amazingly strong he really was – laying down decisions and definitions which I am still carrying out now, 40 years later! Under all my apparent flexibility, there is a really rigid hard control which I have still not come to the end of, though a lot has come out. At first I put it all on to my grandmother and called it 'the Big Granny system', as if she had somehow put it there; but it seems to me now that I did it myself. I just put all that power, which was really mine, into other people, and magnified it out of all recognition. That then made it too frightening to own, so there was no way of getting it back!

30 March 1975: Birthday Trip Tape

These two characters just appeared. They seem very similar to the two from the Marty Fromm group at the very beginning of this episode.

Silly Sally and Wicked Walter . . .

These two come back again later, but most of this trip was about control, and letting go of control.

All those tights and suspenders, all those naughty, naughty. Naughty, naughty snatches of conversation. Between the sequins and the secrets; the sequins and the secrets and the suspenders. Brassières and suspenders.

You see, ladies and gentlemen, while others have visions of the Mystic Orient, inscrutable dreams of the Infinite, our subject, S in this experiment, only ever has pictures of tight bums, and tight suspenders, oozing pudendas, frightfully jolly, frightfully chummy. Frightfully chubby. Cheerful chum chumpney. All pressed up tight and warm. All those nice warm titties . . .

All those amazing visions of little kissing cunts, cranny fannies, pouting mouting opening and closing, all with such lovely little pouting wouting fanny-fannies. Opening and closing. Lips. Like beautiful little lips, opening and closing. What am I really talking about?

I'm really talking about sucking on that lovely, lovely titty. Sucking on that lovely, lovely titty. That's what it's all about. That's what it's all about. Swallowing down that lovely titty. Swallowing that lovely titty. That's what it's all about. That's what it's all about. Swallowing that lovely titty. There! Wasn't that worth it? There! Wasn't that worth it, down all the immensity, and all the evolutions, and all the universes, wasn't that worth it? Just to get back to that lovely big hungry voracious titty, with cats and screaming hags and – Oh God! How awful! I can't describe how hateful it is. Can't describe how horrible it is. It's the most terrifying monster you could ever imagine.

It's the most terrifying monster I, I could ever imagine. [Laughs] It's only, only the most terrifying monster I could ever imagine. No, I can use the imagination of all the others to help me. All the evil and all the horror that all those earth-men could ever help me to imagine. And it's all summed up in that monstrous titty. That monstrous titty that's just waiting to grab me. That monstrous titty that's just waiting to devour me, if only I'd give in to it. Just waiting to grab me. But I'm not going to let it. I'm going to be too clever for it. I'm going to freeze to death. I'm going to freeze to death. I'm going to be so small and so unnoticeable, and so wrapped up in myself, that no one is ever going to notice me.

[Later] I had a little memory there of what it was all about. And then it started to go away again. I knew from the beginning what it was all about. I know what it was all about! I do, I know what it was all about! I really do know what it was all about!! [Cries]

It's about really opening yourself up to somebody, and really doing it [crying] and everything else being just substitutes after that [crying], everything else just being substitutes [crying]. All that nursery talk was just ways of covering it up. [Cries]

[Later] Yes, how close. How close the real thing is, to what covers up for it. All the marmatoast-toast, and septembrianas, and chobby chop-choptermost, chump-chopchuanas, those were all – proptuanas and chumble-tums-chumblemost – just ways of helping me to remember. Ways of getting me back into that feeling, that real feeling. Where it really felt warm.

[Later] Like somehow you're going to make a mess of it. It's all so simple, and you're going to make a mess of it all! I can see it coming! It's all so simple, and you're going to make a mess of it all! [Cries]

[Later] It seems that you desperately want to get back to where it all started from. Maybe until you've dealt with that, you can't deal with anything else. Maybe it's just all that you've got to deal with – oceans and oceans of stuff.

Why shouldn't there be a lot of it? Why shouldn't there be a lot of it? I want there to be a lot of it, Goddammit! That's all my first eight million eternities, Goddammit! My first eight million goddamn eternities, when I knew what it was all about. I don't want to forget all about that, so easily. I had the answer to it all then, you know, much better than I do now. A whole lot better than I do now. [Cries]

I feel as if I have to keep a rigid hold on everything, as if I'm keeping a rigid hold on everything. I'm still keeping a rigid hold on everything. I'm still keeping a rigid hold on everything. That's why I want the light on, and that's why I want the tape on, and that's why I want the watches on, and – I just refuse to let go. I talk about letting go, and I tell other people how to let go, but I can't let go. I haven't got the faintest idea of how to do it! I haven't got the faintest idea of how to let go.

[Laughs] Here I am surrounded by manuals on it. I've got books on it. I've got manuscripts on it. I've got thoughts on it. I've got everything on it except how to do it. I even know how to do it, but I won't. I won't! I won't!! I just *won't* do it! I won't let go! I won't let go of *anything*. Like that's my way of dealing with reality, and I'm going to hang on to it. I'm not going to go into any of your machinations, or any of your skullduggery, or any of your stupid sentimental swindling whining craps. Because they are all a con! All a con!! They are nothing more or less than just a con. They are some kind of a fix, they are some kind of phony rap. They are just going to lure you out, and then they're going to DO you! They're going to shoot all over you! [Cries] They are just going to wait for you to open up and come out, and then they're going to shoot all over you!! THEY'RE GOING TO SHOOT ALL OVER YOU!!! Trample all over you, and tread all over you, and put blood all over you, and scratch you to pieces. Scratch you to pieces in every way. In every conceivable, dripping, horrible way! Whatever that is. Whatever you can imagine. Whatever other people can imagine, whatever the Universe can imagine, whatever anybody can imagine.

[Later] You just rush from one extreme to another. It's all kind of sentimental slop, or it's total hate. I'm sure there must be something else, other
than sentimental slop or total hate. Must sort that one out.

10 April 1975

In the session with Beverly, wanted to follow up the Birthday Trip. Started
with Silly Sally and Wicked Walter. Silly Sally very soppy and nice. Didn't
develop into anything then.

Wicked Walter . . . gradually got into birth thing. Didn't want to be
born at all, said – 'NO! NO!'. Wanted to get revenge for having been born
– it was the worst thing that anyone could do – to take you out of that
nice warm womb into all that pressure and discomfort. I had a very strong
impression of pressure on head at this point, and wanted to press on it,
and did press on it. It was most important to remember that it was mother
who had done it – must never forget to get revenge on her.

At some point this connected up with getting revenge for losing the
breast, or not having it when I wanted it; and with losing that first Mother's
love, or not getting it when I wanted it. And all these connected with the
feeling of 'that's what it's all about' mentioned in previous extract.

Went through whole big catharsis on this, very powerful, leaving me
lying down exhausted but whole and centred. Beverly said: 'Let an image
come into your mind'. My reply:

> There is no image, it's just grey. Grey all round in every direction, and the ground
> is grey too. It's all grey, all round.

Beverly said: 'What is it like?'

> It's not like anything. There is nothing there at all. It is just grey. It is sort of grey
> at an equal distance all round, as if I am at the centre and the grey goes out to the
> horizon. Now it is like a dome. A plain grey dome, very big and covering the whole
> area where I am lying. I am lying in the middle of a grey plain and the grey dome
> is covering the whole.

Beverly said: 'Be the dome'. I said:

> I am protecting him. I am looking after him. I love him. He's done all these stupid
> things, but he's all right. He's all right. He's made some stupid mistakes, but they
> are the kind of mistakes that anyone might make. He confused the womb with me,
> and he confused the breast with me, and he confused Mother's love with me – but
> it's understandable. All the time he thought he'd lost me, I was there all the time,
> and I always will be there.

Beverly: 'Go back to being you. Did you hear that?'

> Yes. [Crying] It's all true, I know now. What a waste! [Crying] I didn't need to
> blame my mother, or get revenge, or create my monsters, it was all a mistake! It
> was all a waste! It was all a misunderstanding.

Beverly: 'Now be the dome again. Does his behaviour hurt you?'

> No, it doesn't hurt me. I care, but I don't mind. I don't add to his bad feelings by
> having bad feelings myself. But I do really care.

We finished up by resolving to remember the dome every day. To take some time to slow down and remember the dome.

It seems to me that this puts together so much, and brings this whole episode to an end – the whole business that started with Marty Fromm and then Big Granny. It was all about destroying my mother, and now I don't need to destroy her any more! And now maybe the whole thing about being either sloppy or hateful can just dissolve. I really hope so, and think so. I feel so good.

It seems to me that this fits very well with the idea of the transpersonal self. The dome felt as if in a sense it was me, but it was also more than me. It couldn't explain itself, because I could only understand in pictures, and no picture could get it right. But it seemed exactly like what I understand of the transpersonal self.

This is presented as a protocol – an unadorned statement of what actually occurred. It seems that it could be explained in terms of various theoretical frameworks. I can recognise a touch of Melanie Klein here, a trace of Otto Rank there, and some Assagioli at the end. But that is not really the point. The point for me is to show that heavy things can be worked through, and are worth working through. A subsidiary point is that it needn't cost very much: this whole episode was mainly done on co-counselling plus two or three LSD trips, and a lucky visit to a friend.

1990 Update

That year of 1975 was a remarkable one for me. I wrote *Ordinary Ecstasy* in just a few weeks after this event; I worked intensively with the Red Therapy self-help group; I developed with John Southgate a new workshop entitled 'Dialectics as a felt experience'; I had three love affairs; I wrote several articles for new magazines which appeared that year; and a social psychology textbook called *The Structured Crowd*; and I lazed on the lawn quite a bit in that lovely Summer. It all seemed very easy.

References

HAIGH, G. (1971). The residential basic encounter group. In H. Otto and J. Mann (Eds), *Ways of Growth*. New York: Pocket Books.

ROGERS, C. (1973). *Encounter Groups*, Chapter 5. Harmondsworth: Penguin.

Additional reading

MEARNS, D. and DRYDEN, W. (1990). *Experiences of Counselling in Action*. London: Sage.

Chapter 20
Spiritual Aspects of Primal Integration

It may be as well to begin by saying something about my own development in this area. In this field it is often relevant to know where the speaker is coming from, and what his or her own experience is.

Perhaps a good place to start is that day in April 1981 when I was walking with Malcolm Lazarus, then organiser of all the Wrekin Trust workshops in the area of spirituality. We were strolling across the Herefordshire hills and talking about the relationship between the Association for Humanistic Psychology and the Wrekin Trust. He dropped a remark which went round my mind for days afterwards. He said: 'Psychology is one realm, spirituality is another'.

This contradicted everything I had been thinking, saying and writing for 10 years or more. My general understanding had been that humanistic psychology had a spiritual component to it, and that everything that was real about spirituality could be incorporated somehow into it. I had been convinced that Jung's four functions of sensing, feeling, thinking and intuiting were all within psychology, and that intuiting dealt with the spiritual aspect. I had assumed that transpersonal psychology was a sort of spiritual upper end of humanistic psychology, and that the higher self (as described by Assagioli (1975) for example) was ultimately to be identified with the real self, and was natural rather than supernatural, human rather than divine.

These ideas which I held – and which I believe are still held by many people in my circle – were held in place by a strong mistrust of organised religion. I had been brought up as a Protestant, but Christianity, Islam and Judaism seemed to me cruel and aggressive dualistic systems which had led to more wars and more suffering than any other single human force. Buddhism, Hinduism, Daoism and Tantra seemed more acceptable,

From J. Rowan (1991). Spiritual aspects of Primal Integration. *Anesthema* 10, 3-20, with permission.

largely because it had seemed to me that whatever was true in them could somehow be incorporated into humanistic psychology.

So when Malcolm dropped his remark, it hit a sensitive nerve. I started to talk to everyone I met about this. I consulted experts. I visited ashrams. I read books. But I did not find what I was looking for until I came across Ken Wilber. He described (Wilber, 1980) *where I had been* so accurately that I felt I could take him as a guide to where I was going next. He says that we are all on a path of psychospiritual development which he calls 'the Atman project', and that this path has a number of describable way stations, which he goes into in detail.

For 10 years I had been saying, with a smile, 'everyone is neurotic', meaning 'everyone has oedipal stuff, family stuff'. More recently, with less of a smile, I had learned to say 'Everyone is psychotic', meaning 'everyone has Kleinian stuff, birth stuff, prenatal stuff'. Now it seemed that if I wanted to do justice to the transpersonal realm (and this is what we shall be looking at for most of this talk) I had to learn to say 'Everyone is divine' and that sounded much more strange, fearful and problematic. It might be all right for Californians, but how about me? How could I live up to the demands of knowing that I had my own Atman project? What does being divine mean? Because this is such a challenging thing. As someone had said 'It's not enough to know about holiness or be an expert on holiness, the point is to be holy'. And that idea scared me very much. I had given lectures on 'the repression of the sublime' and 'the Jonah complex' (both about the *avoidance* of the spiritual life), but this was the first time I had felt these things for myself and in myself. At times I felt like running away from the whole thing.

But I survived and continued, and eventually found my own spiritual path, through a moon group led by a woman who had been trained in the Wicca tradition. This is the old European folk religion. This then linked up with my existing interest in sexual politics and green politics, with the results reported in my book *The Horned God* (Rowan, 1987), where I describe at length the changes which took place in me at that time. Today that group exists no more, but I do continue with my devotion to the Great Goddess and the Horned God. I have linked up with a woman who is very experienced in this field to set up a training in counselling and psychotherapy which follows the lines we had both discovered in the realm of spirituality. It is called the Serpent Institute. As far as I know it is the only one in Britain that deals with the whole gamut of experience from the early prepersonal to the late transpersonal. I was very interested at this conference to see a leaflet from the Primal Integration Center of Michigan, where they say that they too deal with the early material and the transpersonal material, and I think this is a good direction to take.

Now, when we come to look at this whole question of spirituality, we cannot help noticing that one of the most striking differences between primal integration and Janov's primal therapy is that primal integration believes in spirituality and primal therapy does not. As you will know, Arthur Janov (1977, 1983) believes that all religious or mystical ideas are irrational and neurotic, that people who have really been through primal therapy give up all dealings with religious beliefs of any kind, and that religion is essentially socially repressive.

What is not so clear, however, is the extent to which practitioners of primal integration have any use for ideas and practices that might be called spiritual or religious, and what forms these might take. We do not have any one great leader or teacher to speak for us. It might be interesting to conduct a poll among members, to see what kind of forms the basic interest in spirituality might take. Louise Rockman (1986) did in fact try something like this, when she interviewed 14 post-primal patients, and found that 13 of them had some personal interest in spirituality. Well, 14 is not a large sample, but these results are at least suggestive. But because I certainly do not know how many people here are interested, my own ideas are necessarily personal, and put forward in a spirit of sharing, so that we can at least compare notes and make our ideas more concrete and open.

Some Distinctions

So much by way of introduction. Let us now continue on to the main body of what I want to say tonight. To start with, I think it may be useful to make some distinctions, so that we shall have at least something of a shared map of the territory.

One of the most important distinctions, made by many people who have studied religious expression (e.g. Wilber, 1983), is between legitimate religion and authentic religion. (This came up in the session led by Karen Buck and Cynthia Robinson at this conference.) Legitimate religion is about rules and morality and observances and immortality symbols and correct ritual and so forth, and it is usually policed by a formally appointed body of men (less often women, except in organisations for women only) to make sure that the rules are adhered to. Authentic religion is about having certain experiences for ourselves, which change our lives and our outlooks. We may then be acceptable or unacceptable to the men who control legitimate religion – in history, people who have had authentic religious experiences have often found themselves unacceptable to the authorities. In this area, some of the women are just as famous as some of the men – there seems to be less prejudice here. (As Belinda remarked in a session at this conference, this is very similar to the distinction between exoteric and esoteric versions of the same religion.)

The approach of relying completely on authentic religious experiences is called mysticism. The characteristic thing about mystics is that they insist on having the experience for themselves; they are not willing to be told by others.

Now within mysticism there are some important distinctions too. James Horne (1978) says that mysticism can be serious or casual. A serious experience is where we treat it as significant and try to learn from it; it usually has important further results in our lives. A casual experience is one that is dismissed or treated lightly, and that has little effect on later life or behaviour.

He also distinguishes between extravertive and introvertive mystical experiences. In the extravertive, the mystic experiences *the world* as transformed, and discovers the unity that exists in a multiplicity of external physical objects. It usually happens spontaneously, without preparation or seeking for it. The introvertive experience is quite different. Usually it takes place after much preparation and discipline, where the mind is cleared for it to take place, by meditation or by some other means. Here it is *the self* that is transformed.

Now in terms of these distinctions, I want to say that a peak experience, which recent surveys indicate has been experienced by about 60 per cent of the population, is an experience of casual extravertive mysticism. It is a spiritual event, but a commonly available one.

What is a peak experience? I have defined it as the unpredictable occurrence of some kind of ecstasy, most often triggered by nature, music or sex, where I feel one with the Whole. The great writer on this experience is of course Abraham Maslow, who in a number of books and essays argued that peak experiences tend to come thick and fast at a particular stage of development, when the person is ready for them.

But most of the people who have such experiences are not ready for them; they dismiss them as odd, meaningless or even dangerous. They try to forget them. But they are still spiritual experiences, and if we take them seriously and cultivate them they can help us to go further in our own development.

What this means is that the majority of the population have actually had mystical experiences, but that a much smaller number have acknowledged this or done anything about it.

There is one more distinction we must make before we go on, however, because it is so clarifying and helpful. This is a distinction that was originally suggested by Alyce and Elmer Green between the extrapersonal and the transpersonal. This is very similar to the distinction made by Wilber (1980), and also used by Grof (1988), between the lower subtle and the higher subtle.

The extrapersonal has to do with psychic states and abilities such as clairvoyance, contact with the supposedly dead, telepathy, spoon-bending, ESP, walking on fire without getting burned, piercing the skin without drawing blood and so on and so forth. There is a strong connection with the occult and parapsychology, and with a wide range of paranormal phenomena.

The transpersonal has to do with such things as the higher self, the inner teacher, the transpersonal self as taught in psychosynthesis, the archetypes as taught by Jung, the soul as taught by Hillman, the creative self, peak experiences, intuition, certain aspects of healing (which have to be carefully looked at because there is an overlap here with the extrapersonal), the upper chakras and subtle energy systems, and so on. Green and Green (1986) suggest that the basic distinction is that in the transpersonal there is something divine, whereas the extrapersonal is basically non-divine.

In the past this distinction between the extrapersonal and the transpersonal has not been drawn so clearly, and Jung's notion of the collective unconscious includes both. But Stan Grof (1988) finds the distinction useful in his work, which is, as far as I can see, quite close to my own.

The Real Self

Having made these distinctions, which I shall be using all the time, I would like now to talk about the real self. One of the key things that seems to happen in primal integration work is that the person has some kind of breakthrough from the mental ego into an experience of the real self.

This is the feeling of being in touch with my own centre, my inner identity, my true self, my authenticity – that self that lies behind or beyond all self-images or self-concepts or subpersonalities. It is what Assagioli (1975) calls the 'I' – the centre point of the whole personality. It is what Wilber (1980) calls the 'Centaur' – the complete body–mind unity. This often happens in primal work, whether individual or group, but it can also happen in many other ways. It is a developmental step, principally discontinuous, involving step-jump rather than gradual form (Pedler and Boydell, 1981). I have written about it at length in my book *The Reality Game*, showing how the existential tradition has a great deal to say about how it works (Rowan, 1983). This seems to me a very important step in spiritual development, because it is a gateway to the realisation that we *must have spiritual experiences for ourselves,* we cannot get them from someone else. This is the basic attitude of the mystic in all religious traditions – to get inside one's own experience, to commit oneself to one's own experience, to trust one's own experience.

This is also the typical breakthrough experience. It often involves some sense of death and rebirth (Grof, 1988). At each point where we leave one state of consciousness for a higher or deeper or more inclusive state of consciousness, we experience a breakthrough – a peak experience where we suddenly seem to be in contact with the truth. It is like a kind of initiation. All the previous effort now seems dust and ashes, quite irrelevant or even handicapping. Everything now seems clear and true, and there is no fear any more. This happens in primal work quite often, particularly after a cathartic experience. John Heron, a British humanistic and transpersonal therapist (Heron, 1977), has argued that this kind of catharsis makes possible these five things: (1) spontaneous insight; (2) celebration of personal being; (3) break-up of distorted behaviour; (4) living in abundant time; and (5) synchronous events. This suggests at least the foothills of spirituality.

Already we have seen one of the main points I want to make here. We have seen that there are, so far, two different mystical experiences that can be distinguished one from another. The peak experience, as we have already said, is most often an example of casual extraverted mysticism. The breakthrough into contacting the real self is more like an experience of serious introverted mysticism. This is because it is usually part of an intentional process of self-development, and also because in most cases there is a therapist present to underline and interpret the experience as being important, valuable and meaningful for the future.

What we are seeing already at this early stage, then, is that there is more than one mystical experience. As we go along, we shall be discussing several others. What this means is that the very common definition of mysticism or spirituality, which is so often used unthinkingly, is wrong for us, and will not do for our purposes. This is what I have called the 'one-two-three-infinity' definition of spirituality, where we say that one is the body, two is the emotions and feelings, three is the intellect or mind, and everything else is one undifferentiated ocean called spirituality or mystical union. This kind of thinking is very common with New Age people, with EST (or Forum, as it is now called), with the Guru Maharaj-Ji, with transcendental meditation, with some aspects of Zen Buddhism, with the enlightenment intensive, with Rajneesh and many others who should know better. The dangers of it have been discussed very well by Richard Anthony and his colleagues in their discussion of cults (Anthony, Ecker and Wilber, 1987), where they warn against one-step enlightenment as a snare and a delusion. They call this a unilevel approach, and they have a number of arguments against it, all based on bitter experience and history.

What I am talking about *here,* however, is what Anthony and his colleagues call a multilevel approach, which they consider to be much safer and less likely to lead to dogmatism, unreality and danger.

The Deeper Self

What I want to say is that there is more than one spiritual experience, and some of these are very different one from another. One of the most common of these, I suppose, after contacting the real self, is contacting what used to be called the higher self. This is the sense of being in touch with my transpersonal self, my deep self. This often comes about in transpersonal therapy or groups, or in psychosynthesis therapy or groups, but again it can happen in many other ways (see Ferrucci, 1982; Starhawk, 1982; Vaughan, 1982). At first it appears to be outside of us, and may even appear to have a three-dimensional reality. Essentially it has a touch of the divine – it is a symbolic representation of the sacred. I used to say that there were many synonyms for the transpersonal self, depending on the belief system of the participants, but now I am not so sure that all these things are the same. In the years to come I think we shall see much more discrimination and differentiation in this area. Certainly Heron (1988), for example, wants to distinguish between the real self, the transpersonal self and the cosmic self. He says that the real self is self-creating. Contact with it puts us on the road to self-creation, where we can truly take responsibility for ourselves, and say things such as 'I create my world'. He goes on to say that the transpersonal self is self-transfiguring. The person at this level freely chooses to unfold the higher intuitive self and to go deeper into the pre-personal material of their own history.

My own view is that the transpersonal self is best represented, in most cases, by a person. But it does not have to be so. I have known cases where the transpersonal self was represented by a dome, or flowing water, or a jewel (as Barbara Valassis told us at this conference), or a flower, or a light of some kind. For example, Emmons (1978) quotes the example of a 20-year-old woman in a therapy session who said this:

> It was as if there were a bright light encompassing my whole body. My body seemed to inflate and balloon out and 'I', the 'me-ness' of my body, seemed to be filled and carried with this light. . . The light then narrowed into a stream of an intensity I would imagine a laser beam to have and focussed deep down somewhere, no place physical that I can point to, just deep in my 'me-ness'. . . After awhile the light seemed to be focussed on the lump in my throat where I'd tried to hold down my tears. . . The lump in my throat dissolved. . . I feel great.

This symbol of the laser-beam was used in later sessions as a guide, helping to awaken more of the client's potential. This again is serious introverted mysticism.

After having had such an experience I may follow it up in various ways: I may take religious advice and instruction, and most mystics do (Moss, 1981), but even so, I have to decide which instruction and advice to take and which to follow, and there is no way I can put the responsibility for this outside myself. Even if I say that it is a voice inside me, I still have the responsibility for which voice to listen to. Jon Klimo (1988) has a good discussion of this point in his book on channelling.

I do not want to say much more about the deeper self, because I think it is familiar to most of us, but I just want to underline that it is a spiritual experience. More uncommon, however, and much less discussed, is the next spiritual experience I want to talk about.

The Self Open to Others

Stan Grof (1988) talks about two closely related transpersonal experiences, which he calls 'dual unity' and 'identification with other persons'. Both of them, he says, involve the loosening or melting of the boundaries of the body ego. But he is referring mainly to the experiences of the client in therapy; I want to talk about the experiences of the therapist, too. Grof does in fact hint at this when he gives the story of his wife Christina identifying with the dying Gregory Bateson: she felt as if she were inside him, and feeling everything he felt. He says 'It seemed clear that experiences of this kind would be invaluable for diagnostic and therapeutic purposes, if they could be brought under full voluntary control'.

What he obviously did not know was that several people have now begun to do just this. For example, John Watkins, who is an ego-state therapist and makes a good deal of use of hypnosis (Watkins, 1978), describes this as resonance, and likens it to the phenomenon where two pianos are put side by side, and the note A is hit on one of them. The A string in the other piano resonates in sympathy. In the kind of therapy, he says, where this approach is used, what actually happens is that the therapist sets up an ego state corresponding to the client and puts energy into that. In that way the therapist can be with the client from the inside, and share the client's subjectivity. So resonance is that inner experience within the therapist during which he or she co-feels, co-enjoys, co-suffers and co-understands with the client.

At the same time Alvin Mahrer, who is a therapist in the humanistic-existential tradition (Mahrer, 1983), was describing this new approach as experiential listening, and saying that this kind of listening involves a complete sharing of the client's phenomenal world. The therapist becomes part of the personality of the client. The therapist and client can integrate with one another. The personhood and identity of one can assimilate or fuse with that of the other, and then the therapist will have experiencings that are also occurring in the client. Recently, Mahrer has been giving workshops on exactly how to do this, and just this year has produced a short manual (Mahrer, 1989) on how to do it.

Also this year, Andrew Samuels, a British Jungian who has written a great deal on Jungian thought (Samuels, 1989), describes this as 'embodied countertransference', and gives examples of it where he seems to become part of the client's inner world. He says that using the word 'embodied' emphasises that we are talking here of a physical, actual, material, sensual expression in the therapist of something in the client's inner world. Again we may find the words hard to understand or to take, if we have never had this sort of experience.

Similarly, Benjamin Wolman, a psychoanalyst who uses hypnosis (Wolman, 1986) speaks of those times when we become aware of another person's feelings without sensory perceptions and without any possibility of proving or disproving them. He says that such experiences belong in the region of the 'protoconscious'. The protoconscious is not the conscious or preconscious mind, because there things are under control and are available to logic and language. Nor is it the unconscious, because the unconscious is what we are unaware of and cannot simply get in touch with at will. Wolman says that meditation is the best-known method of contacting the protoconscious mind. My own view is that actually the use of imagery is the most common method and, as Jerome Singer (1974) has made clear, imagery is used by many different kinds of therapists.

I think the best account of where all this is taking place is given by Samuels (1989), where he says that it takes place in the imaginal world. This imaginal world is an in-between state, where images take the place of language. It is between the conscious and the unconscious, and also between the therapist and the client. Both persons have access to it and can share it. It is the therapist's body, the therapist's imagery, the therapist's feelings or fantasies; but these things also belong to the client, and have been squeezed into being and given substance by the therapeutic relationship. And Samuels emphasises that these are *visionary* states, concluding that such experiences may usefully be regarded as religious or mystical.

We can see from all this that therapists of several quite different persuasions have all had the same experience and found different ways of talking about it. I think this is something that has been very little discussed, and that now must be recognised as a spiritual experience which can be cultivated or ignored, but which actually does happen. I have certainly found this approach very useful in my own work in primal integration. I have also found that it is possible to give people a taste of what it is like in quite ordinary workshops of an educational kind, by simply asking people to follow Mahrer's instructions.

A Spiritual Approach

I do not think there is is any need to go on making the point that there is more than one spiritual experience. Stan Grof (1988) has a marvellous list of spiritual states, and if you are interested in this, you can read it all up there. What I think is interesting is that there is a credulity problem at this end of the spectrum, so to speak, which is actually very similar to the credulity problem we also meet at the other end of the spectrum. Just as primal people find more and more difficulty in believing memory to be possible the further we go back behind birth, so in the same way many of us find more and more difficulty in identifying with the spiritual experiences as they become more and more esoteric. For example, if we go on to the level of god-forms, and then on to the level of deity as unity, and then on to the level of deity as process, and so on to the ultimate, I find students getting more and more glazed as we continue. And I think this is OK: I would not want people to go beyond their own experience. When you have had the experience, you do not believe, you know. Until you have had the experience, it is right not to go along with something dubious or unlikely or possibly dangerous.

What I would like to go on to now is the question: If we admit that there is a large spiritual realm which we have already entered in many ways, how do we use it in our work?

My own view on this, which I do not think disagrees with anyone else who has worked in this field, is that as soon as we move away from words and into imagery we lay ourselves open to working on this sort of level. Almost all spiritual experiences have this in common, that they cannot be translated adequately into words. We have to abandon that demand, that kind of control, if we are going to move into the realm of the transpersonal. I sometimes feel that the celebrated phrase 'opening the third eye' actually means this intentional entry into the world of the imagination.

But of course we do this all the time. One of the strongest messages I want to give today is that *we are working in the spiritual area much more often than we think.* We just have not given it that label. It is like the celebrated case of the man who was astonished to discover that he had been talking prose all his life.

Let me give an example of something that happened in a primal encounter group a few years back. A woman said she had never felt like a woman, always a little girl. She wanted the group somehow to give her a rite of passage:

> We always asked, 'What do you already know?' She knew she wanted flowers and water. All the women gathered in the pool with music, candles and flowers. We had flowers in our hair. The men were kept out. We all made a line in the pool and she swam between the legs of all the women. The music changed when she became a woman. I think someone was there to receive her. She changed the colour of her flower from white to red. We dressed her in her finery and brought her to show the men, and she danced for the men and women. That affected the others who felt that they hadn't had a transition rite. They didn't need to do it too; hers was powerful enough for everybody.   (Rockman, 1984, p. 38)

This is mythical work, archetypal work at the level of symbol and image. The change from white to red of course comes from the three phases of the Great Goddess, who goes from maiden to mother to crone. This corresponds to the three phases of the moon, waxing, full and waning, and to the colours white, red and black. In Hindu religion this is called the *trimurti*.

In this particular group it was common to organise funerals in a ritual manner to mourn losses that are often unrecognised in our culture: this might include abortions, or the loss of a partner, or the loss of a subpersonality that had been prominent up to its loss in the process of therapy.

> Funerals had set props – a corpse, a sheet, candles. Music, usually Fauré's Requiem. Often a recital of the Kaddish, regardless of whether or not people were Jewish. Usually an object had to get buried, the knife that had killed the person, or some symbol of rage or fear or whatever emotions were being buried. There was a procession to a hole outside. The person was asked to say everything he wanted to say to the dead person, speaking directly, as in gestalt therapy. We repeatedly asked, 'Is there anything you need to do before you say goodbye, or in order to say goodbye?' Often a candle was left burning on the grave. There were post-funeral rites – placing a branch, or flowers daily, or three times a day on the grave.
>
> (Rockman, 1984, p. 39)

Rites of healing and rites of rebellion were also enacted in these groups, particularly when they were led by a therapist who was also an Anglican priest, who seemed to have a gift for this sort of thing, and whose status seemed to help the process.

The people who went through these experiences seemed to become not only more individual, as in the ordinary encounter group, but also more connected with others, more overlapping with others. This is one of the distinguishing features of work at the transpersonal level.

Some might feel that this is all quite ordinary, and that there is no need to mention the transpersonal, but I do not agree. I think we can get a much more accurate sense of what we are doing in group work by recognising that we are working on many different levels all the time.

Even when we think we are just doing quite ordinary work at the level of the real self, it might be better to recognise that we are really going much further. As Hillman and his colleagues have been emphasising recently, we are always working at the level of soul, whether we admit it or not.

Dreams

One of the most important areas where we have choices to make involving the transpersonal is in working with dreams. Some say that Freudians have Freudian dreams, Jungians have Jungian dreams, and so on. There may be some truth in this, but much more true and important is the fact that we can take the same dream in a number of different ways.

When I am lecturing on this in groups I very often give them a simple exercise: to take a dream of their own and get a partner to interpret it first as a message about the past, second as a message about the present, and third as a message about the future. Then they do the same for a dream of the partner's. This only takes about 15 minutes each way, but it is enormously illuminating about the whole question of dream interpretation. Each focus seems to bring out something different within the dream, and to enable the dream to throw light on quite different areas of the person's life.

Ken Wilber has a more elaborate version of this, where he says that a dream can come from any one of nine points along his spectrum model of psychospiritual development. He describes nine fulcrums of development, and refers to them as F-1 (for the first fulcrum), F-2 and so on:

> A middle-aged woman presents a dream which contains a highly charged scenario composed of these central images: she is in a cave (associations: 'hell', 'death'); there is a silver-luminous pole leading from the cave to the sky ('heaven', 'home'); she meets her son in the cave, and together they climb the pole ('release', 'safety', 'eternity').
>
> What, for example, does the pole represent? From an F-1/F-2 level, it might represent a denial of the 'all-bad' mother and a fusion or 'umbilicus' to the safety of the symbiotic 'all-good' mother (splitting). From an F-3 level, it might represent phallic/incestuous wishes. From an F-4 level, it might symbolize the means for more closely communicating with her son. From F-6, an escape or avoidance of existential death. And from F-7, the silver-lined kundalini sushumna (which is said to be the central channel in the spine leading from the first chakra of the physical-hell realms to the seventh chakra of liberation and release in the transcendental Self).
>
> My point is that the pole might have simultaneously represented all of these. The dream symbol, being plastic, is apparently invaded and informed by any pressing issue or level of insistent pathology.   (Wilber, 1986, p. 152)

In the case in point, the dream was actually very significant to the dreamer at two of these levels, but not so meaningful for her at the other levels.

I have done this kind of work myself, and found it very fruitful.

If it is true that dreams can signify at different levels, and if it is true that some of these levels are spiritual or transpersonal, then we are cheating the client if we never ever let them refer to these levels. We are denying that the client has any spiritual life, and in effect cutting it out of his or her experience.

Intuition

One of the most easily accessible aspects of the spiritual life is located, so to speak, in what Assagioli calls the superconscious, that part of the psyche that is closest to the transpersonal self. One of the most characteristic faculties of the superconscious, which most therapists have come into contact with at some time or other, and perhaps frequently, is intuition.

I think it is useful to use this word in quite a broad way, to cover all those ways of getting information that are non-rational. There is a very good discussion of the whole question in the Goldberg (1983) book. But it is easy to make the matter quite concrete. I sometimes suggest an exercise in classes which I teach to illustrate the importance of these non-rational sources. Students divide into pairs, and are asked not to talk throughout the exercise. Each person writes down for the first 10 minutes everything he or she knows about the other person from evidence: in other words, if challenged, there could be some statement in support of that knowledge. Each item is put down in one sentence, which can be adjudged right or wrong.

For the next 10 minutes, the same thing is done, only this time using the imagination. 'Write down everything you can imagine about the other person'. Again in single sentences, each of which can be right or wrong.

For the third 10 minutes, the writing is based on empathy and sympathy and resonance and tuning in to the emotional nature of the other person, using body posture, breathing and anything else available really to get in touch with what is going on inside the person.

For the fourth 10 minutes, students are asked to rely on pure intuition, none of the previous methods. At the end of the time, papers are exchanged between the two partners, and each person marks the other person's sentences: –1 if it is wrong, 0 if it is partly right and partly wrong, +1 if it is right but very general, +2 if it is right and quite specific, and +3 if it is amazingly or surprisingly right.

In every case where I have carried out this exercise, there have been higher scores from the non-rational sources than there have been from the first, rational source. What I think this means is that we are all the time picking up important and valid information about other people in a way that can broadly be called intuitive – it is not based on objective evidence.

Even if a critic said that we were spending more time on the non-rational aspects than on the rational aspects, and so higher scores would be expected, the question would still arise – where does this accurate information come from? Because it is only accurate information that is counted.

Inflation

Having now looked at the practical side of working with the spiritual and the transpersonal, we must now consider two issues that are of crucial importance: ego inflation and psychosis.

One of the classic dangers of working at the spiritual levels is the danger of ego inflation or psychic inflation. This has been best described and dealt with by the Jungians, who seem to be especially knowledgeable in this area. Most of us have come across people who have been affected very powerfully by some spiritual or religious conversion experience, where they have been infused with some sense of the divine, and who have then become quite impossible to live with.

Ego inflation happens when a person identifies with a spiritual being of some kind, such as an archetype (e.g. 'I am Christ'). Archetypes range all over the scale, and some have argued that there are different levels even within the same archetype, but broadly we can say that the archetypes we are concerned with here are god-like in some way. To spell this out more clearly, let us take a concrete example, from the work of a British Jungian, Joseph Redfearn:

> Simply by not resisting, I allowed. . . some sort of flowing in of energy from the 'not-me' into the 'myself'. It was, I think, the experience that people often describe as God entering one's mind and body; an enlightenment filled my mind and brought my body into fresh life and health. The experience was ecstatic at times, similar to the experiences one may have while falling in love, or that which mystics may have.
>
> The 'I' was being inflated by powerful sub-personalities of the 'not-I'. It was felt, sensorially even, as an almost audible inflowing of God. There was certainly a degree of inflation and denial, in that unrealistically unselfish solutions to my personal problems suggested themselves, and later these solutions needed to be modified so as to reconcile themselves with practical reality. . . I would have said I had Christ-like feelings. Long-forgotten passages of the Bible came back to me like joyous illuminations and I felt a new understanding of them. . .
>
> It is important to preserve a sense of humour about these divine experiences, and to be prepared to admit that my God may appear to you to be simply my infantile omnipotence, split off from my awareness of myself and experiences in an inflated way. A sense of humour prevents one from being totally possessed by these 'non-I' parts of the personality, and it prevents the splitting-off from becoming a fixed feature.   (Redfearn, 1985, pp. 42–44)

This is all very British, but the Continental and American Jungians are agreed that working with archetypes carries with it the danger of ego inflation. This seems to me rather like the distinction between infatuation and real love. They look very much alike and feel very much alike, but there is something illusory about infatuation. A further danger is that the person so inflated may for that very reason become very charismatic, and people may follow him or her (usually him). And this may lead to some great disaster. We are not gods, we are human beings, and there is nothing better than a human being for us to be.

This view goes against some views current at the present time, which I (rightly or wrongly) identify with the phrase 'New Age'. Here the view is that we are all gods, or God, but for various reasons deny this. Jean Houston, for whom I have a great respect, has an exercise during the course of which participants are invited to look into a mirror and see there the God-in-hiding. I once asked an advanced exponent of the teachings of Bhagwan Shree Rajneesh whether she was God. There was a long pause, and then she said slowly, 'That is a very interesting question'. It seems to me that this indicated a real confusion as to exactly what is being claimed when one identifies with a guru. (Keith Borden said much the same thing in his workshop at this conference.)

Anyone who has come into contact with the literature of mysticism knows that mystics talk about union with God. What we are saying here is that this does not mean that we become God in the sense of God taking us over and being there instead of us. At all times it is us there, with our experience and history, our unconscious minds, our faults and failings, our aspirations and strengths and resources, our enlightenment such as it is. It is all right to explore the archetypal realms, it is all right to explore the divine realms, but it is not all right to inflate ourselves by confusing ourselves with entities that are beyond us. We can certainly aspire to union with the Divine, and we can certainly have mystical experiences, but we cannot actually be the archetype, we cannot actually be God in the sense of having all the characteristics that are ascribed to that divinity in the spiritual literature. At the minimum, that is inflation of the ego; at the maximum, it is psychosis.

Psychosis

This question of psychosis is very important. My own opinion is that all or most of us are psychotic, just as all or most of us are neurotic, but obviously some people are far worse affected than others, in terms of being able to lead a happy life. If we talk about mystical experiences such as the four we looked at earlier, some of them have things in common with manic experiences or other psychotic phenomena.

Someone who has been writing about the distinction between transpersonal or spiritual experiences and psychosis is David Lukoff. He says that if we ask some very simple questions we can distinguish very readily between pure psychotic experiences, pure mystical experiences, and three or four different mixtures of the two. He says:

> Because of its cross-cultural perspective, attention to unusual experiences and positive attitude towards altered states of consciousness (Grof, 1985), transpersonal psychology can play an important role in re-visioning the psychopathology of manic psychosis.   (Lukoff, 1988, p. 136)

So this is not only a useful area for therapists; it may be necessary if they are to be able to help individuals who are genuinely puzzled about their personal experience and what it means.

Lukoff's work makes it possible to escape from the romanticism of the saying which sounds so good but which I believe is quite misleading: 'The psychotic and the mystic are in the same sea; but the psychotic is drowning while the mystic is swimming.'

Conclusion

If we believe in the importance of the transpersonal, we can say that the contacting and releasing of the real self is just one stage in a process which, as Wilber (1980) has pointed out, goes much further. I have come to believe that someone who has just been through a primal is, in that 'cleared out' relaxed state, open to subtler energies. In my own work on myself, I had an experience of contacting my transpersonal self after a primal (Rowan, 1975) (see Chapter 19).

In other words, dealing in this very full and deep way with the psychological realm enables us to go on and get in touch with the spiritual realm. But if this is the case, why have not more people working in the primal area noticed this? Michael Adzema (1985), as I reported in a previous article, suggests that it is because prejudice gets in the way of it being reported, and creates a myth that nothing of this kind happens. But on the contrary:

> Some long-term primallers with whom I have contact have talked of receiving love, helping, strength or bliss that seemed to be coming from a place beyond the scope of their current physical existence, to be emanating from a 'higher power' of some sort. Their descriptions have many parallels to some descriptions of spiritual experience.   (Adzema, 1985, p. 95)

If this is so – and certainly this agrees with my own experience – then we can eliminate all the projections that come from unconscious material to plague spiritual life, and have for the first time a clean mysticism, not cluttered up with womb stuff, birth stuff, oral–sadistic stuff, oedipal stuff and all the other unconscious bases for phony spirituality.

Not only this, but primal integration therapy also teaches us one of the prime lessons of all spiritual development – the ability to let go of the ego. There are times in our therapy when we have to take our courage in both hands and just go ahead, taking the risk, as it seems, of losing everything in the process. Many times the image of stepping off a cliff or going down into the abyss comes up in primal work; and of course this ability to surrender, to let go, to step off into the seeming void, is crucial for spiritual commitment. If we can throw ourselves, time and again, into the maelstrom of catharsis and still, somehow, be upheld, embraced and enlarged, despite ourselves, then that can give us confidence in a universe that is basically on our side. We learn to trust the process and to trust the universe.

Here we are in agreement with Louise Rockman. I have already quoted her study of 14 post-primal patients, and at the end of that paper she says this:

> Psychotherapy has always dealt with 'religious questions' – the meaning of suffering, fate, injustice, relationship, birth, life, death. This fact is often obscured in the antiseptic pseudo-scientific ambience of psychiatric offices. But for primal-encounter patients, the psychological dimension of religious experience and the religious dimension of psychological experience were always creatively conjoined.
>   (Rockman, 1986, p. 14)

Through primal work we learn how to open up to our inner process. Through spiritual development going on from there, we can learn how to carry on with that same process, into a future which we ourselves help to create.

Note

One issue that is completely missing from this essay, and that came up in questions after the presentation, was the question of past lives. The reason why I did not deal with this is that I have very little experience of it, and thought it best to adhere to issues where I have more competence and experience.

References

ADZEMA, M. (1985). A primal perspective on spirituality. *Journal of Humanistic Psychology* **25**(3), 83-116.

ANTHONY, R., ECKER, B. and WILBER, K. (1987). *Spiritual Choices*. New York: Paragon House.

ASSAGIOLI, R. (1975). *Psychosynthesis*. London: Turnstone Books.

EMMONS, M. (1978). *The Inner Source: A Guide to Meditative Therapy*. San Luis Obispo: Impact Publishers.

FERRUCCI, P. (1982). *What We May Be: The Visions and Techniques of Psychosynthesis*. Wellingborough: Turnstone Press.

GOLDBERG, P. (1983). *The Intuitive Edge*. Los Angeles: Tarcher.

GREEN, E.E. and GREEN, A.M. (1986). Biofeedback and states of consciousness. In B.B. Wolman and M. Ullman (Eds), *Handbook of States of Consciousness*. New York: Van Nostrand Reinhold.

GROF, S. (1985). *Beyond the Brain: Birth, Death and Transcendence in Psychotherapy*. Albany: SUNY Press.

GROF, S. (1988). *The Adventure of Self-discovery*. Albany: SUNY Press.

HERON, J. (1977). *Catharsis in Human Development*. University of Surrey, Guildford: Human Potential Research Project.

HERON, J. (1988). *Cosmic Psychology*. London: Endymion Press.

HORNE, J. (1978). *Beyond Mysticism*. Waterloo: Wilfred Laurier University Press.

JANOV, A. (1977). *Primal Man: The New Consciousness*. London: Abacus.

JANOV, A. (1983). *Imprints: The Lifelong Effects of the Birth Experience*. New York: Coward-McCann.

KLIMO, J. (1988). *Channeling*. Wellingborough: Aquarius.

LUKOFF, D. (1988). Transpersonal perspectives on manic psychosis: Creative, visionary and mystical states. *Journal of Transpersonal Psychology* **20**, 111-139.

MAHRER, A.R. (1983). *Experiential Psychotherapy: Basic Practices*. New York: Brunner/Mazel.

MAHRER, A.R. (1989). *How to Do Experiential Psychotherapy: A Manual for Practitioners*. Ottawa: University of Ottawa Press.

MOSS, D.M. (1981). Transformation of self and world in Johannes Tauler's mysticism. In R.S. Valle and R. von Eckartsberg (Eds), *The Metaphors of Consciousness*. New York: Plenum Press.

PEDLER, M. and BOYDELL, T. (1981). What is self-development? In T. Boydell and M. Pedler (Eds), *Management Self-development*. Farnborough: Gower.

REDFEARN, J.W.T. (1985). *My Self, My Many Selves*. London: Academic Press.

ROCKMAN, L. (1984). Ritual enactments in primal-encounter groups. *Aesthema* No. 4, 36-43.

ROCKMAN, L. (1986). Creativity, spirituality and therapy: Fourteen post-primal patients explore their experiences. *Aesthema* No. 6, 8-14.

ROWAN, J. (1975). A growth episode. *Self and Society* **3**(11), 20-27.

ROWAN, J. (1983). *The Reality Game: A Guide to Humanistic Counselling and Therapy*. London: Routledge.

ROWAN, J. (1987). *The Horned God: Feminism and Men as Wounding and Healing*. London: Routledge.

SAMUELS, A. (1989). *The Plural Psyche: Personality, Morality and the Father*. London: Routledge.

SINGER, J.L. (1974). *Imagery and Daydream Methods in Psychotherapy and Behaviour Modification*. New York: Academic Press.

STARHAWK (1982). *Dreaming the Dark: Magic, Sex and Politics*. Boston: Beacon Press.

VAUGHAN, F. (1985). *The Inward Arc: Healing and Wholeness in Psychotherapy and Spirituality*. Boston: New Science Library.

WATKINS, J. (1978). *The Therapeutic Self*. New York: Human Sciences Press.

WILBER, K. (1980). *The Atman Project*. Wheaton: Quest.

WILBER, K. (1983). *A Sociable God*. New York: McGraw-Hill.

WILBER, K. (1986). Treatment modalities. In K. Wilber et al. (Eds), *Transformations of Consciousness*. Boston: New Science Library.

WOLMAN, B.B. (1986). Protoconscious and Psychopathology. In B.B. Wolman and M. Ullman (Eds), *Handbook of States of Consciousness*. New York: Van Nostrand Reinhold.

Chapter 21
Four Hills of Vision:

Working on Men's Consciousness in Groups

Introduction

For some 15 years now I have been working with men in groups, specifically on issues of male consciousness in a patriarchal society, or what Eisler (1990) is now calling, perhaps more helpfully, a dominator model of society. If humanity is to survive, we have to move away from a dominator society towards a partnership society, such as has existed at various times in the past, but now with a much better chance of being understood and being successful.

This is difficult work, because it involves encouraging men to face the oppressor in themselves, as well as the hurt child, the inner person with feelings, the inner female and so forth. So it is rather like working on racism and other uncomfortable topics of that kind.

The type of work I have been doing is group work, specifically experiential group work. In this kind of work, I set an exercise for a group of men, and when they have completed it, we work through the feelings aroused by it in a spontaneous and unstructured way, trying to do justice to the feelings that emerge.

For example, I might say: 'Please find a partner, and when you have done so, look into your partner's eyes for one minute, without saying anything'. Some men will find this quite easy, others will be unable to do it at all, others again will find various feelings arising, which may be stronger or weaker. For a few men, this is a very threatening exercise, which makes them feel weak, and which they can then avoid in various ways: for example, one man might say 'I couldn't look directly into the eyes, so I looked instead at the eyebrows, and I found that easier'. We will then explore the implications of this.

From J. Rowan (1991). Four hills of vision: Working with men in groups. In J. Matthews (Ed), *Choirs of the God: Revisioning Masculinity*, Unwin Hyman, London, with permission.

As I have gone through the years, and have worked with different types of men in different contexts, I have come to believe that this work can be done in terms of four different positions. These are as it were four hills, standpoints from where we can survey the scene before us. Some of us may find it helpful to think of each hill as higher than the last, while others may find it better to think of each as simply separate and distinct from the last, without any idea of higher or lower. For that reason I have referred to them as positions, rather than as levels or stages.

The first is the conscious position, where we are going into matters like how men treat women, how men relate to other men, how men talk about women with other men, and so on.

The second is the unconscious position, where we discover possibly surprising things about how men relate to their mothers or fathers, how internal conflicts arise and how they function, how the dominance model gets into the bones, so to speak.

The third is the transpersonal position, where we go into the question of the anima, the shadow and other archetypes, and also such things as rituals of death and rebirth, of initiation. What is our myth, our legend, our fairy story about men and women? The discoveries here are again often surprising or disturbing.

The fourth is the position of god-forms, where we meet the Horned God and the Great Goddess, and try to do justice to what we may discover there. Actual experiences of wells, of standing stones, of tree circles and so forth can come in. Here the surprise and the disturbance are likely to be greater, because these things are even more hidden from our daily lives.

Let us look at each of these in turn, and see if we can come to terms with the phenomena which arise in each of these positions.

Position 1: Conscious

There is a useful distinction, which Daniel Cohen made in a newsletter article many years ago, between *male chauvinism* (a type of behaviour that is usually fairly easy to change once the awareness of it is made conscious); *sexism* (a more fixed attitude that is much more resistant to change, but can certainly move if tackled in the right ways); and *patri-archy* (an underlying pattern affecting people on many different levels and extremely hard to shift).

Male chauvinism

In the kind of groups that I most often organise, it is quite common to work successfully on male chauvinism. This is a point of view from which one simply takes it for granted that everything masculine is better than everything feminine, without ever examining it very closely.

One of the best people to discuss this is Bob Connell (1987) who has talked about 'masculine hegemony' in a way that I think must be convincing to anyone willing to consider a political analysis of gender and power. He argues the case for feminism with great attention to the way in which men actually think and believe. He challenges successfully the notion that males are, and should be, on top. This is thorough sociological work.

Once the male chauvinist assumptions are challenged, they quite quickly give way in the group setting, and change can come about reasonably fast. One of the exercises I do to explore this is called *the disappearance*. Here I tell the group of men: 'Two hours ago all the women in the world disappeared. There are no women any more. And this includes girl children and babies, fetuses and embryos and ova kept for research purposes, and so on'. Then I just leave them to discuss that scenario for one hour, an hour and a half, or two hours, depending on the length of the workshop. This is a powerful exercise, because the men can see for themselves how they talk and behave: it is not a question of telling them.

Usually what happens is that they talk a great deal about sex – how can they possibly get on without it; will marauding bands of men from other countries have to be dealt with; how can women be replaced somehow by biological research. Sometimes the men form themselves into a committee and have definite offices. This can all be discussed in the light of the idea of male chauvinism. (In my book *The Horned God* I tell the story of the Minzies and the Frongs, which casts some light on this – Rowan, 1987.)

Sexism

This is more deeply engrained, and harder to get at. It often requires a real change in the whole attitude structure of the person before it can shift. So this is more long-term work. Sexism is often based on low self-esteem, so that the man in question is able to boost himself up by putting women down, or so it seems to him. So the whole pattern of low self-esteem has to change before sexism can go, and this is a long-term therapeutic operation.

However, all these things are kept in place by social assumptions about the male ego and how it should be. It is often stated in articles and books that the male ego needs a lot of support and boosting (and this job is of course mainly done by women) in order to keep it functioning at all. This seems a bit suspect. One of the most striking statements I came across in the early days of the men's movement was a quote from Keith Paton (later Mothersson) in a newsletter which said 'The healthy male ego is oppressive and wrong'.

In a group, one way to explore this is to ask two men to share one sheet of paper and to make a picture. The way in which they do this is very revealing about the male ego and how it works. Usually there is competition rather than cooperation, the two men each seeing how much of the paper they can dominate. This simple demonstration is more convincing than any amount of instruction or research evidence.

So we have to work on this level quite consistently to achieve any real change, because the social reinforcement of sexism is always there. This is also the reason why group work is much more effective than individual psychotherapy in this sort of area – the real presence of other men working on the same issues makes it clear that this is a social, not just an individual, problem. I shall be coming back to the male ego later.

Patriarchy

When we come to the patriarchal level, we find a much more difficult pattern to deal with, because it is reinforced from so many different angles. Someone who has spelt this out very well is Elizabeth Dodson Gray in her spirited and readable account of patriarchy and what it is all about (Gray, 1982).

Eisler (1990) speaks of the dominator model of society as another way of talking about patriarchy, because the word 'patriarchy' can be taken so literally by some people. She emphasises how the dominator model is deeply embedded within each one of us, and hard to reach because of the continual social reinforcement that it receives.

So to deal with this is very hard, and here we may need even more to go into the unconscious and into the transpersonal, if we are to deal with it successfully and bring about real change.

Position 2: Unconscious

One can only go so far by simply working on the conscious level. Ultimately it is necessary, in any real attempt at change of dominance patterns, to go to the unconscious level. One of the key things here, of course, is the original family pattern from which the man emerged.

How the man related to his father as a child is crucial. What kind of a model of masculinity did the father represent? All kinds of positive and negative messages come from this early relationship.

Feelings about the father may often be closely related to sexuality. Perhaps the father was too sexual, or not sexual enough. Often the father's sexuality is quite mysterious, because of the absence (physical or mental) of the father from the family. Coming to terms with this may be a very important step in discovering one's own sexuality.

Similarly, a man's relationships with women are very strongly influenced, at an unconscious level, by how he related to his mother as a child. Did he love her? Did she love him? These are surprisingly often very loaded questions. They may carry a big charge, and be quite salient in the man's development.

One of the key exercises in this area is to ask the man to get in touch with his inner female. This is almost invariably a revealing and opening-up experience, which can bring some very important insights. This can be done through a guided fantasy, but I usually prefer to do it like this:

A contrasex exercise

Breathing, grounding and centring.

Now find a space where you can have a cushion or a chair in front of you. Cushion facing another cushion or chair facing another chair.

Sit on one and face the other. Close your eyes if you find that helpful. Now find in yourself the opposite sex. See if you can concentrate on finding a woman inside yourself, a woman in every physical sense, and in every psychological sense. See if you can allow yourself to be this woman. Really experience what it is like to be a woman. But it must not be a woman you know in the outside world. It has to be a woman from inside you. Really be that woman.

And then put that woman on the other seat – imagine her as completely as you can. Get as full an image or impression as you can. How is she dressed? What age is she? What expression does she have on her face? What is her hair like? How is she breathing? And then start to speak to that woman. What would you like to ask her? What would you like to tell her? What would you like to demand from her? Perhaps think of times in the past when you have been aware of her.

And when you have done that, and got some sense of how it goes, switch over and be that woman. And start to speak as that woman. What does that woman say? What do you say as that woman? Let her talk to you, respond to what you said to her. Have a dialogue with that woman. Get to know her, relate to her, find out how things go with her. Visualise her, concretise her, be with her. Go back and forth as you may need to. You have ten minutes for that.

This can be done in a very shallow way, or in a very deep way: it depends on all sorts of factors which it will be. But such an exercise should not be offered by anyone who is not a therapist or counsellor, or has a great deal of that kind of experience in groups, because of the depth of feeling that can sometimes come up with this exercise.

This is of course not the only exercise that can be done at the unconscious level – we also work on dreams, use guided fantasy, encourage regression to earlier ages, use certain kinds of massage to stimulate early memories, bring in art work and so forth.

Position 3: Transpersonal

Another way of seeing the deeper relationship with women comes from the collective unconscious. Such an archetype as the anima is highly relevant to the whole way in which the man perceives women. The anima is the woman inside the man. Very often the details of her appearance or character are derived from the mother, but this is not a mother complex, this is a deep archetype.

Also found in this area are the rituals of initiation. All real change in the personality takes the form of initiation into a different state. Very often this initiation takes the form of death and rebirth.

Group work lends itself to ritual, and new rituals seem to arise quite spontaneously in many groups. But they can also be devised consciously, as in the following example of a ritual which was used by Sue Mickleburgh and me in a workshop we did for a big conference on 'Sexuality and Spirituality' on the island of Lanzarote in May 1987.

As people arrived, there was music playing, earthy and simple. We divided the participants into two groups, 20 men and 30 women. Sue took the female group, and I the male group. The female group occupied the main space with Sue, and the male group went outside with me.

The women were told that what we were going to do was to create a powerful space, full of energy – female, goddess-type energy and hold on to it, even when the men re-entered the group. The first thing they did was to form a circle and introduce themselves by saying their names and, at the same time, performing a movement or gesture which expressed how they were feeling, or wanted to feel.

Then came a series of breathing exercises. Breathing unites body, feelings, thought and spirit by operating on all four of those levels.

Then Sue asked the women to hold their arms in front of them, with the palms of their hands about two inches apart, and gave instructions for a ball of energy to appear and grow between them. Then they slowly lowered their hands down to their sides and joined hands. They stayed silent and still for a while, holding hands and feeling the energy being transmitted around the circle. Sue then explained that they were going to use this energy, in a joyful way, to remind themselves where it had come from and to give thanks for it.

They danced around in a circle, still holding hands, singing 'The earth is our Mother, we must take care of her, the earth is our Mother, we must take care of her'. As they went round and round the singing got louder and louder and there was a feeling of energy and joy.

The joining

They stopped, and the men quietly entered the circle, stooping low to get underneath their linked hands. As they entered in this way their bent bodies and hunched shoulders seemed symbolic of the saddened and chastened men of the world realising how much pain and suffering they had caused women and feeling humbly grateful that they were still, after all the bad things they had done, accepted and welcomed into a joyful place where the strength and power of the women was quite different from anything they had ever experienced.

As they did so, the women faced into the centre of the circle, and extended their arms and hands into the centre, raising them as they breathed in and lowering them as they breathed out. They breathed in unison, making a constant wave of female energy directed towards the centre of the circle.

The important thing now was for the women to keep the atmosphere as it had been before the men entered the circle, and not to seek to comfort them and give away everything they had spent time raising. The men were in the circle, lying on the floor, seeming very miserable, and the women were standing tall and proud giving them attention in a strong and loving way. Slowly the men started to make contact with each other, and after a while the women linked hands again and danced around in the circle. Some of the men joined in the dancing and soon everyone was dancing.

The male group

When the men were outside I told them about the whole question of initiation, and explained that it was like death and rebirth.

> There will be three steps in this initiation. The first step is to give up everything that makes us male – to divest ourselves, one by one, of each thing. The second step is to go into the Goddess space and feel what it is like to be surrounded by female energy, not keeping it out and not defending ourselves against it, but accepting it and relating to it. And the third thing is to go deeply into ourselves and find the deeper masculinity within the Goddess space.

There was then some explanation of the Orphic Mysteries, and some discussion of this. I went on to explain the ritual itself.

> You are going to pass through ten gateways, and at each one you will give up something masculine. See if you can allow yourself to experience what life would be like without this thing. And remember that this is cumulative – once you lose something it is gone, and so you lose first one thing, and then two things, and then three things, and so on, until they are all gone.
>
> Now. Take one step forward, through the first gateway. Here you lose the male attitude to emotions and feelings. This is the attitude that says that emotions and feelings are rather a nuisance, they only get in the way of what is really important, they are irrational and timewasting. [Here there is a pause of 2 minutes. This does not sound very long, but in fact it does seem a very long time. This 2-minute pause is kept throughout the ritual, between each of the gateways.]
>
> Now take one step forward, through the second gateway. Here you lose the male attitude to children. This is the attitude that says that children are not very interesting unless they can talk sensibly about things and enter into proper conversations. Before this they are messy and inconvenient, or perhaps sometimes cute and adorable, but not really to be taken seriously. [Pause]

Take one step forward, through the third gateway. Here you lose the male attitude to work. This is the one that says that work is the most important thing in life, and that it must take precedence over everything else. If anything else conflicts with work, the work comes first. Be aware of what it is like not to have any more the male attitude to feelings and emotions, or the male attitude to children, or the male attitude to work – try to make it real to yourself. [Pause]

Then take one step forward, through the fourth gateway. Here you give up the male attitude to relationships. This is the one that says that relationships should take care of themselves; I do my part, the other person does their part. It is something like a contract; each person carries out what they have agreed to do. And that is really all there is to it. [Pause]

One step forward again, through the fifth gateway. Here you surrender the male attitude to women. This says that women are there to be used. They may be used to cook or keep house, they may be used to look up to or have sex with, they may be used to look good on one's arm or play hostess to one's friends and contacts, but the key is to use them well, and never to be used by them. One must be in charge at all times, or run the risk of looking weak and foolish. Be aware of what it feels like not to have this any more. [Pause]

Now another step forward, through the sixth gateway. Here you lose the male attitude to science and technology. This is the one that says that science and technology are the answer to everything. Everything that is now unknown and uncontrolled can one day be known and controlled through science and technology, and that would be a very good thing. These things have been successful in the past and will only be more and more successful in the future. [Pause]

One step forward, now going through the seventh gateway. Here you give up the male ego. The male ego continually needs to be stroked and looked after and protected; it inflates and deflates very easily, and it is important to keep this under control. It continually thinks of itself as being very important and very worth while. It very easily becomes impatient. It is very keen on appearing masculine and desperately afraid of been seen as feminine. It likes showing off, but it hates and can't bear being criticised. Now is the time to let go of this, and really allow yourself to feel what this is like. [Pause]

One step forward, through the eighth gateway now. This is where you have to give up your male body hair and beard. All those types of body hair that are typically masculine, including bald heads too. Imagine having nothing to declare you masculine in the way of hair. When we get to these last three, there is sometimes a tendency to laugh or giggle. See if you can do it without laughing, just feeling it directly, and breathing through it if necessary. [Pause]

One step forward, now going through the ninth gateway. Here you have to give up your testicles. This is the act of castration, which the priests of Attis always used to do as a sacrifice to the Great Goddess. No testicles, no testes, no balls now. Feel what that is like. [Pause]

One last step forward, and now this is the tenth and last gateway. Here you lose your penis, your phallus is gone now. The last masculine possession goes too. See if you can stay with that experience, of having nothing left at all.

Now here we have to pause until the Goddess space is fully prepared. It was only a matter of 3 or 4 minutes before we could go in, waiting for the cue that I knew was going to come. But the men did not know how long it was going to be, and the sun had now set, and the wind was beginning to get cold, so that the weather echoed very well the feeling of loss and deprivation.

The joining

Now the men were asked to blindfold themselves or shut their eyes, and hold hands in line. I led the way, and bent down to go under the arms of the women in the circle. All the men bent down as they came in, and we circled in around the inside of the women's circle until all the men were in. They lay on the ground at first, taking in the fact of being in a circle of female energy. I encouraged them to take it in, not to resist it or compete with it. I reminded them that their task now was to get in touch with their deeper and truer masculinity, as we had discussed earlier, along the lines of my book *The Horned God*.

Then I encouraged them non-verbally to make contact with other men, just stroking their hands and joining hands. Some of them made closer contact, in twos and threes, others just stayed in contact as they were. This felt much better.

Then I encouraged them, non-verbally again, to stand up together. When they were all standing up, I started the music. This music was South American dance music, again rather folky and unfamiliar. They began to move in response to the music, and so did the women.

The final phase

The next phase started spontaneously; we gave no lead at all as to what should happen, apart from starting the music. The women started to dance round in their circle, and the men danced their way into an inner circle. Then all at once the men began to turn outwards, so that the two circles were facing one another. As the music became louder, the circles became more irregular, and eventually broke apart, and people were dancing on their own or forming and reforming small groups of dancers all over the room. This dancing went on for quite a while.

We had thought that people might like to talk in small groups about the experience at this point to digest it, but the energy was much too high for that.

We asked people to sit in a circle, and brought out the bread and wine we had ready. We got people to pass it from one to another: as they passed on the wine they said 'May your spirit be strong' and as they passed on the bread they said 'May you have sustenance'. (These phrases come of course from the Wicca tradition.) Someone had found a candle and put it in the centre of the seated circle. It was just getting dark and the little light shone brightly for us. We grounded the energy we had raised. We parted with many expressions of feeling. The workshop came to an end.

Next day several people came up to us and said how much they had enjoyed it and how much they had got out of it. One man shaved off his beard, which was an unintended side effect! The organiser told us later that he had had some glowing reports about our workshop. We certainly felt that we had learned a great deal.

Some questions

But of course this raises a great many questions. A woman who had read an account of the workshop said she felt uneasy about the negativity of the approach to men. Also one or two men have said the same thing – could I not be more positive, more celebratory?

I have experienced a number of efforts for men to discover themselves on their own, in men's groups of various kinds – consciousness-raising groups, therapy groups and spiritual groups. I have not been impressed with the results. So often the group, no matter how it started and with what intentions the men got together, slides into some kind of warm self-congratulation or some kind of cold break-up. I referred to some of the reasons why that might be in *The Horned God*. Reports of the Bly groups in the USA reveal much the same picture. Such groups can be very moving experiences for the men, but they do not seem to help much in changing the patriarchal set-up between men and women, and that is what interests me. The best clues I have got about the latter has been from disciplines such as paganism and Tantra, where the relationship between the male and the female is directly referred to. Here is a quote from Arthur Avalon's *Shakti and Shakta*:

> A glorious feature of the Śākta faith is the honour which it pays to women. And this is natural for those who worship the Great Mother, who representative (Vigraha) all earthly women are. . . 'Women are Devas; women are life itself', as an old Hymn in the *Sarvollasa* has it. It is because Woman is a Vigraha of the Ambā Devī, Her likeness in flesh and blood, that the Śākta Tantras enjoin the honour and worship of women and girls (Kumāriś), and forbid all harm to them such as the Sati rite, enjoining that not even a female animal is to be sacrificed. With the same solicitude for women, the *Mahānirvāna* prescribes that even if a man speaks rudely (Durvācyam kathayan) to his wife, he must fast for a whole day, and enjoins the education of daughters before their marriage. The Moslem Author of the Dabistan (ii 154, ed. 1843) says 'The Āgama favours both sexes equally. Men and women equally compose mankind. This sect hold women in great esteem and call them Śaktis, and to ill-treat a Śakti, that is, a woman, is a crime.' The Śākta Tantras again *allow of women being Guru*, or Spiritual Director, a reverence which the West has not (with rare exceptions) yet given them. Initiation by a Mother bears eightfold fruit. . . A high worship therefore which can be offered to the Mother today consists in getting rid of abuses which have neither the authority of ancient Śāstra, nor of modern social science and to honour, cherish, educate and advance women (Śakti).
>
> (Avalon, 1978, p. 172)

There is a lot more, but you can see the drift. This seems to me very compatible with Western paganism, as promulgated for example by Starhawk (1979) or Sjöö and Mor (1987).

Coming now to the question of how this applies to the psychology of masculinity as worked out in men's groups, it is as if there are at least three models of maleness and how to work with it. First of all there is the standard phony social model, where the male has to be a proper man, and not effeminate or cowardly. Here it is OK to be male as long as one stays within the bounds of socially stereotyped masculinity. If one strays outside it in the macho direction, that may be a cause for punishment or treatment, but basically it is acceptable or winked at. If one strays outside it in the feminine direction, however, that is much more suspect and condemnable. We need not say too much about this model – it is too familiar. It is well worked out and defended in that dreadful book (Baumli, 1985) about the so-called 'Free Men' in America.

Secondly there is what one might call the monistic model, which is usual in personal growth and the kind of psychotherapy I normally do, where we say that the man has to go down into his depths, finding perhaps first a bad layer of self-putdowns, and then a layer of pain, and then a layer of deeper truth which is OK – or whatever model of layers is being used here. It is OK to be male, and just a question of finding the deeper, truer version of it.

Then thirdly there is what one might call a dialectical model, which is much more rarely used by group leaders, where we say that the first 'bad' layer is found to be bad or harmful only because separated from female energy and female power. Connected up again in a proper relationship with that energy and that power, the 'bad' transforms into a deeper truth which is OK. One familiar symbol for this is the Yin-Yang diagram, where the white area has a black spot at its centre, and the black area has a white spot at the centre, indicating that opposites interpenetrate each other.

Now there are one or two ways of talking about masculinity that are quite compatible with this dialectical model. I heard it said in one workshop that the male was like an electron circling the female nucleus, and that this was the healthy state; to split that atom could be destructive. This is a very similar point to the one I have been trying to make. I have also heard it said that what was most vulnerable and precious in the person could actually be seen as the vital centre of the person. Again this seems quite compatible with what I am saying here. But very often in groups the leader seems to be adhering to the monistic model, asking people simply to own and to rejoice in their own masculinity.

Now it seems to me that these three approaches are not necessarily contradictory. I think they correspond to three different types of work in this area.

Three types of work

The one type, which uses the model of adjustment to social reality, is the position of most of the psychotherapy that is generally available. The highest aim is to be able to play one's role in society properly.

The second type, which takes the monistic approach, is the position of personal growth. Table 21.1 shows how this relates to the adjustment model, which is detailed in the first column. Looking at the second column now, it can be seen that here one is interested in the personal unconscious, in the healing of the splits (such as mind/body, left/right, intellect/emotion, topdog/underdog, but in particular here the split between the male and the female), and generally in the integration of the person as a social and psychological being. This is what Ken Wilber (1980) calls the centaur position, and what he and others have called the position of the existential self or the real self.

The other type, which uses the dialectical approach, is the position of spirituality and the transpersonal (the third column on Table 21.1), seen through the eyes of paganism. It says that the male and the female must be related through the *hieros gamos* if the male is not to be destructive. This is not about healing the split between the male and the female, but about enabling them to relate together in an appropriate way – a way that actually works in today's world.

So one way of putting this point would be to say that we have three positions from which we may work: in the first position we stick to adjustment, helping the person to make changes at the conscious level to make life more bearable and successful; in the second position we are concerned with the unconscious and with deeper changes that involve real self-discovery and owning up to one's inner reality; and in the third position we are concerned with the spiritual and the transpersonal. One way of putting this is to say that we have here three layers: on top the conscious, under that the unconscious, and under that again the transpersonal.

Another way of putting this, which I now think is more useful for some purposes, is to see the three layers as circular, thus:

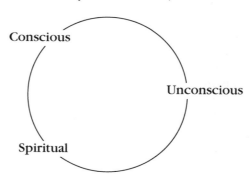

Table 21.1 A comparison of four positions in personal development

	Position 1	Position 2	Position 3	Position 4
Wilber level	Persona/Shadow	Centaur	Subtle self	Causal self
Rowan position	Mental ego	Real self	Soul	Spirit
Self	I am defined by others	I define who I am	I am defined by the Other(s)	I am defined by the Other
Motivation	Need	Choice	Allowing	Surrender
Personal goal	Adjustment	Self-actualisation	Contacting	Union
Social goal	Socialisation	Liberation	Extending	Salvation
Process	Healing – ego-building	Development – ego-enhancement	Opening – ego-reduction	Enlightenment – questioned ego
Traditional role of helper	Physician Analyst	Growth facilitator	Advanced guide	Priest(ess) Sage
Representative method	Hospital treatment Chemotherapy Psychoanalysis Directive Behaviour mod. Cognitive–behavioural Some TA Crisis work RET	T-Group method Gestalt therapy Open encounter Psychodrama Horney etc. Bodywork therapies Regression Person-centred Co-counselling	Psychosynthesis approach Some Jungians Some pagans Transpersonal Voice dialogue Wicca or magic Kabbalah Some astrology Some Tantra	Zen methods Raja yoga Taoism Monasticism Da Free John Christian mysticism Sufi Goddess mystics Some Judaism
Focus	Individual and group	Group and individual	Supportive community	Ideal community
Statement	I am not my body I am not my emotions I am not my desires I am my intellect To say anything more would be presumptuous	I am my body I am my emotions I am my desires I am my intellect I am all these things and more	I am not my body I am not my emotions I am not my desires I am not my intellect I am a centre of pure consciousness and will	I am (am not) my body I am (am not) my emotions I am (am not) my desires I am (am not) my intellect I am That
Questions:	Dare you face the challenge of the unconscious?	Dare you face the challenge of freedom?	Dare you face the loss of your boundaries?	Dare you face the loss of all your symbols?
Key issues	Acceptability Respect	Autonomy Authenticity	Openness Vision	Devotion Commitment

In this way of seeing it, we go from the conscious to the unconscious, and from the unconscious to the transpersonal, and from the transpersonal back to the conscious, and so on round and round in a spiral of growth. (Perhaps you have seen Jill Purce's (1974) book, which I think is excellent, on the spiral.) The advantage of seeing it in this way is to underline the point that Starhawk (1979) makes, that it is only the pagan view of the transpersonal which has a political significance in making the male safe for the world. Because it is only in paganism that the male is in the right relationship with the female. And this entails using what I have just been calling the dialectical model of the male.

This would be to take male-in-relation as safe and to be the focus of attention, and male-out-of-relation to be dangerous or suspect. I feel that the monistic can all too easily become the autistic, and that the autonomous can all too easily become the overweening – as in the story of Inanna and Dumuzi, as told by Perera (1981). This is what I am saying all through Chapter 10 of *The Horned God,* of course.

I hope that this discussion will make it clearer what the reasons are for envisioning the ritual in this way. It very firmly grasps the third position, and works entirely from there.

Position 4: God Forms

But if we really want to understand death and rebirth, we have to be prepared to go into an even more difficult area, the realm of the god forms. The Horned God is the consort of the Great Goddess, and can form an ideal image of how the male can relate to the female.

This goes beyond the archetype into an area of religion proper. It is only here, I believe, that men can realise that the question of female power is crucial to their own development; and this takes us back to politics. Politics is about power, and we have to understand about female power before we can shift male power from its present dangerous position.

Men are really afraid of female power, I have discovered, and find it very hard to come to terms with. But the way to come to terms with female power is to worship it.

It was an exciting day for me when I came across the seven-page entry for Kali-Ma in Barbara Walker (1983) and found that it said things such as:

> Kali was the basic archetypal image of the birth-and-death Mother, simultaneously womb and tomb, giver of life and devourer of her children: the same image portrayed in a thousand ancient religions. . .
>
> Kali stood for Existence, which meant Becoming because all her world was an eternal living flux from which all things rose and disappeared again, in endless cycles.
>
> The Nirvana Tantra treated the claims of male gods with contempt: 'From a part only of Kalika, the primordial Shakti, arises Brahma, from a part only arises Vishnu,

and from a part only arises Shiva. O fair-eyed Devi, just as rivers and lakes are unable to traverse a vast sea, so Brahma and other gods lose their separate existence on entering the uncrossable and infinite being of Great Kali. Compared with the vast sea of the being of Kali, the existence of Brahma and the other gods is nothing but such a little water as is contained in the hollow made by a cow's hoof. Just as it is impossible for a hollow made by a cow's hoof to form a notion of the unfathomable depths of a sea, so it is impossible for Brahma and other gods to have a knowledge of the nature of Kali.'

The Yogini Tantra said of Kali, 'Whatever power anything possesses, that is the Goddess.' Shakti, 'Power', was one of her important names. Without her, neither man nor god could act at all. . .

As a Mother, Kali was called Treasure-House of Compassion (karuna), Giver of Life to the world, the Life of all lives. Contrary to the west's idea of her as a purely destructive Goddess, she was the fount of every kind of love, which flowed into the world only through her agents on earth, women. Thus it was said a male worshipper of Kali 'bows down at the feet of women', regarding them as his rightful teachers.

This was extraordinary stuff for me to read, because it overturned all the ideas I had had up to that time about Kali, who I had thought about if at all as a thoroughly destructive and nasty entity. Our modern consciousness has split apart the benevolent and the destructive aspects of Kali: as Sjöö and Mor (1987) succinctly put it: 'Paradox is split into dualism, an act characteristic of patriarchical consciousness.' Soon after reading this I saw a film called 'Indiana Jones and the Temple of Doom', which underlined all the old errors about Kali, and even added some new ones: for example, the threat to the heroine of being sacrificed to Kali. Kali never had female sacrifices of any kind, not even female animals.

Now the consort to Kali is Shiva, and I read on avidly to find out what Barbara Walker said about him. Here is some of it:

Shiva was called Lord of Yoga, i.e., of the 'yoke' that bound him to the Goddess. . . Among Shiva's many other titles were Great Lord, Lord of the Dance, Lord of Cattle (Pasupati), Beneficent One (Sankara), Lord who is Half Woman (Ardhanarisvara), God with the Moon in His Hair (Candrasekhara), He Who Belongs to the Triple Goddess, He Who Gives and Takes Away, Consort of the Goddess Uma, Condemned One, Destroyer, Howler. . .

Tantric yogis insisted that their supreme Shiva was the only god and all other gods were only inferior imitations of him. He was certainly older than the Vedic heaven-gods. . .

As Lord of the Dance, Shiva represented one of Hinduism's most subtle concepts . . . Shiva performed this dance in a place called Chidambaram, the 'Centre of the Universe'; but the location of this place is within the human heart. . . therefore the god is located within the core of man's own self. . .

Shiva was seldom depicted alone, for his power depended on his union with Kali, his feminine energy, without whom he could not act. The puzzling vision of Shiva as Shava the corpse, under the Goddess's feet, illustrated the 'doctrine that Shiva without his Shakti can do and is, so far as the manifested is concerned, nothing.' Yet joined to the Goddess, he became the Bindu or spark of creation.

> Every human orgasm was believed to share in this creative experience as 'an infinitesimally small fragment and faint reflection of the creative act in which Shiva and Shakti join to produce the Bindu which is the seed of the universe.'

Again I found this was exciting stuff. It seemed to offer a mythological account which made perfect sense of the dialectical relationship that I had found to be so important. When I came to investigate, I found that the relationship between Shiva and Kali in the Eastern religion was paralleled in the relationship between the Great Goddess and the Horned God in the Western traditions.

This is now spelled out in a masterly work which has only recently become available from the Farrars (Farrar and Farrar, 1989). Here we can see how the Horned God Cernunnos, or Herne in the pagan traditions of our own area, has all the characteristics we have found in the East.

> He is usually portrayed with horns and accompanied by animals. He usually either wears or has looped on his horns the torc (circular necklet) of Celtic nobility. Often, as on the Gundestrup Cauldron, he holds a serpent with a ram's head or horns.
>
> (Farrar and Farrar, 1989, p. 97)

This is exactly how he is also portrayed in the Mohenjo-Daro representation of Shiva Pasupati, Lord of the Animals. The serpent is of course the representative of female underworld wisdom in myth and legend world wide. But the ram's head indicates that this is a specifically masculine version of serpent wisdom. It is a way of saying that the relationship between the male and the female is particularly close and particularly important for the Horned God.

The Farrars note that the Ulster hero Conall Cernach, whose name has cognate roots with the other names of the Horned God, goes to relieve a castle which has been invaded by a terrible serpent, where the serpent submits to him without resistance, 'jumping into his girdle, where Cernunnos's attendant serpent is often found'. Such familiarity with the underworld, the space of the Goddess, is very characteristic for the Horned God. He is not afraid of the underworld, but connects with it in a lively way which does it honour and respect.

The Horned God, like the Great Goddess, has many names: they include Dionysos, Pan, Dumuzi, Tammuz, Osiris, Orpheus, Adonis, Attis, Mithra, Quetzalcoatl, Hu, Dis, Hades and Hermes, among others. All these can be studied with advantage. And the Farrars suggest a useful ritual for getting in touch with him in his guise of the stag.

Conclusion

At the end of this examination, we have come up with some disturbing news for men. They have to re-evaluate their assumptions radically if they are to come to terms with a more adequate vision of how males and

females can relate. It is not easy for men to do this. One very sophisticated and knowledgeable man wrote to me, after reading some of this
material, and said that it looked to him as if I were saying that women
should be given precedence in all matters. This felt to him as if I were
saying that he should agree to be hurt or wounded by women, and 'to lie
down and be prepared to be run over by every passing steamroller'.

I replied by saying that unless men agree to be wounded nothing much
is going to change. Any man who says 'I refuse to be wounded – this thing
can be tackled by intelligence and good will and positive thinking' is
highly suspect to me. Suspect because feminism is in a way all about hurt,
and unless men actually feel some kind of hurt, rather than sympathising
with it in a patronising way, they are not going to experience the message
of feminism on any real kind of human level. Many men seem to get the
message of feminism only as far as their heads, which means that they get
the words but not the music, not the real dance. If we are going to get a
response that is anywhere near adequate, we have to accept that we are
hurt too, we do actually feel something ourselves. The refusal to lie down
under every passing steamroller is the refusal to be broken. The 'healthy
male ego' has to learn how to be broken by feminism. This is not an easy
lesson or an easy option – it is hard and has to be hard, because of the
resistance that gets in the way. But unless this lesson is learned, men are
going to continue to play the 60/40 game.

The 60/40 game was first identified in the early days of the anti-sexist
men's movement by Keith Paton (later Keith Mothersson). This is where
a man living with a feminist admits that she is most often right about
feminist issues, particularly when she confronts him on his own actions.
He sees that she has more insight, more feeling, more motive in such
things. But in his head this gets translated into a kind of proportion or
percentage. She cannot be right all the time – no one can be right all the
time. So maybe she's right 90 per cent of the time, or 80 per cent, or 70
per cent, or 60 per cent. Of course, this means that every issue still has
to be argued and fought out, because this might be one of the – admittedly minority – cases where he is right.

> And all the other cases the same (funnily enough) so you don't give an inch. The
> 60/40 game is a heap of shit. You know it but you won't break. You insist on
> fragmenting your POWER, your BLOODYMINDEDNESS, into a hundred little issues
> – on each of which (once safely parcelled out) you are prepared to argue ratio-
> nally, it's just that she gets so worked up.   (Paton, 1973)

I think this rings as true today as it did then.

This goes with my belief that the male as such is suspect. Men are
continually coming up with apparently reasonable notions such as that
they are not there to be run over by every passing steamroller, and then
using them to avoid even the most obvious changes in their behaviour.

Men can be incredibly awful – I haven't told even the half of it in my chapter, or in my book. Whenever I hear men talking about sexual politics, I cringe, because what they are saying is generally so dreadful. If it is not dreadful in the direction of getting off the hook and avoiding all the issues, it can be dreadful in the direction of making the challenge of feminism so bad and so demanding that no one can live up to such a challenge, and so we all retreat into guilt and inaction. This is one of the points that Lynne Segal (1990) has made so powerfully in her new and excellent book.

The precise point of all my work – and of course I may not have succeeded in my aim, but anyway this is the aim – is to go fully into the guilt and despair, but not to rest there. In this it is rather like the Joanna Macy (1983) approach to nuclear war. Being a man is like being the pilot who dropped the bomb on Hiroshima. Perhaps more for me, who cheered the dropping of the bomb on the two grounds that it was a marvellous step forward in the mastery of Nature and would also get me back home from India that much quicker, than for those readers who are too young to have had such an experience. Believing something so terrible is important, but equally important is not being paralysed by that belief. These are the two steps. I think the only real, genuinely well-based and grounded kind of hope is the hope that comes on the other side of despair, and that actually grows out of the despair. I spit on the phoney hope which believes that all is basically OK, and that all we have to do is to celebrate the excellence of men and the marvellousness of women.

If any man says to me that 'We do sometimes need to protect ourselves' my answer is that obviously we need to protect ourselves from being killed or having our houses burned down, or something irreparable like that – I am not urging some absurd abandonment of all our interests. But what we do not need to protect, and what it is very important not to protect, is our ego. It is the ego that we are protecting whenever we indulge in the 60/40 game. The male ego has to be broken. It can then come into existence again on a deeper level, where it is in the right relationship with the female, and does not need the self-protection which was so important before. A man can be strong and vulnerable at the same time: they are not opposites, they are all part of the same thing. It is the openness, the non-defensiveness, that is so important and so hard to learn.

If any man says to me that 'Men have to come to their own understanding' of course I agree. Some women's formulations, while excellent for them, just cannot be used in the same form by men. For example, women can totally exclude any contact with men, for short or long periods, and this may be a useful stage in their own development; but men do not have this option – we have to remain in contact with at least one man!

If any man says to me 'We can't prescribe for other men' of course I have to agree. I hold to the general ethical belief that 'you can't lay your trip on someone else', which I learned in the LSD culture of the 60s. But

I have also become very impatient with the avoidance practised by so many men in relation to feminism. So I prefer to say things in a rather challenging way that sounds rather pushy and prescriptive, just to arouse some response. Then when I get the response, I can come back with some more detailed examination of the answers.

If any man says to me 'You sound very self-righteous' I am worried and think it deserves some examination. Self-righteousness is 'righteousness for which one gives oneself credit'. Righteousness is 'Justice, uprightness, rectitude; conformity of life to the requirements of the divine or moral law; virtue, integrity'. I don't know why stating the obvious about patriarchy should be self-righteous. For example, when Bob Geldof told some of the United Nations people that they were a bunch of hypocrites, he seemed to me righteous but not self-righteous. I really do not know how to say some of the things I want to say without taking the risk of seeming self-righteous to some people. I suppose Bob Geldof seemed self-righteous to some people.

It seems to me that in a million ways you, and I, and all of us, support and maintain the system that dropped the bomb. This is just a sober recognition of the way in which we all subscribe, in our daily purchases, in our taxpaying, in our media consumption, in our work, in our leisure, to the horror world. If I counted up, in the course of one day, the number of actions of mine that supported patriarchy and the number that opposed or questioned it, the first number would be larger than the second number. And I suppose the same would be true of you. So that is one way we drop the bomb on Hiroshima. And to the extent that we perpetuate the linear thinking and competitive attitude that we were brought up with, that would be another way in which we drop the bomb all over again: I myself feel that I have dealt with quite a lot of that at a deep level, and I assume that some readers at least would feel the same, but I wonder, if push came to shove, whether we have quite eliminated it all?

So I leave you, the reader, with some unanswered questions and some painful issues. That is what happens sometimes in my workshops too. This is because masculinity is such a difficult issue now, and in the immediate future. But it is an issue that we have to deal with successfully, or die.

References

AVALON, A. (1978). *Shakti and Shakta*. New York: Dover.

BAUMLI, F. (1985). *Men freeing Men*. Jersey City: New Atlantis Press.

CONNELL, B. (1987). *Gender and Power*. Cambridge: Polity Press.

EISLER, R. (1990). *The Chalice and the Blade*. London: Mandala.

FARRAR, J. and FARRAR, S. (1989). *The Witches' God*. London: Robert Hale.

GRAY, E. (1982). *Patriarchy as a Conceptual Trap*. Wellesley: Roundtable Press.

MACY, J. (1983). *Despair and Personal Power in the Nuclear Age*. Philadelphia: New Society Publishers.

PATON, K. (1973). Quoted in Rowan (1987).

PERERA, S. (1981). *Descent to the Goddess*. Tornoto: Inner City Books.

PURCE, J. (1974). *The Mystic Spiral*. London: Thames & Hudson.

RAWSON, P. (1973). *The Art of Tantra*. Greenwich: New York Graphic Society.

ROWAN, J. (1983). *The Reality Game*. London: Routledge.

ROWAN, J. (1987). *The Horned God: Feminism and Men as Wounding and Healing*. London: RKP.

SEGAL, L. (1990). *Slow Motion: Changing Masculinities, Changing Men*. London: Virago Press.

SJÖÖ, M. and MOR, B. (1987). *The Great Cosmic Mother: Rediscovering the Religion of the Earth*. San Francisco: Harper & Row.

STARHAWK (1979). *The Spiral Dance: A Rebirth of the Ancient Religion of the Great Goddess*. San Francisco: Harper & Row.

WALKER, B.G. (1983). *The Women's Encyclopaedia of Myths and Secrets*. San Francisco: Harper & Row.

WILBER, K. (1980). *The Atman Project*. Wheaton: Quest Books.

Chapter 22
The Downward Path to Wholeness in Transpersonal Psychotherapy

Height springs to mind as an image that has the same meaning the world over. We talk about aspiring to higher things, or about being one-up on somebody; we think of the Royal Family as more exalted, superior; we use phrases such as 'onward and ever upward'; we speak of being up to it (or not being up to it), or of rising above it; we all know what we mean by soaring intellect or high ideals; some of us even talk about height psychology, the higher self, reaching the heights and having peak experiences; a few of us even think of the spirit in the sky, God in His Heaven – even of the various grades of heaven, ending up in the seventh heaven, which is the highest of all.

But there is a whole other, contrasting vocabulary, a whole other way of seeing things, which we used to have and lost long ago. In the days of the Goddess, before the patriarchal sky-gods took over, the underworld was the womb where everything happened. Down there in the darkness – for the Goddess was usually approached through caves – the miracles of birth and creativity were honoured and adored. The most sacred ceremonies of death and rebirth took place down there in the depths. At the entrance to the cave there was a maze, a labyrinth, presided over by a mythical woman. The initiate had to find the way through the underworld – the womb of the Mother – going through symbolic death to be reborn again through her on a deeper psychic level. Monica Sjöö and Barbara Mor, in their wonderful book on the Goddess, say: 'Simultaneously, by dancing the winding and unwinding spiral, the initiate reached back to the still heart of cosmos, and so immortality, in her' (Sjöö and Mor, 1987, p. 75).

The terrible days of the patriarchal takeover changed all this. Much of the history is lost to us because of the success of the patriarchy in

From J. Rowan (1989). The downward path to wholeness in transpersonal psychotherapy. Paper delivered at the 1989 International Conference on Transpersonal Psychotherapy.

destroying all remnants of the Goddess worship. Some of the worst stories of how the culture of the Goddess was wiped out are recounted in the Bible, although the truth of the matter is hidden by the fact that the scribes were reluctant to mention the Goddess at all, and usually referred to Her through Her less important consort, Baal. Merlin Stone (1976) has written the account of all this in her book *The Paradise Papers,* where she also makes it clear that the story of the Garden of Eden was specifically written, at quite a late date, to turn people off the Goddess and Her worship. The snake and the tree were both sacred to the Goddess: the snake lives in caves and holes in the earth, and the tree has its roots underground.

In psychology today the underworld is being rediscovered. James Hillman, in particular, has spoken out for the importance of the under-world as a clue to our deepest humanity (e.g. Hillman, 1979). It is precisely through our illness and our woundedness, he says, that we may seek doorways to the depths of soul. We do not need to 'rise above' our ego and our human nature – rather do we need to go inwards, down into the centre of our ego, and find our self there. At the still centre of the turning world lies the secret of our existence, not in some distant region beyond the stars.

Jocelyn Chaplin, a feminist psychotherapist living in London, has written very well about how in psychotherapy we have to go down into the under-world. She says:

> The middle period involves going 'down' into previously hidden parts of the psyche. Often these are parts of ourselves that we symbolically describe as dark. These qualities, and death, were associated with the goddess in her form as old woman or crone, e.g. Hecate, who was the goddess connected with the centre of crossroads in ancient Greece. She is also associated with winter, when the previous harvest has been cut down and the new growth is still under the surface. Winter is also a time of holding in energy, of consolidating inner strength, before moving into spring, when it can be expressed outwardly.   (Chaplin, 1988, p. 86)

Any real wholeness must do justice to the depth within, and not get seduced by the attractions of the sky. In order to do this, I have found in my own case that I have had to break through layer after layer of patriar-chal conditioning, questioning important things that I had taken for granted, not even realising that I was doing so. I had been looking to the sky for freedom and spirituality without being aware of my own gestures. I had been avoiding the underworld, not even knowing or wanting to know of my own avoidance. Even Hillman, who is so eloquent about the importance of the underworld, somehow manages to make it seem unpleasant and menacing. He calls it the world of death, but it is just as much the world of life and generation and creativity and ecstasy.

There are two directions, not just one. Even if we wish to speak of transcendence, there are still these two directions, up and down. Rolf von

Eckartsberg (Valle and von Eckartsberg, 1981) makes the distinction between open-eyed transcendence as height-awareness and affirmation of self, and closed-eyes transcendence as loss of selfhood and depth-awareness. Both are essential to any full attempt at wholeness or completion. But whereas the upward path is the path of aspiration, the downward path is the path of letting go.

Once we see the richness and value of the downward path, accepting that what is down there can be positive, everything changes. We lose our fear, carefully instilled by the patriarchy, of what is underneath, behind and below. The vortex becomes positive, the blood becomes positive, the darkness and silence become positive.

And looking upwards we become uncomfortably aware of what Freud said about the phallus – how it was always rising up, how it conquered gravity, how it related to dreams of flying. How many of the images of height are phallic, when we look at them with these newly opened eyes. How many of our highest images really speak of looking up to the phallus and worshipping it. Our whole civilisation is unaware of the extent to which it idolises the phallus. If we want to think and feel and sense and intuit as whole human beings we have to do better than this. It does not help us to put all the good things up and all the bad things down.

Think of the images we have been brought up with. All the evil was put down in the pit. Sheol, Gehenna, Hell; Pluto, Hades, Dis; the fires, the sulphur, the prongs; all down there in the depths under the earth. Something inside many of us still falls for this today. The fear we feel seems instinctive, untaught, natural; a victory for patriarchal propaganda. With the Good God forever at one pole, and the Bad Devil forever at the other, the human mind is locked forever into a battlefield of dualistic antagonisms, with no hope of resolution. The forbidden fruit of the Goddess gives knowledge of good *and* evil – knowledge of the reconciliation of opposites in the experience of the still centre. Monica Sjöö tells us that:

> If human beings eat this fruit, patriarchal religion is out of business. A world free of psychic alienation would need no Christian salvation, or 'salvation' of any kind. When dualistic opposites are allowed to fuse in the mind, the psyche saves itself.
> (Sjöö and Mor, 1987, p. 174)

What we have to do now is to 'reclaim the night', reclaim the depth, reclaim the underworld. We have to reclaim and re-vision the whole world down there that has been lost for so long.

The Labyrinth

In my work in psychotherapy, both in the actual work and in the training of psychotherapists, I have found the image of the labyrinth to be a powerful one.

The modern maze is something to get lost in, and we have all but forgotten the original form of the labyrinth, which was a ritual path of going to the centre and coming out again, having covered all the paths within the labyrinth. Every path was traversed, every part of the labyrinth was met twice – once on the way in, and once again on the way out. At the centre there was a turning, a ritual turn where the mystery happened. Still today the Hopi Indians have the labyrinth as one of their sacred symbols, and call it 'Mother Earth'.

First of all this explains the basic form of all psychotherapy – the journey to the heart of the matter. Many traditions of therapy have many different ways of putting this. The Kleinians talk of going to 'the point of maximum anxiety' (Isaacs, 1939); the object relations school talk of discovering 'the basic fault' (Balint, 1968); Janov (1991) speaks of discovering 'the primal trauma'; Laing (1983) speaks of 'recession' into the centre of our being; and so on. Jocelyn Chaplin, whose work I admire greatly, has spoken of silence as being at the centre of the labyrinth. She says:

> The silence is a powerful space for the client to discover a genuine self. It can be seen as the gap at the centre of the spiral or labyrinth. In that 'nothingness' or hole is in fact the whole being of the person. The 'empty vessel' they feared is actually full, of themselves. The hole is indeed holy.   (Chaplin, 1988, p. 78)

The labyrinth is very ancient, going back at least to the second or third millennium BC. It develops out of the basic mark of the spiral, and in later times a spiral mark could refer to the labyrinth as a sort of shorthand. The spiral is a symbol of the Goddess before it is a symbol of anything else. But it is important to realise that it is not a picture of the Goddess, but a picture of a ritual. It is the ritual which brings us to the Goddess, and it is a ritual which is basically danced. Jill Purce says:

> However, the essence of the labyrinth is not its outward form, its delineating stones and hedges, but the movement it engenders. The spiral, mandalic movements of the dance predate even the labyrinth itself.   (Purce, 1974, p. 30)

As we know, the spiral later became a symbol of life and growth.

But in classical times the most powerful myth of the labyrinth was that of the monster at the heart of the maze; the monster who must be wrestled with and overcome; the dreaded Minotaur.

And this brings us to the second thing that the labyrinth can teach us in relation to psychotherapy. Elinor Gadon (1989) thinks that the tale of the Minotaur is a subversion, a radical change in the ritual, because instead of going to the womb of the Mother for rebirth, the person going into the labyrinth meets danger and possible death. But I see this as an extension of the myth, not a denial of it. After all, how can we have rebirth if we do not have death first? In psychotherapy we know that the womb in not the warm, safe place we once thought it must be. Quite often it is a place of danger, of emergency, of terrible feelings of being powerless and at the mercy of whatever happens (Lake, 1980). We always speak of initiation when we speak of the labyrinth: and what is our real initiation into this world but in the womb, and in leaving the womb, the same way we came in? This, then is the second thing we can learn: therapy is initiation.

But the person in the myth who knows the way out is Ariadne. In the late forms of the legend, and in the novels of Mary Renault, Ariadne is just a person, the daughter of the king. But she is really a Goddess. Kerenyi (1976) says that she was a Great Goddess. She was the mistress of the labyrinth, and he tells us that 'the dancing ground, on which the figure of the dance was drawn, represented the great realm of the mistress'. Her name means 'utterly pure'. She was a moon goddess, and a goddess of the underworld. Always there is a connection, it seems, between the moon and the underworld. Outside of Crete, Ariadne took the form of the Great Goddess of love, Aphrodite. But on Crete, she was the wife of Dionysos.

Here we come to the third thing that the labyrinth has to teach us: how to deal with the borderline case. Dionysos is mainly a god of women. His cult was mainly a woman's preserve. Though he is male, and phallic, there is no misogyny in this structure of consciousness because it is not divided from its own femininity. Dionysus is man and woman in one person. Dionysus was bisexual in the first place.

James Hillman (1972) has made some very important points about this god. One of the names for Dionysus was 'The Undivided', and one of his main representations was as a child. The child refers to a view of reality that is not divided. Asked if it wants ice cream or jelly, the child says 'both'. A Dionysian perspective towards therapy would not exclude the child for the sake of maturity, because the child is the synthesis itself. The childish may not be put away, but shall be retained within consciousness for the sake of 'both'. This is of course terribly important in psychotherapy: some of our most important efforts consist in doing justice to the wounded child within, as David Grove (Grove and Panzer, 1989) and Alice Miller (1985) have recently been reminding us.

But Hillman takes us further. In one of his most convincing and well worked out essays, he says:

> In Dionysus, borders *join* that which we usually believe to be separated by borders. The philosopher is also a lover; Socrates is a drinking Silenus; the riotous Dionysus has but one wife, Ariadne. Dionysus presents us with borderline phenomena, so that we cannot tell whether he is mad or sane, wild or sombre, sexual or psychic, male or female, conscious or unconscious. Kerenyi says that wherever Dionysus apppears, the 'border' also is manifested. He rules the borderlands of our psychic geography.   (Hillman, 1972, p. 175)

So he can help us in some of the most intractable cases, the borderline condition, which is neither fully psychotic nor familiarly neurotic, but between the two.

.hing the labyrinth can teach us is something about how the
 ɔ relate to the female in a non-dominant culture. Dionysus
adne as a consort, not as a dominant boss.

.s a horned god, with such forms as bull, goat and stag. Thus
he ...... n the horned god of witchcraft, who also operates as a consort
to the Great Goddess. His totem was a panther (*Pan-theros,* the beast of
Pan). His emblem was the *thyrsus,* a phallic sceptre tipped with a pine
cone. His priestesses were the Maenads, or Bacchantes, who celebrated
his orgies with drunkenness, nakedness and sacramental feasting. Yet he
is always on the side of women, and his phallus was always in the service
of women.

Identified with many other saviour-gods, Dionysus was also called
Bacchus, Zagreus, Sabazius, Adonis, Pentheus, Pan, Liber Pater, or 'the
Liberator'. In the Wicca tradition, as I have explained elsewhere (Rowan,
1987), he is Cernunnos, another horned god, another god of the underworld, another god of animals and of life.

His later hero-incarnation, Orpheus, star of the popular Orphic
Mysteries, was the same sacrificed god, torn to pieces by the Maenads. So
we come again back to the underworld, by a different route. Orpheus had
a particular relationship with Persephone, goddess of the underworld,
who was herself identified sometimes with Ariadne.

The Serpent

But one of the main benefits of going into the underworld and accepting
it is that there is where we find the serpent. The serpent is an extraordinarily powerful symbol for us in psychotherapy. Its sheds its old skin and
renews itself, and speaks to us of death and rebirth. It wriggles about and
around obstacles, and speaks to us of flexibility and the refusal to get stuck
in one place. It belongs equally in the sunshine and in the shadow, on the
mountain and in the cave. It takes us where we want to go in psychotherapy.

But it is much more than this. In ancient times, the cosmic serpent was
everywhere known as the energy source of life, connecting with earth and
water. Oracles called upon the serpent, and wherever you have oracles
you have serpents.

But going deeper again, the ageless serpent was originally identified
with the Great Goddess herself. In the East she was known as Kundalini,
the inner female soul of man in female shape. Barbara Walker tells us about
the serpent 'coiled in the pelvis, induced through proper practice of yoga
to uncoil and mount through the spinal chakras toward the head, bringing infinite wisdom' (Walker, 1983, p. 903).

So the serpent represents wisdom, transformation, connections between
the worlds and even the spiralling shape of the primal universe and human

energies themselves. It is willing to be our helper, and to be used on the staff of Hermes to go backwards and forwards between the unconscious and the conscious, between the feelings and the intellect, between the body and the mind.

There is now a whole magazine, called *Snake Power*, which calls itself 'a journal of contemporary female shamanism', devoted to nothing else but showing how important this serpent energy actually is in the world today.

But this is equally important for men. The serpent is often taken to symbolise the phallus, male sexual energy. In the earliest times this was understood to be contained within the Goddess, born from her, and returning to her again, when at the end of each world-cycle she curls up in dark sleep. So there is nothing necessarily aggressive or misogynistic about such images: rather they seem to represent the phallus serving the Goddess, women, and the life processes of all (see Sjöö and Mor, 1987, p. 61).

Jocelyn Chaplin (1988) has pointed out how science now accepts the idea of interconnected opposites, constant change and transformation, rhythm and the self-regulation of the universe, as in the work of Fritjof Capra (1975), for example. This is to understand the ancient serpent with our conscious analytical minds. She points to the connection between all this and the dialectical thinking that comes from Hegel and Marx.

In conclusion, then, it seems as though the underworld, the labyrinth and the serpent have much to teach us, and as if the journey into spirituality, into the transpersonal, is not necessarily an upward one, moving into the light. It can equally well be a downward journey into the sacred darkness.

References

BALINT, M. (1968). *The Basic Fault*. London: Tavistock.

CAPRA, F. (1975). *The Tao of Physics*. Berkeley: Shambhala.

CHAPLIN, J. (1988). *Feminist Counselling in Action*. London: Sage.

GADON, E. (1989). *The Once and Future Goddess*. San Francisco: Harper & Row.

GROVE, D.J. and PANZER, B.I. (1989). *Resolving Traumatic Memories*. New York: Irvington.

HILLMAN, J. (1972). *The Myth of Analysis*. New York: Harper Torchbooks.

HILLMAN, J. (1979). *The Dream and the Underworld*. New York: Harper & Row.

ISAACS, S. (1939). Criteria for interpretation. *International Journal of Psychoanalysis* **20**, 148–160.

JANOV, A. (1991). *The New Primal Scream*. London: Abacus.

KERENYI, C. (1976). *Dionysos: Archetypal Image of Indestructible Life*. London: Routledge.

LAING, R.D. (1983). *The Voice of Experience*. Harmondsworth: Penguin.

LAKE, F. (1980). *Studies in Constricted Confusion*. Oxford: CTA.

MILLER, A. (1985). *Thou Shalt not be Aware*. London: Pluto Press.

ROWAN, J. (1987). *The Horned God: Feminism and Men as Wounding and Healing*. London: Routledge.

SJÖÖ, M. and MOR, B. (1987). *The Great Cosmic Mother: Rediscovering the Religion of the Earth*. San Francisco: Harper & Row.

STONE, M. (1976). *The Paradise Papers*. London: Virago.

VALLE, R.S. and VON ECKARTSBERG, R. (Eds)(1981). *The Metaphors of Consciousness*. New York: Plenum Press (for articles by Marlan and Eckartsberg.)

WALKER, B. (1983). *The Woman's Encyclopedia of Myths and Secrets*. San Francisco: Harper & Row.

Index